THE
ROOSEVELTS

*All happy families resemble each other;
every unhappy family is unhappy in its own fashion...*

Anna Karenina
TOLSTOI

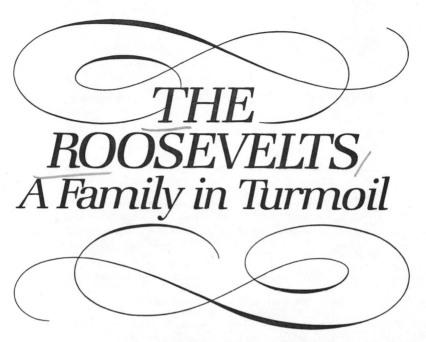

THE ROOSEVELTS
A Family in Turmoil

by Lillian Rogers Parks
in collaboration with
Frances Spatz Leighton

PRENTICE-HALL, Inc., Englewood Cliffs, N.J.

Book Designer: Linda Huber
Art Director: Hal Siegel

10   9   8   7   6   5   4   3   2   1

Library of Congress Cataloging in Publication Data

Parks, Lillian Rogers.
The Roosevelts : a family in turmoil.
Bibliography: p.
Includes index.
1. Roosevelt family.   I. Leighton, Frances Spatz.
II. Title.
E807.1.P37   973.917'092'2 [B]   81-992
ISBN 0-13-783043-2   AACR2

Contents

A Note to the Reader

I don't know why Americans can't stand thinking that presidents and first ladies are mere humans. They can accept that a president was a mere man *before* he came to the White House, but once he is there, they insist on draping him with some cloak of saintliness. And if it doesn't fit *they* have a fit.

And not content with building a saintly figure out of the man they have voted into office, they insist that his whole family must be a family of saints.

I know that FDR did not appreciate the worship of the general public after his first flush of excitement. As a matter of fact, he grew weary of it, and he once commented that he hoped to heaven there would be no statuary of him after he was dead and gone for people to continue worshiping.

We, who worked at the White House, would have died of boredom had first families not been human. We were human and we wanted them to be. We loved unraveling the mysteries of the Roosevelt family, loved helping keep their secrets. We just wished that Eleanor and Franklin were closer and happier together—and more romantic with each other. We were sorry each had to lean on others for whatever happiness they could find.

But "life is life," as Eleanor herself once said, in regretting that so many unhappy things had happened in her family. She had added ruefully that one cannot lead anyone else's life, one just made the best of it.

To Jimmy Roosevelt, the Roosevelt son whom we,
backstairs at the White House,
adored for his unfailing kindness to us and for
his great and touching devotion to his invalid father.
We never told him how we felt but we saw
and were moved...

Acknowledgments

I would be selfish not to acknowledge publicly
how much I owe the White House servants with whom
I exchanged backstairs stories and insights for our ears only.
Now the temper of the nation is such that the public
has the right to know what we knew then
and kept confidential among us for fully 50 years.

I'm sorry that most of that loyal army
are no longer alive to see the truth told at last
but they hold my undying gratitude.

I also wish to acknowledge the valuable
assistance on this book of our dedicated helpers—
Kaye S. Becker and Sylvia Stewart.

Who's Who in This Book

THE ROOSEVELT FAMILY

Franklin Delano Roosevelt: Democratic President, 1933–1945, spanning the Great Depression and World War II; born 1882, died 1945.

Eleanor Roosevelt: his wife; the first First Lady to lead a life of her own, commanding complete freedom through a writing career and an active political life; born 1884; died 1962.

Anna: only daughter; kept FDR's secrets; born 1906, died 1975.

    First husband: Curtis Dall, stockbroker

    Second husband: John Boettiger, newspaper reporter Anna met at White House; he later committed suicide after divorce

    Third husband: James Halsted, medical doctor attached to Veteran's Administration

James: eldest son, FDR's favorite; born 1907.

    First wife: Betsey Cushing, socialite daughter of famous brain surgeon

    Second wife: Romelle Schneider, nurse he met while patient at Mayo Clinic

    Third wife: Irene Kitchenmaster Owens, receptionist in his Congressional office before he married her

    Fourth wife: Mary Winskill, former teacher of his young son, Hall Delano

Elliott: most married son, Eleanor's favorite; born 1910.

    First wife: Betty Donner, steel heiress

    Second wife: Ruth Chandler Googins, Texas socialite

    Third wife: Faye Emerson, glamorous movie star

    Fourth wife: Minnewa Bell, California oil heiress

    Fifth wife: Patricia Whitehead Peabody, Arizona real estate agent

Franklin D. Jr.: handsomest son, resembled father; born 1914.

    First wife: Ethel du Pont, beautiful daughter of Pierre du Pont; she eventually committed suicide after their divorce

    Second wife: Suzanne Perrin, interested in farming

    Third wife: Felicia Schiff Sarnoff, former wife of Robert Sarnoff, head of RCA

    Fourth wife: Patricia Oakes (an equestrian wedding)

John: youngest, tallest, only son not to run for office, and only offspring to turn Republican; born 1916.

> First wife: Anne Sturgess Clark, North Shore socialite; she went to Majorca after her divorce from John and lived with Faye Emerson, Elliott's divorced wife

> Second wife: Irene Boyd McAlpin, New York socialite who shares his life as a gentleman sportsman on his Tuxedo, New York, estate

FDR's Grandchildren: These are the 13 grandchildren of the President at the time of his death. Many more have been born since, including a James Roosevelt, Jr.

> Anna's children:
>> "Sistie"—Anna Eleanor (III)
>> "Buzzie" —Curtis Dall, Jr., who changed his name legally to Roosevelt
>> John Boettiger, Jr.

> James' children:
>> Kate
>> Sara Delano

> Elliott's children:
>> Billy—William Donner
>> Ruth Chandler (II)—"The little peacemaker"
>> Elliott Jr.
>> David Boynton

> Franklin Jr.'s children:
>> Christopher du Pont
>> Franklin Delano III

> John's children:
>> Haven Clark
>> Anne Sturgess (II)

Sara Delano Roosevelt: FDR's mother, adored by the President; feared and sometimes avoided, sometimes catered to, by the First Lady in a love-hate relationship.

Hall Roosevelt: First Lady Eleanor's younger brother, who was an alcoholic; even so, he was the closest and most adored person in her life.

Aunt Polly: actually, Laura Delano, FDR's maiden aunt who hovered in the wings all his life and was there when FDR died at Warm Springs.

Daisy Suckley: actually, Margaret Suckley, distant cousin of FDR and almost constant companion of Aunt Polly; gave Fala to FDR.

Who's Who in This Book

PEOPLE CLOSE TO FDR

Louis Howe: lived at White House, FDR's political wizard

Harry Hopkins: originally Eleanor's satellite, defected his loyalty to FDR

Missy LeHand: a most unusual private secretary; lived in the White House

Lucy Mercer Rutherfurd: Eleanor's social secretary, who almost broke up Eleanor's marriage when Eleanor discovered her love letters to FDR; with FDR at Warm Springs when he died

Princess Martha: Eleanor was very jealous of the attention FDR gave her in and out of the White House after Missy's death

Henry Morgenthau: FDR's neighbor and Treasury Secretary; butt of FDR's gags

Harold Ickes: survived all through FDR's administration as Secretary of Interior, in spite of Eleanor's dislike

"Cactus Jack" Garner: FDR's Vice President for the first two terms; FDR liked the humor but not the man

Henry Wallace: FDR threatened to refuse the third term nomination if he couldn't have Henry

Gus Gennerich: FDR's favorite bodyguard, victim of a mysterious death

Steve Early: FDR's press secretary; guarded the Boss' secrets

"Pa" (Colonel Edwin) Watson: FDR's secretary and buddy; was supposed to be a tower of strength but he died before the term was up

Louise Hackmeister: FDR's switchboard operator; most closemouthed woman in the White House

Colonel E. W. Starling: FDR's favorite Secret Serviceman on whom he played tricks

PEOPLE CLOSE TO ELEANOR

Lorena Hickok: Eleanor's masculine looking, live-in guest

"Tommy" (Malvina) Thompson: Eleanor's personal secretary and keeper of her secrets, they shared a cottage, each leading her own life

Earl Miller: the touching romance of younger man and older woman started when he was Eleanor's bodyguard at the Governor's Mansion in Albany and continued on and off until Eleanor's death in 1962

Edith Helm: Eleanor's social secretary at the White House

Henrietta Nesbitt: Eleanor brought her to Washington from Dutchess County, New York, to be her housekeeper and refused to part with her, no matter how much FDR protested about the food she served

Mary McLeod Bethune: black educator who greatly influenced Eleanor and taught her to fight segregation

Marion Dickerman: associated with Eleanor in running Todhunter, private school for girls

Nancy Cook: associated with Eleanor in running the Val-Kill furniture cottage industry; for a time Marion, Nancy, and Eleanor spent all their spare time together, but by the time Eleanor became First Lady, the close relationship had cooled and they had divided up their ownership of things—still, the two could come to the White House whenever they liked

Joe Lash and Trude Pratt: a young couple Eleanor took under her wing; both were involved in the youth movement of the 30s and much of their courtship took place at the White House; they later married and Joe became one of Eleanor's biographers

Mabel Haley Webster: Eleanor's personal maid; Eleanor sought her out for White House duty because she knew all the Roosevelt secrets and was not easily shocked; worked for Eleanor once before, in the old days on R Street, when Eleanor had discovered her husband's love affair with Lucy Mercer

THE HOUSEHOLD HELPERS

MAIDS

Maggie Rogers: my mother, head maid at the White House

"Little Girl," "Little Maggie," "Little Lillian": I answered to all those names as I did my work, mostly sewing, and moved around the White House with the aid of one crutch; FDR and I were both victims of polio and it was a special bond between us

Lizzie McDuffie: she had been the Roosevelt's maid at the Governor's mansion and had a bantering relationship with FDR, she could take liberties with him the others of us couldn't; FDR's favorite household helper, her loyalty was to the President rather than to Eleanor

Mary Foster: personal maid who came into the White House with Eleanor and died before the first year was up

Annie and Nora: two white maids who had to leave the Roosevelt White House because they weren't black

Lily Carter: bath maid

Bluette Pannell: live-in maid; helped look out for Lorena Hickok

Katurah Brooks: quit while she was ahead

Who's Who in This Book

Margaret Sykes: a lively girl who took Mama's place when she retired; Eleanor took a liking to her, helping her get fine jobs in the welfare field after the White House years

Ella Sampson: a live-in maid; a lovely looking schoolteacher who came to work at the White House because of the Depression; formed a lasting friendship with Margaret

Wilma Holness: a distant cousin of mine, she found romance at the White House

DOORMEN

John Mays: tragedy came his way

Samuel Jackson: he comforted Mama on her deathbed

BUTLERS

Alonzo Fields: chief butler when the Roosevelt administration began

Charles Ficklin: followed Alonzo Fields as chief butler (later, the title was changed at the White House to maitre d'); wonderful friend, lived to help celebrate my 75th birthday

Armstead Barnett: opened his own catering business after leaving the White House

John Ficklin: Charles' brother, now the maitre d' at the White house

COOKS

Jimmy Carter: the first Jimmy Carter of the White House

Mary Campbell: when FDR's mother died, the President brought Mary from Hyde Park to cook the kind of gourmet food he liked

Loretta Deans: went often to Hyde Park with the Presidential White House entourage

Daisy Bonner: FDR's cook at the Little White House at Warm Springs, she cooked the President's last meal

VALETS

Irvin McDuffie: Lizzie's husband; both lived at the White House until the twenty-four-hour duty broke McDuffie's health and he suffered a nervous breakdown; even when he left, Lizzie continued working for the President

Cesar Carrera: the second valet to have his health break in service to the President; for seventeen years he shared the home of Maggie and me

George Fields: brother of Alonzo Fields; served in World War II

Arthur Prettyman: the valet who took McDuffie's place; present at FDR's death

"Isaac" (Irinea) Esperacilla: by fate, it was Prettyman and not he who went to Warm Springs that fateful April

MISCELLANEOUS PERSONAGES

Murray, the Outlaw of Fala: a dog who was almost human; called simply "Fala" by the President; FDR's constant companion during the war years, they travelled everywhere together, including to war strategy conferences

Diana Hopkins: daughter of Harry Hopkins, who was semiadopted by Eleanor Roosevelt and came to live at the White House at the age of five

King George VI and Queen Elizabeth: they ate a hot dog and made history, but their visit had deeper significance

Winston Churchill: British Prime Minister who acted as if he belonged at the White House—and FDR seemed to feel he did

Alice Roosevelt Longworth: the famous socialite daughter of President Teddy Roosevelt and first cousin of Eleanor Roosevelt; the thorn in Eleanor's side for all of Eleanor's life; FDR did not want her around the White House parties

Marian Anderson: the Daughters of the American Revolution (DAR) would not permit her to sing at Constitution Hall because of her color, so Eleanor countered by inviting her to sing for the King and Queen of England

Kate Smith: business came first

Madame Chiang Kai-shek: a most difficult house guest

Carole Lombard and Clark Gable: a Hollywood couple who wowed the White House staff

Fanny Hurst: one of Eleanor's favorite writer friends, she came quite often

Gertrude Stein: another writer who came but once and did not please Eleanor

President Harry Truman: he hired Eleanor

President Dwight "Ike" Eisenhower: he fired Eleanor

I

NOTHING IS AS IT SEEMS

Nothing Is As It Seems...

There are no secrets in the White House. Only secrets from certain people. But somebody knows. Somebody sees. Somebody eventually tells.

Servants are always lurking nearby. It is part of the job. When I was working in the White House as a maid, I couldn't fall through a trap door just because a first lady or president was near.

And Eleanor told the household help much more than she realized. Her high voice was penetrating, and since she couldn't hear too well, she tended to talk a little louder than necessary. We didn't eavesdrop. We just couldn't help but overhear.

Anyway, the First Lady didn't worry about what she said. She would run ahead of Tommy Thompson, her secretary, as Tommy tried to catch up, and Eleanor would talk to her over her shoulder, saying exactly what she thought of this person or that or of what the President was doing.

Whether she was angry or happy, we knew it. Most of the time, thank goodness, Eleanor was happy and cheerful, bubbling about her many plans.

The only secrets she seemed anxious to keep from the public, those early days at the White House, concerned son Elliott's marriage, which was on the rocks. She had told people Elliott's wife, Betty, and his son, Billy, were just staying with her a little while and were going to follow Elliott as soon as he found a place for them to live.

But we knew differently. We knew Elliott and a buddy were having fun roaming around out West, and the chances of finding Elliott and Betty living together again were about as good as finding an icicle in Hades.

Nothing Is as It Seems

There are two families that occupy the White House at any given moment of history: the showcase family and the hidden family of retainers. (I could say the "silent" family of retainers because they never speak in public, but behind the scenes they speak plenty and have their own strong opinions.) The presidential family, of course, is the showcase family, closely related to one another. I was part of that very vocal hidden family, related to one another only in our love of the White House and its occupants.

When Franklin Delano Roosevelt came to the White House, there were seven members of the showcase family: the President, age fifty-one, his wife, forty-nine, and his children—Anna, James, Elliott, Franklin D. Jr., and John—ranging in age from twenty-six to sixteen.

I was thirty-two and the daughter of the head maid, which certainly helped my ranking in the silent family that stood behind the Roosevelts, helping them put up a good front. Besides Mama Maggie and me, there was a veritable army of retainers—ushers, doormen, cooks, butlers, maids, electricians, engineers, plumbers, carpenters, housemen, valets, and even some men tucked away in the bouquet room, fixing flowers.

I want to tell the story of the Roosevelt family as we, who worked for them, saw them. The public speculated, but we, who saw them night and day, really knew what they were like. And our lips were sealed.

Now the stars of the story are gone from the scene—Babs and the Boss. Even Mama is gone. And so, I must tell the rest of the story of the Roosevelts before it is too late and paint *my* picture of history, correcting some portions of the canvas and adding some brushes of color.

It was a relief when the hale and hearty Roosevelts moved in and everything seemed so normal after the silent Hoovers. Or was it? Gradually we learned that nothing was as it seemed.

There was no end to surprises. The President's female secretary, Missy LeHand, was to live in the White House. Such a thing had never happened before. And what was more, the word quickly spread that she was to be treated with the same deference given to Eleanor.

If she asked for anything—any service—staffers jumped, as if the First Lady was asking. What's more, she was no old crow. She was young, vivacious, and pretty, and she seemed perfectly at home in the President's bedroom suite. Soon she was dashing down from third floor to second in her robe.

We knew that Missy was taking up residence on the third floor. We knew that Lorena Hickok was Eleanor's more or less permanent guest on the second floor. FDR was spending his evenings with Missy LeHand. Eleanor Roosevelt was spending her evenings with Lorena Hickok.

White House servants looked at each other and said, "What goes?" It soon became obvious that there was some kind of platonic relationship between FDR and Eleanor and each searched for happiness and affection elsewhere.

How close Lorena Hickok and Eleanor already were became obvious to some servants on the very day of the inaugural ceremonies. Eleanor and Hicky, as we were soon calling her, spent a lengthy time together in Eleanor's bathroom and came out claiming that was the only place they could find privacy for a press interview. It was hardly the kind of thing one would do with an ordinary reporter. Or even with an adult friend.

Meanwhile, FDR was busy with his own friends. And that night Eleanor became the first First Lady to attend an Inaugural Ball without her husband. If they had wanted to be together, surely they both would have gone, after a "barbeque" for the Roosevelt family at the White House.

But FDR went his way and Eleanor went hers. There was even some talk backstairs that FDR might have had a short visit from a mysterous beauty whom Eleanor Roosevelt did not know was attending inaugural ceremonies as FDR's guest, the lady the world would come to know as Lucy Mercer, or Lucy Mercer Rutherfurd. She was hidden in the shadows that day.

Like the Mad Hatter's tea party in *Alice in Wonderland,* things were getting curiouser and curiouser.

When you have so many people tied together in one household—the famous family and the little known family—it is like a steaming teakettle: Now and then a little pressure must escape.

There were feuds and there were sore spots. There were marriages and divorces among the household staff. We had weddings, births, sicknesses, funerals, all of which brought us closer together. We had every kind of problem. Alcoholism. Romantic dalliance. Accidents. Nervous breakdowns. Even a war!

We had a mysterious death of one aide close to FDR, a death that was glossed over and never investigated. Life at the White House in the Roosevelt days was one long soap opera, and as one tragic or humorous episode ended, another began.

Generally, the staff knew more about the Roosevelt's problems and feuds than they knew of ours. But they were such a warm family that sometimes they got involved in our lives.

An example, but one that was not funny, brought Eleanor into the life of the doorman, John Mays. One day, soon after the Roosevelts had come to the White House, but long enough for Eleanor to have become very fond of the warmhearted Mays, the doorman told her he needed to go home to check on his wife, who had just had a tooth extracted. He assured her he would be back in time to work the reception she was giving that night.

Mays arrived home to find his wife dead in bed. Mrs. Roosevelt was so upset she could hardly concentrate on her duties at the formal party. Until she could rush there herself, she sent her personal maid, Mabel, and Mama to sit with Mays at his home.

I was standing at the water pitcher tray near the entrance as they hurried by, telling me where they were going. Eleanor had become quite attached to Mays, though their skins were of different colors.

Mays was a part of the silent family, the supporting cast that surrounded the Roosevelts as they moved in on March 4, 1933. But the first and foremost member that day was Maggie, my indomitable mother, who had a life of her own and had been estranged from my father for many years.

She had worked her way up to head maid at the White House and she was there to greet the new first family in spanking clean white uniform, when they stepped inside after watching the Inaugural Parade. Mama already knew their belongings, having helped get their possessions moved in and unpacked in the course of a hectic few hours.

Next, there were the top attendants to FDR and his wife, who arrived with the Roosevelts and had been with them since FDR had been governor. Irvin and Elizabeth McDuffie owed their allegiance to FDR.

Mac, as the President called him, was the valet, a handsome and congenial man. Lizzie—as she soon told us to call her—was fun-loving and helpful. She was always eager to give us a hand as well as look after the needs of the President. Between them, they knew all there was to know about the Roosevelts, their marriage, their family history, their skeletons in the closet.

But there were others who knew the First Family intimately. Gus Gennerich, who came from New York to be FDR's bodyguard, was one. And, of course, there was Missy and all the daughters-in-law.

If you heard the whole Roosevelt family at dinner together—Eleanor and Franklin and all the offspring with their spouses—it was hard to believe that there could be any unhappiness there. They laughed. They shouted—they even outshouted the President. They seemed to delight in their noisiness.

It was only when you stopped to listen that you realized it was only the Roosevelts who were making all the happy commotion. The young in-laws were strangely quiet. In that household, if you wanted attention, you had to fight for it.

Mays, the doorman, once said, "Everybody doesn't fit into this family. It's hard to fit into the Roosevelts." Judging by the number of Roosevelt divorces, he was certainly right.

Initially a bride would be brought home to the White House and she would look radiant. Then she would return to the White House looking downcast. Roosevelt sons thought they were doing their duty if they dropped their wives, children, and maids off at the White House and left them there while they went out to have a good time.

For some strange reason, marriage to a Roosevelt scion was devastating. Maybe the mates they chose simply couldn't adjust to life in the public eye. Each of the Roosevelt children had at least one divorce. The mates of two committed suicide sometime after being divorced.

While they sat around the White House waiting for their husbands to come get them, some of the wives of the Roosevelt sons would occasionally talk about how awful their lives were.

Eleanor was easy on her sons, but FDR was so tenderhearted with them that he wouldn't discipline them at all. They got into their scrapes. The word was that once, when Eleanor insisted he at least take away a son's driver's license as punishment, FDR squealed on her, saying that he was taking the license only because Eleanor had requested it. It was clear that FDR always wanted to be the good guy.

Word was the President was a "fanny pincher." As one butler put it, "The Boss is just as normal American as apple pie." Some of the White House help got a big kick out of it when FDR proved it by making the most of his attendance at FDR Jr.'s wedding, kissing all the bridesmaids and a lot of the pretty young guests for good measure, and fanny pinching right and left.

When we saw how undisciplined the Roosevelt dogs were, we said that was an indication of how the children would be, and it certainly turned out right. They were an unruly crew, each doing whatever he or she wanted without asking anyone's permission.

Usually, it was speeding tickets and minor accidents that hit the newspapers. One was so careless that he set the bed afire in the Queen's Room. Fortunately only the blankets were ruined. He escaped without a singed hair—the luck of the Roosevelts, we said.

Sons frequently turned up to ask for money. Even as married sons, they dared seek subsidies. The word around the White House was that the President didn't want the wealthy families to think he couldn't keep up with them. From what we servants heard, it was a hardship to keep giving out money with all the personal expenses the President had. The government allowances didn't begin to pay for the Roosevelt expenses, such as entertainment.

Take the case of Anna. When the Roosevelts came to the White House, Franklin and Eleanor had not only Anna but her two children, Sistie and Buzzie, living there, and the Roosevelts were hardly the kind of family to ask an offspring to kick in a little for the support of the household. While Anna came and went, Sistie and Buzzie, the most famous of the Roosevelt grand-children, stayed at the White House.

One of the first things Sistie and Buzzie did for attention at the White House, during one of their grandmother's receptions, was to decorate the Grand Staircase, where the guests passed by, with long streamers of toilet paper.

Among the first things that happened to Eleanor was a run-in with the Park Service of the Interior Department. The First

Lady had requested that a swing be installed on a certain tree for Sistie and Buzzie, aged six and two, when they arrived to live at the White House.

Immediately the Interior Department was up in arms and it was as if Mrs. Roosevelt had sounded an alarm. Men swarmed over the White House grounds. Mrs. Roosevelt was told that putting up a swing could injure an historic tree.

Now Eleanor was up in arms. I remember she rushed down a hall saying loudly to her secretary Tommy, "History will survive a swing and so will the tree."

Eleanor got her swing.

People who see the happy Christmas photographs of the Roosevelt family don't know the drama behind the scenes. Elliott's third wife, Faye Emerson, had a child by a previous marriage, a little boy everyone called "Scoop." He would usually stay close to his mother. Eleanor loved the child and tried to make him feel at home.

However, we noticed that whenever a family picture was being taken, little Scoop wasn't included. He was tactfully sent to play elsewhere with a maid until the picture session was over.

The maids would laugh about those picture-taking sessions and say that every time a cameraman came in sight, FDR Jr.'s wife Ethel would plop one of her little boys on the President's lap.

When the Roosevelts came to the White House, we were amazed at their handsome children. Anna, who at twenty-six had already made the President and First Lady proud grandparents, and four sons, all tall and strapping. John, the youngest, was taller than all the rest. He was six-feet-four—at 16.

Franklin Jr. was eighteen, Elliott was twenty-two, and James was twenty-five.

We were curious about them. The nation was curious about them. Meanwhile, the White House staff, Secret Service, and their parents carefully hid their constant pranks and problems—some with the law—from the public.

All that showed was the tip of the iceberg.

Every now and then something would be hushed up about one of the sons—usually Elliott, the hothead of the family—punching someone in the nose. They took personal offense when someone called the President a "bastard" or their mother a "nigger lover." Over and over the President and First Lady assured them that such things were par for the course, and though it was flattering to be protected with derring-do, it wasn't needed or asked for.

Still it was a strange feeling to know that FDR was one of the most loved and hated presidents in history.

It hurts us, backstairs, to hear how Eleanor was abused for trying to help blacks, inviting some to the White House as honored guests. Reactionaries said she was just doing it to help her husband get votes. I knew she heard one nasty jingle in which FDR is supposedly talking to her. She suffered over it as much as we did backstairs:

> *You kiss the niggers*
> *I'll hug the Jews*
> *We'll live in the White House*
> *As long as we choose.*

Once James turned around in a train after listening to a passenger make obscene comments about his parents, and shoved the man. Another time, columnist Westbrook Pegler insulted the First Family in print. Elliott and James both went to their father and seriously suggested they follow Pegler until they caught him in an unguarded place and horsewhipped him. FDR again tried to explain the facts of political life, then bragged to his cronies over drinks about the "grand plan" of his sons that he had had to veto.

John was a few days from his seventeenth birthday when he came to the White House. But he felt very mature and went out on the town on Inauguration night. As we heard the story the next morning, he had driven up to the gate alone in the wee hours, driving a clunker of a car, and honked to get in after exploring Georgetown.

The guards at the gate asked for his identification and he didn't have any. He said he was John Roosevelt. They looked at him skeptically and asked if he wanted to go to a phone booth somewhere and call the White House. They had no instructions about any missing Roosevelt who was to be let in.

It was obvious that they didn't believe him, and in fact, a guard had said that if he were the President's son, he wouldn't be driving a car like that, he'd probably be in a White House car.

Poor Johnny sat in a hotel lobby until morning, not wanting to wake up his parents. His mother hadn't known he was missing or she would have had Cox's Army out looking for him, as we used to say. When Eleanor found out, she was upset, but by then it was a great joke to John and his brothers. The sons took their White House connection lightly and had as much fun with it as they could.

When they were new to the White House, the two teenagers, Johnny and Junior, loved to grab White House telephones and have fun answering them, in the name of some company or fish market. Their father didn't hear about it, usually, but the help got a good laugh.

One day FDR Jr. picked up a White House phone out of boredom and the person calling asked for the President.

FDR Jr. said, "May I ask who's calling?"

"Pershing," said the caller, who sounded young.

Nobody was going to put anything over on Junior. He knew the World War I general wouldn't be calling the White House even if he was still alive. Somebody must think he was dumb.

"The President is not here at the moment, but this is Jesus Christ," he said. "I'll tell him you called."

"Wait a minute, wait a minute," said the caller. "I'm not trying to be funny. I'm the son of General Pershing."

The story made the rounds at the White House, and it was so funny FDR did not have the heart to scold Brud, as FDR Jr. was called. But he did caution him to be respectful if someone named Jesus Christ called.

At first I wondered why FDR did not use crutches the way I did. We were both victims of polio. It would have made his life so simple, and I longed to tell him this. But though he did single me out to talk with in friendly fashion, now and then, encouraging me to talk freely, I didn't think he would appreciate this kind of advice.

I was very glad I had kept my mouth shut, because from the staff close to him I soon learned that FDR wasn't that stable, and besides he feared that if he were to walk on crutches, everyone would know how crippled he really was. His greatest fear, next to fire, was that the public would think he was not physically up to the job of the presidency. His own mother had put that notion in his mind, and he spent a great deal of time proving something to her and hiding his infirmity from the general public.

As he saw it, as long as he had a strong cane on one hand and a strong arm to lean on with the other hand, no one could really tell how afflicted he was. Only we knew what agony those few steps were. His legs were hopeless. The twenty-pound braces hurt.

But the top part of his body was truly magnificent and strong. He could swing himself from his wheelchair into a regular chair easily. And as long as he was seated behind his desk, he was so handsome and strong looking there was not a sign that he was crippled.

Another thing I longed to tell the President was to quit letting his valet and housemen push him and to use his own arms to turn the wheels of his wheelchair, just for the exercise. The reason he never pushed himself was that it just wasn't the proper thing to do. It was their job, and it wouldn't look right for him to be pushing and them to be walking.

I was amazed at all the tricks used to give the illusion that FDR was not as helpless as he was. Some thought he walked with just the help of a cane, and many fine ones arrived as gifts. FDR kept a collection of pearl-handled and fancy carved canes in a big urn.

But in reality, the cane wasn't enough to keep the President upright. The important support was the arm of a strong man he was leaning on. And the shuffling along that FDR could do on ceremonial occasions, with the cane on one side and the good strong arm on the other, could only last a few minutes. He needed that wheelchair.

It was a burly, strong Secret Serviceman who would carry FDR from automobile to wheelchair, or wheelchair to train. I would sometimes watch this transfer and would be amazed at how quickly and neatly it was done. Mike Reilly, chief of the White House Secret Service detail, would usually be the one to scoop up the President, but other men would cluster around them like a human wall, so it was hard to see what was going on.

People nearby might not even realize what was happening— the transfer of the Boss from one seat to another.

When FDR was getting his new plane built—the "Sacred Cow"—he was afraid he would look too conspicuous being carried up a long ramp or else he would have to be loaded and unloaded far away from the crowd. But he hadn't reckoned with American ingenuity. Douglas Aircraft engineers came up with an inconspicuous wire mesh elevator that zipped him right up.

And again, the public did not know the whole story. They were seeing only the staged effect.

We knew that we were expected to keep the secret about the wheelchair that was always around the corner, out of sight of the public. We had to go along with the illusion that the Boss could walk.

It was just part of the whole pattern around the White House where nothing was as it seemed.

But then, as far as Roosevelt went, things were not always what they seemed away from the White House, either. I remember so well what happened to Bill Simmons, FDR's receptionist, who was part of the intimate Roosevelt life.

Simmons was stationed outside FDR's Oval Office, but he would come to the Mansion now and then. I liked him very much. We maids said he looked like a "walking Roosevelt." He was tall and handsome and had the same build as FDR.

One day the story made the rounds of the White House about how FDR had given Simmons an acting lesson. He asked Simmons if he'd like to be President for a while.

Simmons was speechless, thinking FDR had gone mad. But FDR laughed and told Simmons to sit down, putting his pince-nez glasses on his receptionist's nose. Simmons was very nervous when FDR jammed his famous cigarette holder between Simmons clenched teeth and said, "Now act like me."

Poor Bill managed a weak smile and bobbed his head around a little. "Again. Watch me," said FDR. Simmons tried again.

"Splendid," said FDR, laughing delightedly. "You are now *the President* on the train. I'm tired of waving at crowds." FDR then taught Simmons how to wave to the crowds and throw back his head and do all the things FDR did for the benefit of the throngs that assembled in every town and hamlet the presidential train passed through.

Nothing Is as It Seems

When people would tell me they had waited for hours and were rewarded by seeing the President wave to them as his special train passed through, I did not disillusion them. I let them have their dream. I didn't tell them that maybe they did and maybe it was just a mirage—a mirage named Bill Simmons.

In Their Majesties' Service

Few people realize how ready the backstairs crew is to do everything for a first lady. Actually, all she need do is lift her spoon to her mouth. There's someone to do everything else.

There are butlers to bring the food to the table—serve from the left, remove from the right. There is a doorman to open the door. There is an usher to escort in her next guest and introduce the guest to her. There's a housekeeper to receive her orders of the day and also dream up menus.

There are cooks and kitchen helpers galore.

There are people to pack and unpack suitcases, and to clean house.

There are housemen to look after male guests.

There are chauffeurs.

There are maids and personal maids.

When Eleanor Roosevelt came to the White House, she already had a personal maid to help her dress. Nor was she used to cleaning rooms, cooking, or looking after her husband. She had grown up pampered by servants, unlike other first ladies I had known, such as Mrs. Calvin Coolidge.

In fact, I would hazard an opinion that Eleanor was the least domestic first lady we have had, even up to and including today. Much is made of the fact that Eleanor Roosevelt had a tradition of serving scrambled eggs and sausages to all the guests at Sunday night suppers. Everyone assumed she cooked other things.

The truth of the matter was that Eleanor had, as a grown woman, taken cooking lessons, paying a good fee. But through disuse, she'd forgotten most of what she'd been taught and was timid about the rest. Her triumph was scrambled eggs, which everyone seemed to like, so she continued to make them. Besides, as she commented to us, it gave her a good feeling to be cooking and serving something herself.

Stirring would be a more appropriate word. She did not break the eggs at the table. The scrambled egg mix would be brought in by a butler, and Eleanor would scramble the eggs in the silver chafing dish, right at the table. That was the extent of her much-publicized cooking. It would be too hard to cook the sausages properly in the chafing dish, so those would be cooked in the kitchen and brought in by the butler.

Every Christmas holiday there would be one of the scrambled egg nights, but such a crowd of people gathered that it was too much for Eleanor to cope with. She would have a cook scramble a huge supply of eggs in a double boiler, and they would be rushed to the chafing dish as needed.

The personal maid who came with Eleanor in 1933 was Mary Foster. One of our first tragedies in the Roosevelt White House was her death soon after. A woman named Mabel Haley of Catlin, Virginia, was handpicked to take her place.

Mabel did everything. Mabel washed Eleanor's underwear, stored her dresses between wearings, found the dresses Eleanor decided to wear, made suggestions on which dress to wear, repaired and pressed her clothes and underwear every day. Made her bed. Kept her closets and dresser drawers in perfect shape.

Shopped. Made small Christmas gifts for Eleanor to give away. Ran errands. Rushed around, did a million things. Packed and unpacked her suitcases. Took her shoes—including the riding boots that would frequently be muddy from Eleanor's misadventures with her horse—to the bench in the attic where Irving Holly, a houseman, would make them like new. He even polished and shined the soles. Once Holly shined a pair of mine, and I almost fell on the floor because the soles were so slick.

It was true that Mabel did a lot of dirty work, but when she appeared among the other maids of the White House, she was treated with great care and caution because she had the ear of the First Lady. Nobody wanted to get in trouble with her—especially since it was the policy of Mrs. Roosevelt to fire servants who couldn't get along together, no matter who was right.

We knew why Eleanor had picked Mabel and sought her out. It was because Mabel already knew all of the family skeletons, having worked for the Roosevelts years before, when FDR was assistant secretary of the Navy. Mabel knew everything and was shocked by nothing.

She knew about Lucy Mercer's affair with FDR when Lucy was coming to the house on fashionable R Street off Connecticut Avenue to work as social secretary to Eleanor. Mabel told me what an irresistibly handsome rogue the Boss had been when he was still on his feet, even going out dancing without his wife. That was back in the days when Eleanor was still sleeping with her husband.

Mabel knew this because Eleanor had told her so, outright, when Eleanor was showing her around the rooms on the first day. They had come to the master bedroom, and Eleanor had pointed to the double bed and said, "You know, I sleep with my husband." It was Eleanor's way of explaining that she did not have a room of her own, and that Mabel would only have one bed to make.

Eleanor and Mabel had a perfect understanding and Eleanor trusted her personal maid completely. Around the White House you knew who was really important to Eleanor by noticing who Mabel looked after. We knew that Lorena Hickok, Eleanor's live-in friend, was especially important, because Mabel started doing Hicky's mending and washing her underwear. Hick, incidentally, was the only person around the White House who mended silk stockings. Even the maids threw theirs away rather than appear with mended runs.

But as the maids said, Hicky was unique.

Another thing a first lady didn't have to do was turn on the electric lights herself. A maid would go through the White House family rooms turning on the lights. Someone else would turn them on in the public rooms downstairs. Usually lights went on at five P.M.

We turned on all the lights except those in Mrs. Roosevelt's rooms. She loved the twilight in winter. She would say, "Come back and pull my blinds later," then sit, looking out the window.

And of course a first lady does not turn down her own bed. Or draw her bath. We maids ate supper at five. Eleanor would like to take her bath at six and have it be cool. Mabel would draw the water hot and go to dinner in the servants' dining room. By the time she was back, Eleanor would be bathing in water exactly suited to her. Afterwards, Mabel would take out the wet towels and put in fresh ones.

Eleanor loved bathing and took several baths a day. She loved to be immaculate. But she had met her match in Mabel. Mabel was more than immaculate.

In fact, she carried it to the point where it would amuse the rest of us—but sometimes, not Eleanor. Mabel hated to touch things. She was very germ conscious. She went to such extremes, that often she would use her elbow instead of her finger to ring for the elevator, so that she would not have to touch the button someone else had touched on her way to lunch or dinner. And her food had to be covered if she was a moment late in arriving at the dining room.

Eleanor didn't want anyone to be a bother to anyone else. She was very consistent about that, often hesitating to ask a servant to do something if that wasn't that person's specific job.

Incidentally, a first lady's clothes are not put away after a wearing until they have been pressed. That way they are always ready for the next wearing.

As maids came and went, almost every one of us got a turn now and then to take care of Eleanor Roosevelt. For several years, it was usually Margaret Sykes who filled in when Mabel was on vacation or had a day off.

Mabel married while at the White House and became Mabel Webster. It was her second marriage. Eleanor became so fond of her, that when Mabel's son by her previous marriage died, Eleanor went to the funeral. The son had been studying to be a minister and had contracted TB. Eleanor had been warned that she would be the only white person attending, but she didn't care.

It endeared her to us forever after. In the 30s it was almost unheard of for a white woman to appear at an all-black gathering of any kind. And this was a first lady.

But this did not blind us to her flaws. She was too fussy at times. The lady who did not have to lift a finger at the White

House because of her small army of servants was quick to complain the one time she found some dust in her own room.

Once in a while she'd get on her high horse, and like a top sergeant, go charging around, doing the equivalent of a white glove inspection.

I still have one of Eleanor's *My Day* columns, which starts off, "THURSDAY—I have just made the rounds of every room in the White House with Mrs. Nesbitt, the housekeeper. We even inspected the third floor..." The column goes on to tell how, when the grandchildren are in residence on the third floor, she tells Mrs. Nesbitt "to get in touch with the nurses to find out what food should be ordered for the various children..."

All of this special food was a financial burden to the Roosevelts. We used to marvel at how Eleanor spoiled everyone and didn't make them bring their own special foods or just eat standard baby foods.

From the very start, my own mother, Maggie Rogers, head maid of the White House, was in a position to get to know Eleanor Roosevelt very well. She was one of two maids taking care of the second floor living quarters at the time the Roosevelts came to the White House.

Mama Maggie took care of the West End, and Katurah Brooks took care of the East End. Mama's most important job was to take care of Eleanor Roosevelt's room. Eleanor's bedroom was directly over the State Dining Room. The President's room, near hers, was above the Red Room. The President also used the second floor Oval Room as his study.

Actually, there are three oval rooms in the White House, four, if you include the Oval Office used by modern presidents. However, the Oval Office is not in the White House proper but in the West Wing, which was added on and connects with a long, glassed-in passageway. The three I am talking about begin on the ground floor with the Diplomatic Entrance. This is the South Entrance to the White House, and years after the Roosevelts, First Lady Jacqueline Kennedy would paper it with old historic wallpaper that had been scraped off the walls of a Virginia estate.

Then on the first floor, the public floor of the White House, is the oval Blue Room, often used for reception lines during formal entertainment and for the huge annual Christmas tree donated by a different state every year. FDR's oval study, where he ate many of his meals and entertained his friends at cocktails, was directly above this room.

Mama did not have to take care of the President's bedroom because FDR was so fond of Lizzie McDuffie, the wife of his valet, that he wanted only her to have free access to his bedroom. They had known each other a long time—from the New York days—and he had no secrets from her.

Lizzie treated FDR like one of her own family, kidding him and teasing him by kissing the bald spot on top of his head. Since she knew all his secrets, she also took care of Missy LeHand's bedroom suite, which was not too far away on the third floor.

Missy dashed up and down between the President's suite and her own and presided at his afternoon cocktail parties, often eating dinner with him alone in the Oval study.

Katurah, Maggie, and Lizzie knew and saw everything but kept silent outside of the White House. When the family went to Hyde Park, Katurah and Lizzie followed, but Mama, as head maid, stayed to look after the family quarters. Someone had to be ready to take care of Mrs. R, who would show up suddenly from her travels at any time of the day or night, and someone had to be there who knew how the family wanted drop-in guests to be treated.

Anyway, Lizzie preferred to go to Hyde Park, since Mac, her husband, was going to be there. And let's face it, she preferred to be wherever the President was. FDR counted on Lizzie for her sense of humor, her sense of the outrageous. Even when he had guests—the old intimate friends, that is—FDR might send for Lizzie to liven things up a bit. Lizzie had show biz in her veins so she loved it. She had two Early-Muppet-style dolls and she would put on a show using various voices.

One of the dolls was named Suicide and the other, Jezebel. FDR loved their fights and misadventures and roared with laughter.

Lizzie McDuffy was well-read, a graduate of Morris Brown University at Atlanta. I think this is one of the things that annoyed

Henrietta Nesbitt, the housekeeper, who didn't like anyone knowing more than she did. Lizzie tried to tease Henrietta, but the housekeeper did not have her sense of humor. Lizzie would take everything seriously and just be annoyed.

Also, it may have galled Mrs. Nesbitt that Lizzie had such influence with the Roosevelts and would take it upon herself to bring in certain famous black entertainers for some of the formal parties. I seem to recall that Todd Duncan was one who came because of his friendship with Lizzie.

Temporarily, this put Mrs. Nesbitt in an inferior position as simply the housekeeper, instead of the friend of the honored guest and entertainer.

FDR also had every service. They lifted him into bed. They lifted him out of bed. Into chairs, out of chairs, into cars, trains. They handed him his toothbrush with paste on it, his shaving gear. Turned down his bed. Sat with him. Ran his errands. Made his phone calls. Handed him anything out of reach—and everything was. Forced themselves to stay awake.

Eventually, two valets had nervous breakdowns in "his majesty's service." Even to the end, sick as they were, they worked devotedly and loved the Boss very much.

FDR was that kind of man. You loved him or you hated him. We, who worked around him and for him, loved him.

Irvin McDuffie was the one who helped the President with his crawling exercises. This was a self-help program that made the President feel less panicky about escaping in case of fire or enemy attack. FDR had powerful shoulders and he gave them a good workout. McDuffie said FDR never wanted his wife or children to see him crawling, so the exercises were super secret.

Why didn't he just rely on crutches for emergencies? Because they weren't absolutely safe if he lost his balance. Once, behind the scenes, FDR had been walking to the podium on crutches at a public event, and he had fallen. He joked with those who helped him up, but the inside story was that he was very upset. He never relied on crutches again.

FDR had gotten acquainted with McDuffie and his wife Lizzie when he started going to Warm Springs for his polio. McDuffie had been a successful barber, and he had given up his shop to hitch his wagon to FDR's star. They were more than valet and President—they were confidants.

McDuffie knew everything about FDR and loved him more for it. Lizzie came to be trusted with all of FDR's secrets as well, and she was warm and motherly with him. The McDuffies were among the few people who always knew the state of FDR's romances with Lucy Mercer and Missy LeHand, and they protected him from any prying eyes—especially Eleanor's.

We could see that the strain of taking care of FDR and being on twenty-four-hour call was taking a terrible toll on McDuffie. He started to drink to calm his nerves. One night, though, relaxed from a few too many drinks, McDuffie didn't hear FDR's bell. FDR happened to be all alone for a little while, and by the time he was rescued, he was terribly upset. Someone went to McDuffie's room and found him zonked out and asleep. The next day he was terribly sorry. FDR forgave him, but Eleanor heard of it and had a conference with some of her sons and decided McDuffie was no longer reliable enough—and worst of all, could not to be counted on—in an emergency.

It was the beginning of the end for McDuffie. He had worked for ten years around the clock for FDR, and suddenly in 1939, his career with Roosevelt was over.

Eleanor wasn't unhappy to get rid of McDuffie, because she knew his only loyalty was to Franklin.

The second valet to have his health broken from the long hours and utter fatigue of serving a president trying to keep his wheelchair condition a secret was a man very close to Mama and me. The reason I knew him so well is that he lived with Mama and me—in our house, that is—for seventeen years. He was originally from San Juan, Puerto Rico.

Cesar Carrera was one of the finest men I ever knew, and one of the most interesting. He was proof that having a menial household job didn't preclude refinement and culture. Cesar started out at the White House as only a houseman, but he was a graduate of Tuskegee and had been involved in the Sears Art Gallery before going to the White House.

At first we arranged for him to work in the White House Cloak Room at evening parties, but the housekeeper, Henrietta

Nesbitt, was so impressed with his knowledge and personality that she tried to steal him away from the gallery—and succeeded. One of the housemen got sick and Nesbitt hired him as a permanent replacement. Eventually he took Maggie's place. My mother had been head maid, but Cesar was called head houseman though his job was to supervise all the second and third floor maids.

When Cesar suffered his nervous breakdown and was taken to Bethesda Naval Hospital, President Roosevelt arranged for a Navy man to sit by him around the clock. The reason was twofold. He wanted to make sure Cesar was well-treated, and even more important, that he did not leak secrets.

The possible leakage of White House secrets was always a problem. I think we kept the Roosevelt secrets well, and though we talked among ourselves, we did not talk to outsiders. Though I wrote a book in 1961 about my life in the White House, *My Thirty Years Backstairs at the White House,* I did not decide to reveal the real secrets of the Roosevelts until their own children started talking.

Cesar recovered from his breakdown, but had to take time off to rest, and Roosevelt, who had grown very fond of him, said that if he needed a change of pace, he could have a job in any place in the world where there were American offices.

He decided to go to Puerto Rico and held a job in a post office there. He didn't like it as much as he thought he would and came back to Washington. But he still wasn't strong enough for the White House, and he went to work in a Washington post office instead.

At last, love came into his life when he met Louise Proctor, a practical nurse at St. Elizabeth's Hospital. At this point Cesar was again living with me and Mama, who was, by then, retired. When he and Louise married, they moved into an apartment. After mother died I lived alone.

I missed the pleasant life we all had together. Therefore it was a red letter day for me when Cesar and Louise came to tell me that they were buying a two-family house so that we could all be a family again.

How wonderful it was that first year in the lovely little house. But it was too good to last. Cesar, that wonderful man, would sit at the window looking at the flowers outside and say, "Lillian, I am memorizing God's real life painting for when I must go to the hospital." He died of cancer before the year was quite up, and I still look out the window at God's painting. Louise and I continue to share the house.

After Cesar's health broke and he said goodbye forever to the White House, two men took his place as valet to the President. Never again would just one man be on twenty-four-hour duty until he collapsed from exhaustion.

Katurah Brooks had no intention of working until she dropped in her tracks. She eventually got tired of bouncing back and forth between Hyde Park and the White House like a bouncing ball. And she wearied of the long White House hours— a ten-hour day was standard. Her husband, Phil, encouraged her to give it up as well, so she suddenly transferred to the Bureau of Engraving for an "eight-to-four," as we called cushy government jobs.

FDR had no qualms about getting involved in the lives of his household staff. Now and then he would take a minute to make sure I was all right, and he would even ask, "Are you happy, little girl? Are you being treated all right? We have to stick together, you know."

His concern, I knew, was due to that crutch he saw me using, but he would get interested in anyone who looked unhappy, too. Once the President had an attendant he particularly liked, but who always acted upset on the same day of every week. FDR had an aide he trusted do a little sleuthing and learned that a woman was at the bottom of it. Every time he saw this particular girl he would fall apart. Roosevelt had him temporarily transferred to another job in another state, and when FDR heard, from his own sources, that the fellow had gotten over his infatuation and was dating other women, he brought him back to Washington. Soon he was dating a Washington girl and he married her and lived happily every after. End of story.

And FDR was simply delighted and bragged to his cronies when Lizzie McDuffie was being considered for the role of Scarlett's maid in *Gone with the Wind*. I do believe the Boss arranged for her to have the audition. At any rate, he gave her time off to make her screen test.

For a glorious few hours, we all thought she had gotten the role because it was announced over the radio that the White House had produced a new star. But the report was a mistake, and Lizzie settled back down to making beds and trading fruit for flowers.

It's hard to realize today that there was a time when in fine homes like the White House, guests were provided with a bowl of fruit in their rooms at night, as a routine thing. By day, there would be flowers, and each night, when the maids turned down the beds, the flowers would be put outside the room, and the bowl of fruit substituted. Ah well.

After McDuffie's nervous breakdown, Lizzie lost her White House quarters and became a day worker, just like me.

One day Lizzie, in a rare serious and even melancholy conversation with the Boss, told the President that if there was life after death, in the way Hindus believed, she would pray to return to earth as a canary.

By strange coincidence, this was the last day of the President's life. Lizzie would talk about it afterwards. She had been standing in the doorway of his bedroom at Warm Springs, that morning of April 12, 1945, and FDR, with the morning newspaper in his hands, had paused to engage her in conversation, as he frequently did.

At first FDR had looked at her with dismay, almost a haunted look, as if pondering why she or anyone would want to be a caged creature. His own dream, as she well knew, was to rise from the wheelchair and be free.

Then the President got tickled at the thought of Lizzie, who was no canary but firmly earthbound with much excess weight, seeing herself as a tiny bird, and he started laughing. Lizzie could never get insulted at the President making fun of her, and she joined his laughter.

But then, after he was through joking and pointing at her rotund figure, Lizzie again became serious and asked FDR if he believed in reincarnation. He looked at her and grew quiet. Lizzie waited for his answer. He seemed not to want to answer. Instead, he asked Lizzie if *she* believed in reincarnation.

Confronted with the question, Lizzie felt strange. She said she didn't know.

The moment was over. The mood changed. FDR, still thoughtful, lifted his newspaper and resumed reading.

I always wondered what his answer would have been, what he was really thinking. And I often wondered how it happened that on his last day, Lizzie, who was so close to the President, was thinking about reincarnation.

It was eerie.

The Backstairs Gang

We were like a family, we maids and housemen and butlers, sometimes sharing a laugh and sometimes sharing a tear. One day found us comforting a maid whose husband had committed suicide. He had been despondent, and a friend had taken him for a ride to cheer him up. As they crossed the Anacostia River, the maid's husband opened the car door and leaped out, jumping into the water. Some fishermen tried to save him but he fought them off.

That's what had hurt her the most—he had *wanted* to drown.

Servants were used to shocks. Once a maid opened a door only to see a male guest involved in oral sex with a female guest—not his wife. Another time, a servant opened a door of another male guest and found a nude woman casually walking around. We always knocked on doors but some people just didn't care.

Before the White House got the good idea of making a real motion picture theater out of the old cloak room in the East Wing, we had a projection screen installed in the archway of the Center Hall of the family quarters on the second floor. FDR and some of his guests would watch a movie, sitting in the Center Hall, facing toward the West Hall. They didn't know that we, the help, had already seen the movie and that it was old hat to us. The day of the showing, Johnson, the electrician, would test run the movie and he would send word around. We would drop anything we were doing and rush to watch, dust rag in hand or sewing in our laps.

I remember when the movie was "It Happened One Night," with Clark Gable and Claudette Colbert. When Gable stripped to his underwear, Mrs. Nesbitt, the housekeeper, got so indignant that she jumped up and left in a huff.

We doubled over in laughter and it added to our already overflowing supply of Nesbitt stories.

Nothing Is as It Seems

There was a lot of gambling going at the White House, both in the servants quarters and upstairs on the family floor. Harry Hopkins, when he lived on the second floor, had the racing form delivered every day. The cooks sat at the kitchen table studying the racing form and the racing news in the daily newspaper.

I placed my own bets on the public telephone at the White House. Some, like me, played the horses, and some played the numbers as well. There was one horse I watched from its birth, because it had been born with a bad foot. Since I used a crutch, I could sympathize with Assault's attempt to measure up to and be better than any other horse.

The Trumans had followed the Roosevelts into the White House, and Assault was scheduled to run in the Kentucky Derby. I was as thrilled as if I had triumphed over my crutches. Margaret Truman had been invited to the Kentucky Derby, and Julia Sharp, one of the maids, was helping her pack.

I told Julia to tell Margaret to be sure to bet on Assault. "Tell her I said so," I said. But Margaret took the advice of her hosts and bet on a different horse. Assault won.

In Eleanor's day, we had very little money for luxuries like sending furniture out to be cleaned or hiring cleaning services to come to the White House to do a professional job. We just learned to cope.

I remember when a dignitary was arriving from South America, and at nearly the last minute, housekeeper Henrietta Nesbitt discovered a large stain on the sofa in the honored guest's suite. We had so many guests, it was hard to keep track of the condition of all the furniture between visits.

Henrietta asked me to do something, and fast. I grabbed some old wash cloths and got to work with cleaning fluid. The sofa turned out so well that two other maids, Wilma and Julia, caught the fever and started cleaning sofas in other rooms.

Only a few of the help lived in. The rest of us descended on the White House daily from every corner of town. Mama and I had to arrive by 7:30 A.M. in order to have breakfast before starting work.

We ate better than the first family at breakfast time—eggs

and bacon always. Sausage now and then. Scrapple sometimes. Always several kinds of toast and jelly. Hot cereal daily—oatmeal, cream of wheat. Sometimes even pancakes.

About fourteen of us maids and housemen ate in the servant's dining room. The butlers ate in the pantry because they were on duty and had to take trays to rooms. They would eat on the run. Only on special occasions would they take turns on duty and eat with us. When they did they were most welcome because they brought lots of news concerning the personal lives of the First Family—the comings and goings of children and in-laws. In turn, we shared any funny or surprising tidbit we knew.

Once the report was that Franklin Jr. had complained to his mother that his bed had not been properly made and that the bottom sheet had not been tight enough. White House beds were important, of course, and they were made to look beautiful every day. Katurah Brooks and Margaret Sykes were the best at this fine art, and everyone else was trained to be at least excellent at making a bed, so we laughed off FDR Jr.'s complaint as that of a spoiled darling—just an amusing White House anecdote to pass along. "Hey, did you hear, Junior may get us all fired for incompetence in the bedroom?"

The cooks ate at their own table in the kitchen. Lunch was our big meal. We ate at twelve o'clock sharp because the family ate at one, and some of us would be needed to serve them.

Again, we were sure that aside from state dinners, we servants had the best meals at the White House. Lunch might be roast beef, pork, stewed chicken, or baked ham. On Friday we always had fish. Every day we had hot vegetables and various pies and ice creams for dessert.

Summer we had watermelon, which I didn't eat. I would be accused of being prejudiced against Negroes—a little ethnic joke.

One cook was a whiz at spoon bread, and she would frequently make it for us. One day Harry Hopkins, who was living at the White House, shocked us by popping into our dining room at lunchtime. We thought he had taken a wrong turn and was lost. No, indeed, he assured us. The odor of the chicken we were eating had driven him crazy, and he was wondering if he could have that instead of what they had sent for his lunch upstairs. The smiling cooks fixed him up with some doggy bags and off he went, taking chicken and all the fixings.

I don't know how the maids dress at the White House now, but in Eleanor Roosevelt's time, the rule was white uniform with black shoes in the daytime. For evening, it was black taffeta uniform with white collar and cuffs and organdy embroidered apron. We thought we looked pretty good.

In the old days before World War II, no lady was seen walking outside her home without a hat. All of us wore hats and gloves to work daily. Mrs. Nesbitt was the first to break precedent. When she stopped wearing her hat to work, we maids almost had a fit. It was indecent. Soon we saw in the papers that Rosie the Riveter was going to her wartime job wearing a scarf around her head instead of a hat—it was the new badge of the war worker.

Henrietta Nesbitt was a mystery to us from day one. We used to kid each other and say, "How did we get so lucky?" Ava Long, her predecessor, had been skillful at handling a huge staff and it was a smooth operation. Suddenly it all changed.

Mrs. Long was out as housekeeper, and Henrietta Nesbitt took over, bringing with her—a husband. Mrs. Nesbitt didn't know beans about running a White House. She had just been a lady who ran a bakery in Dutchess County, New York, where she met Governor and Mrs. Roosevelt.

She would send over boxes of little cakes to help FDR's gubernatorial campaign.

And the mighty tree from the little cookies grew. When the Roosevelts moved to the Governor's Mansion, they sent for some of her baked goods. Mr. Nesbitt was unemployed and Henrietta had to earn a living for both of them.

This was just the kind of situation that brought out the mother in Eleanor. She gave Mr. Nesbitt the job of keeping track of the food supplies at the White House, handling the time sheets of the household help, and making sure the Interior Department, which paid us, sent the right pay.

Poor Mr. Nesbitt did not live too long after they came to the White House, but Mrs. Nesbitt survived the whole Roosevelt administration and continued to work a while for Mrs. Truman, who had considerable trouble letting her know who was boss. Eleanor Roosevelt had no interest in being the boss of the White House and she was perfectly content to delegate all responsibility to Henrietta. The only trouble was that Henrietta had little idea of what needed doing, but had a huge ego. She simply had to have her own way. Our only defense was to ignore her and do what we knew was right. But she was a perfect demon about checking up on us to make sure we were doing something wrong.

For example, Mrs. Nesbitt decreed that maids could no longer carry feather dusters. She did not like their looks. However, that was the only way we could dust the tops of highboys and chiffoniers. She would catch us hiding the feather dusters. We brought them out when she wasn't looking.

Getting around Mrs. Nesbitt became a way of life. When Madame Chiang Kai-shek came to the White House without her husband, she brought two nurses with her, since she did nothing on a small scale. She was going to hold a press conference with the ladies of the press in spite of how she felt.

Mrs. Nesbitt gave me instructions on how the Monroe Room was to look for this press conference. I was told to arrange three pillows on the sofa to help support Madame Chiang and make it easy on her anatomy.

I could not believe that this woman would want people to know that she didn't feel well, and so I checked it out with the nurse. The nurse told me that Madame Chiang would certainly not want the pillows until after the press had gone.

I went back to the housekeeper and told her what the nurse said.

Mrs. Nesbitt said, "I don't care what she said. Put them on the sofa anyhow."

I said I was sure that Madame Chiang Kai-shek didn't wish to appear as an invalid at her press conference, but Mrs. Nesbitt waved me off and said, "Hurry and put them on."

I hurried, but I didn't put the pillows there and nothing was ever said about it.

Another time Mrs. Nesbitt went in the opposite direction and decreed that a certain Latin chief of state did not warrant the best bed linen. She told us, "Don't bother to put the good linen sheets

Nothing Is as It Seems

on the beds for these people." We knew that Mrs. Nesbitt was bigoted and that her only reason for the order was because the man's skin was brown. Around Mrs. Roosevelt she would not have dared to let her prejudice show, but she knew she was safe because we wouldn't squeal on her.

We maids simply looked at each other then marched right into the guest room and put on the finest sheets we could find. But it was Cesar, a fellow Latin, who went out of his way to have the last word, though it was a subtle one.

When the honored guest came, Cesar simply took one of the man's shirts into Mrs. Nesbitt's office and said, "Isn't this the finest linen you've ever seen?"

Mrs. Nesbitt just looked and went, "Humpf," but she got his point.

We just never knew what she was going to dream up next. One time she got carried away and spent a small fortune on special, finest quality sheets, buying 144 of them, to take care of only three or four beds, which required special king size sheets. The fine, hemstitched, percale sheets were more than twice the cost of ordinary sheets at the time.

Those among the help who did not cotton to Mrs. Nesbitt kept their feelings well hidden, but this was not the case with Mrs. Nesbitt, who let her dislikes show, especially in the case of Lizzie, the maid.

It did not help the atmosphere that Lizzie felt she could afford to ignore the housekeeper's directives. Lizzie liked to make full use of working in the White House to meet the beautiful and powerful people of the world, and so she would, against Nesbitt's orders, stand on the first floor with a pincushion in her hand, watching them come and go. The pin cushion was nicely displayed so that guests would assume she was there to help them if a shoulder strap should break or a button pop.

I don't know if one ever did but the next day Lizzie would be laughing and bragging about all the famous people she had met.

All of the White House maids were black. The first thing Eleanor Roosevelt did upon entering the White House in March of 1933 was to decree that all household workers would be Negro.

The white maids she fired—Nora and Annie—were devastated. They had worked with Mama in the second floor family quarters. And there were also about six other various cooks and backstairs helpers.

It was the first time it was great to be black. It meant you could hang on to your job at the White House. Everyone let go was helped to find another job somewhere in government or in the city of Washington. Annie got a good job with a foreign embassy. Everyone ended up somewhere in a good position.

All of the maids and black cooks who had kinky hair had a monthly standing date at their beauty parlors to get their hair straightened. I sometimes wonder what Eleanor Roosevelt would have thought of Afro hairdos. It's just a thought!

She probably wouldn't have minded how we wore our hair, as long as it was neat. But no girl with pride would think of letting her hair get nappy or frizzy, even though it was a burden to have it straightened on the small Depression-time salary we received—a salary that was cut still further during one of FDR's economy binges.

I was lucky that I didn't need to have my hair ironed. Since I had Indian blood, my hair was only slightly wavy. My maternal grandmother was a Cherokee Indian.

Not only did the Roosevelts have only black servants at the White House, but the President also had a black cook at Warm Springs. She was Daisy Bonner, and she lived for the times he came to Warm Springs, because then she could be near him. He was very fond of her, too, and he would have long conversations with her in a way he didn't have time for with the help at the White House.

Daisy cooked for FDR from the time he built his Little White House in Warm Springs until he died 20 years later. She served his first meal there, and his last meal, on April 12, 1945. She lived exactly fifteen years longer and died in the same month, April, as her hero.

Eleanor had her favorite maid. FDR had his. Bluette was Eleanor's. Lizzie was FDR's.

We never knew what Lizzie would be up to next. Hollywood, Hyde Park, Warm Springs. She moved around.

Once Lizzie McDuffie decided she was a great campaigner and insisted on going out to make speeches for FDR among the blacks. It was her own idea, but FDR didn't stop her.

Backstairs, as we did her work as well as our own, we muttered that Lizzie was probably disobeying the Hatch Act and would probably get herself arrested for campaigning for a *certain* candidate while being paid by the government. The Hatch Act had passed in 1936.

It didn't happen. Nothing happened except that Lizzie's stock was soon even higher with Franklin Roosevelt, while Mrs. Nesbitt fumed.

We noticed in the papers that when Lizzie was campaigning, she was called "Special Assistant to the White House." We teased her a lot for that, telling her we didn't know whether we dared ask a "Special Assistant" to make a bed. She would just laugh good-naturedly. She had a most wonderful personality that kept her on an even keel and cheerful, even in the dark days of her husband's illness.

FDR once said to her, "Doll, I swear I see that halo you're wearing."

FDR gave one of his canes to Lizzie McDuffie, and she was very proud of it because he parted with precious few from his collection. Many of his dearest friends and cronies would have given an eyetooth for one of them.

Bluette was a part-timer, then a regular, then a live-in. Bluette's husband had worked in the Oval Office in the West Wing, serving many Presidents. He died suddenly and left some debts behind. A colleague of the husband got the bright idea of asking Mrs. Nesbitt if she could give Bluette just six months' work to clear up the debts.

She remained ten years, a lovely, elderly lady whom everyone leaned on. Mrs. Roosevelt liked her so much that in 1937, when Diana Hopkins moved in, Eleanor asked Bluette to live-in and sleep on the third floor where she would be handy in case little Diana Hopkins needed something in the night.

Diana's father wanted her to be independent, even though Diana was only five when she came to the White House. But Eleanor could not be that severe and felt Diana needed some mothering.

Even Lorena Hickok, Eleanor's special friend, leaned on Bluette and felt great affection for her. Hickok would never ring the bell for service, but she didn't have to anyway when Bluette was around because Bluette could almost read her mind and bring her whatever she needed before she asked.

Hickok, with her great sense of humor, named her car after their favorite maid, and she and Eleanor would often be riding around in the car called Bluette. I don't believe Bluette ever knew she had been so honored. Bluette was sweet and gentle, but she did not share their kind of humor.

When Katurah, Mama's second floor helper, left, Ella Sampson came to work and live-in at the White House. She was actually an out-of-work schoolteacher and she was—and is—a lovely looking woman with fine features and a regal air.

When my mother Maggie retired in 1939, a pretty little spitfire named Margaret Sykes replaced her. Eleanor Roosevelt took a liking to her for her spirit and her fine mind, and always took an interest in her welfare, even helping her get jobs in the New York area after the White House years. One job I know of had to do with helping problem boys in a special school.

Margaret had the kind of personality that made her a favorite around the White House. She and Ella formed a fast friendship that continues today.

Margaret really hit the work jackpot when she came to the White House. It was just when we were getting ready to receive the King and Queen of England—George VI and Elizabeth. Maggie was supposed to have left before the visit, but Mrs. Roosevelt asked her to stay until after the royal visit, and gave her Margaret to help her. "Bring Margaret in now so she can get used to excitement," Mrs. Roosevelt said. And excitement she had.

The royal couple required constant work and attention. Backstairs they, and their entourage, who we also attended to, were quickly labeled "a royal pain." Even Eleanor frowned when she received orders on how the royal beds were to be made. I recall she pretty well ignored the edicts, but I saved them for laughs:

Nothing Is as It Seems

"The King prefers two lightweight blankets covered with a silken coverlet. At the foot of his bed should be placed a down puff, not folded but pushed in the manner of accordion pleats.

"The Queen also prefers two lightweight blankets covered with a silken coverlet but she does not care for the down puff. Instead she prefers a second silken coverlet placed at the foot of her bed with one corner folded back to form a triangle."

I remember the maids looked at the directions and said, "What are they talking about?" and "This makes no sense," and it made still less sense when the ladies-in-waiting arrived at the White House in the sweltering June heat carrying the King's and Queen's personal water bottles.

When Katurah was leaving the White House, Mrs. Roosevelt said, in words so typical of her, "What can I do for you? Would you like money or would you rather I make something for you?"

Katurah said, "Money I would spend, but if I had something you had given me, I would have it forever." She thought she would get one of Eleanor's famous hand-knit sweaters, but when the time came to say goodbye, the First Lady gave her a lovely wooden bowl that had been made at her Val-Kill factory.

When Mother left, not too much later, Eleanor gave her a beautiful gold watch from herself and the President, with Mama's name and "30 years faithful service" inscribed—the last six of which had been with the Roosevelts. After Mama had been retired for some time, Eleanor Roosevelt invited her to come to Hyde Park as a guest. Mama wasn't feeling well enough and declined. It's the one thing missing from her career as head maid. It would have been such a triumph. I know how nice it would have been for her because Mays was invited on another occasion and came back saying, "I can't believe the royal treatment I got. The woman is a saint. She makes no distinction between black guests and white."

I was partially responsible for at least one happy ending at the White House. It concerns a distant cousin of mine, Wilma Hughes. It started when a maid left the White House, and Mrs. Nesbitt thought she would like to hire a young girl to take her place because she would be easier to train, being young and pliable. Henrietta said, as she brought a mere slip of a girl to me,

The Backstairs Gang

"Lillian, give her a uniform and tell her to keep her mouth shut and not tell anything she sees or hears about the family."

In this case, I don't think the girl would have understood enough to blab any secrets about the White House. She couldn't get the hang of anything I tried to teach her, and she chewed gum so loudly that a houseman in another room once called in to ask her to please stop.

Time and again I reminded the girl that nobody who works in the White House chews gum on duty, but five minutes later she would forget and start chewing again.

A real disaster occurred when she brought the navy blue crepe dress that the new Mrs. Harry Hopkins had just worn for her marriage ceremony into the sewing room to press before putting it away. I told the girl to be sure to use the pressing cloth and went ahead with whatever I was doing. The girl put a hot iron on the dress without a pressing cloth and it burned a hole right through.

I was beside myself but there was nothing I could do. The new Mrs. Hopkins didn't say a word but I could tell she was hurt. Later I heard that she had wanted so save her wedding dress. It took four months for Mrs. Nesbitt to agree to get rid of the new girl and to admit that not everyone young is trainable. She sighed and suggested I pick the next replacement. I suggested my cousin Wilma Hughes, and she was hired.

Meanwhile Ivan and Katy Holness, who had worked for Anna Roosevelt at the White House and elsewhere, came back from Seattle and bought a home. They had gone there with Anna after she married John Boettiger but had not liked the troubled atmosphere.

Instead of coming back to the White House full time, Ivan got a job in the Treasury Department and then at the World Bank, but served at White House parties as an extra waiter. In this way, he got to know Wilma. After his wife died, Wilma and he eventually got married. Both later retired—Wilma after 34 years at the White House—and had a lovely home.

As I was editing this book, I received word that Wilma's husband, Ivan, had just died. And almost at the same time came a message that my brother Emmett Rogers, who had served as a lieutenant in France in World War I, had died in Coronado, California.

As a child, Emmett had worked at the White House as a yard boy, during the Wilson administration. He became a fine linguist in French and Spanish and married a Peruvian girl, Fidelia Galardo, who also took pride in a Roosevelt connection. She arranged and cooked for the parties of the Roosevelt sons—James and John—when they resided in Coronado, California, with their wives during the war.

Her big moment came when FDR, himself, had visited Coronado and she served him. On learning that Fidelia was "Little Lillian's" sister-in-law, he asked her, "Why aren't you working for the government?"

My sister-in-law replied, "Because I'm busy taking care of your children, Mr. President."

And right on the heels of all the bad news came good news. Alonzo Fields, former maitre d' and brother of valet George Fields, was marrying again, after losing his wife of many years, Edna. I received an invitation to the wedding and to meet the new bride, Mayland McLaughlin, in Medford, Massachusetts.

I sent a note telling my old friend how happy I was at his newfound happiness and put off meeting his bride until I had recovered from the sadness of my own loss.

There were other marriages involving the White House gang backstairs. Charles Ficklin, the chief butler, or maitre d', who replaced Alonzo Fields, married early in the Roosevelt administration.

It was hard for a man who had a high position in the running of the White House to adjust to his own marital household. Charles would come into my sewing room, fold his arms, and sit at the sewing table. I knew he wasn't happy. We would talk things over and I would tell him how women think. I remember he wanted to buy a better house and was working long hours doing extra work in private homes to get up the down payment.

This meant he spent very little time at home and he couldn't understand why his wife wasn't delighted with this situation because, after all, it was to benefit her as well.

The White House staff still has a Butler's Club that caters to social Washington in its spare time. A hostess is very proud to hire a White House butler for a party, and of course, he is the best trained helper she could find.

I remember when Mrs. Eisenhower was most annoyed about the fact that White House butlers were busy around Chevy Chase and Foxhall Road. She told her housekeeper, "Mrs. Walker, everywhere I go I see my butlers working. Can't you stop these men from leaving the White House at night and going to these parties?"

Mrs. Walker said, "I'm sorry, Mrs. Eisenhower, we don't have anything to do with their lives when they leave here."

Eleanor Roosevelt was too busy to worry about what her bulters were doing in their off-hours. But had she complained, they had the perfect answer for her already. Her husband had cut their salaries as part of his economy drive, and they were most annoyed.

When war broke out, the White House butlers and housemen were as patriotic as anyone else. I remember so vividly when butler Armstead Barnett and valet George Fields went marching off, and how thrilled we were when each came marching back in one piece. Armstead continued as a butler, but George Fields came to the White House only to pick up his things. He transferred to Chicago, where he married a very nice girl named "Gonni" Gonzalez. We have remained friends through the years, and I have visited them in Chicago.

Armstead Barnett retired some time after the Roosevelts were gone from the White House and opened a most profitable catering business. He married Viola Carpenter, who was a part-time helper at the White House, and we all are still friends.

Another butler, Charles Ficklin, eventually retired on disability. He lived a year in the house I share with the widow of FDR's valet Cesar. In fact, he presided at my seventy-fifth birthday party, at which I was surrounded by my whole White House backstairs crowd, all telling stories on each other. I told about the day Charles Ficklin had deserted me on the roof of the White House. He had escorted me up to watch one of the many parades and had said, "I'll be right back to get you."

Nothing Is as It Seems

He forgot. I waited and waited. I looked at the iron steps that went straight down and hated to think of having to navigate those with crutches. They were used only by Eddie, the engineer who came up daily to raise the flag.

In Roosevelt's day, the flag on the White House meant the President was in residence. Eddie would watch from the rooftop for the President to enter the White House, and the moment his wheelchair rolled under the South Portico, up the flag would go. The war in 1941 ended this practice because it was feared the enemy would know when the President was home and when he wasn't. So the flag was kept flying daily.

At any rate, I eventually descended from the roof—an inch at a time—and never let Ficklin forget it. At the party, he was still protesting that he was really coming up to get me, but had been detained by the President.

Speaking of flags, I remember that Mama used to be the maid who mended the frayed flags after the wind had whipped and shredded them. In my time, they had changed to a kind of flag that was a little less destructible. In the White House, we so respected the flag, whether anyone was watching or not, that we never let it touch the floor.

I remember when, one day, Mrs. Nesbitt brought a flag to me to be ironed. She said, "And be sure not to let it touch the floor." I stood there looking at her and feeling hurt to be reminded. Before I could come up with a retort, another maid said, "But, Mrs. Nesbitt, Lillian learned that in the cradle."

Charles Ficklin died in March of 1978. His brother, John, another wonderful man, is now maitre d' at the White House.

John Mays, the doorman, though tall and dignified, could always be counted on for a laugh, and once the laugh was on him. He had gotten married, and soon after he came to work with a long face. He walked into my sewing room muttering to himself.

"What's troubling you, Mays?" I asked.

"Would you believe my wife expects me to wash windows?"

The shock in his voice broke us all up, and indeed, the thought of the elegant White House doorman washing windows was hilarious.

P.S. He didn't wash the windows.

Because of his height, Mays was enlisted during the next administration of President Truman in a little practical joke on Margaret Truman and her friends. They were spending the night in the Lincoln bedroom to be able to talk about it to their school chums.

Good old Harry wanted them to have something they could really talk about. There was a White House ghost story that now and then Lincoln's ghost stood staring out the window of his bedroom. Mays was supposed to put on a Lincoln-style tall hat and stand at the window, and Harry, himself, would make a noise in the hall to awaken the girls.

Mays told us later, with a long serious face, that he didn't think anyone would be dumb enough to mistake a black man for Lincoln, even in the dark. One of the maids asked him how he said no to a president. "I didn't say no," he said, "I was a no show— I took sick leave."

Speaking of Mays reminds me of Samuel Jackson, who came to work at about the same time as he, during Taft's administration. He, Mays, and Mama were dear friends. Mays and Jackson were both doormen when hired, but Jackson got shifted to the President's office to help look after his needs, holding the title of clerk. Jackson did all kinds of odd jobs for FDR, running errands that the President wouldn't trust anyone else to do, handling some mail, and even operating the mimeograph machine. Mama and Jackson were both members of Shiloh Baptist Church. I followed my own path and became an Episcopalian.

Jackson was so close to Mama that when she lay on her deathbed, he came and spent much time on his knees beside her bed. I choke up even now as I think of those two men, who were once so big a part of my life.

The Hidden Third Floor

The third floor was the place to be.

I worked in and around and spent time on every floor of the White House but nothing could compare with the third floor. It was like a little village. A hidden village. Even standing outside on the street, you would have to be an architect to know it is there, so well hidden is it by porticos and balustrades.

But it was there all right, and it was the hub. Everyone brought the news there. I would sit in my sewing room, sewing or mending, and know what was going on all over the house.

Mrs. Roosevelt's personal maid had a room there—first Mary Foster and then Mabel Haley (Webster), after Mary's death from an operation. Lizzie and McDuffie, the President's favorite maid and her husband had rooms there until McDuffie's nervous breakdown. All the live-in help had rooms there—Bluette and Ella and the cook Mary Campbell that FDR brought down from Hyde Park after his mother died, so he could finally get his way on food.

There was a special kitchen on the third floor called the diet kitchen. It had been installed for Louis Howe. FDR so loved the little man who had masterminded his career that he would do anything in the world to keep him comfortable in the White House. Since Howe was a sick man with serious respiratory problems, his sleep was erratic and he ate strange foods at odd hours.

The valets dashed by with the President's clothes, on their way to the pressing room, where male servants did ironing. Housemen who took care of male guests also swung by on their way to the iron. Sometimes they stopped in the sewing room to chat a moment or check the day's schedule of White House activities that was tacked to the wall every day.

Nothing Is as It Seems

The social secretary dashed back and forth all day on a path between Eleanor Roosevelt and Tommy Thompson's office and her own office, adjacent to mine on the left. The quarters of Eleanor's personal maid adjoined my office on the right.

Edith Helm was Eleanor's social secretary, but she didn't deign to go over to the East Wing of the White House, where the teeming social office was, on the opposite end of the building from the President's official Oval Office in the West Wing. No, indeed, the social office had to come to Edith Helm. Every morning a Miss Andrews would come over from the East Wing to Helm's office, next to my sewing room, and take dictation and orders to be delivered to various persons in the East Wing.

One of my East Wing favorites was Harry Charlton, who had been a social aide for many years. He led a busy life because Eleanor entertained every day she was at the White House—at least with a tea. Harry, who was white, would amuse us with tales of how he used to deliver White House invitations on bicycle when he came to the Executive Mansion as a young man.

Another favorite of mine was Frank Sanderson, FDR's administrative officer, and a kindly man who was forever using his spare time to help disgruntled maids or housemen find better jobs in government. When White House salaries were cut 25% because of one of the Roosevelt economy kicks, Eleanor could not understand why so many employees wanted to transfer to other, better paying jobs. She gave a pep talk to a few of us about the honor of working at the White House.

She didn't have to convince me. I loved the feeling of historic places and people and I had no dependents, but some were attempting to raise three or four children on less than seventy-five dollars a month.

The White House pet among the men was a stately old white-haired gentleman, Jules Rodier, who had come to work in the attic telegraph office of the White House in 1900. As he told us, Eleanor's uncle, Teddy Roosevelt, ran him out of the attic because his energetic kids needed the space to sleep and roughhouse in. In those days of Teddy Roosevelt, he recalled, there was just one telephone in the White House and whoever was nearest it answered when it rang, from domestic help to the President himself.

In 1941, when Jules was 70 years old, Franklin Roosevelt,

very fond of the old gentleman who still handled secret messages sent and received by the President, told him his job was secure—and that he was giving him a "lifetime extension." We at the White House surely thought FDR would outlive old Rodier, but it was the other way around. The President died in office, in 1945, at the age of sixty-three. Jules, the oldest living White House employee continued coming to the White House until he died at age ninety-one in 1962. He hadn't continued working all that time, but he never missed returning every year for the annual White House Christmas party, where he was the star of the show. He decided he'd had enough work in 1949, and voluntarily resigned. As he told me, "I don't want to be like Franklin Roosevelt and die young." At the time he said it, he was seventy-eight.

It was said that Eleanor was the first "liberated" First Lady. We maids had our own women's lib in the Roosevelt administration. We simply took off our badge of serfdom—our little white caps—and nothing was said about it. So we used our own judgment and in the evenings, to make the First Family look good, we simply wore a little token cap or decoration made of lace with a taffeta ribbon woven through it occasionally. I made many of them for whoever was serving the night parties and receptions.

At parties, no one ever could tell who the Secret Servicemen were. They dressed like the guests in white tie and tails. This was still the day of formality, and even for a family get-together of sons and daughters-in-law, the Roosevelts dressed for dinner in dinner jacket and black tie. White tie and tails were the order of the day for formal parties.

Almost any evening when Eleanor was hostess to a few friends, whether her husband was there or not, she changed into a long hostess gown of some sort. She liked to wear a particular long black lace gown that I recall.

I remember when the President was deciding where he would eat, Oval study or family dining room, Missy would always ask, "Do we dress for dinner?" When just the two of them dined in the study, there was no need to dress. If FDR had cronies who had just come from their offices, they did not dress for dinner.

Missy looked tall and radiant in her slim low-necked and sleeveless gowns of various blue shades that FDR loved. I used to hem her gowns. They were always beautiful.

One woman who probably knew even more secrets than the

household staff was Louise Hackmeister, who was in charge of the President's switchboard, a position she kept for twenty years. She was the most closemouthed female in the White House—and she had to be. In war and peace she knew what was going on and who was in and who was out with the President.

Hackmeister's nickname was Hackey, and we used to laugh that between Lorena Hickok and her, the White House was being run by Hicky and Hackey. Mary Eben, who was in charge of all gifts sent to the President, shared an apartment with Hackey at the Wardman-Park Hotel. I often went there after leaving the White House to sew for Mary Eben. There was a great deal of segregation in Washington, D. C., at this time, and blacks had to use the tradesmen's entrance. But Mrs. Eben would have none of that. She told me the first time, "Go to the front desk and pick up the key to my apartment."

I said, "What door do I use?"

She said, "The front door, of course."

I went through the front door, and evidently she had paved the way at the front desk because I never had a bit of a problem. I believe the Roosevelt White House was the catalyst for the whole civil rights movement that would eventually open all front doors.

Col. E. W. Starling was one of our favorites around the third floor. He was head of the Secret Service detail, and the President liked to have his fun with him. He would say, "Where is that Bird?" and the bird, who was Starling, would be sent for. We were all "Bird" watchers.

An embarrassing trick FDR would play on Starling was to outrace him on country roads, during their trips to Hyde Park, and then hide his car behind trees. FDR's special hand-controlled car was small and could outmanuever the Secret Service limousines on the narrow roads. Then FDR would pull off the road onto some hidden lane and watch the big cars go by. When Starling finally figured out where he was, he would be in a cold sweat. But FDR would beam at him and say, "What kept you?"

The word would come back to the White House that Starling had been outwitted again. But Starling had the last laugh. He outwitted FDR, getting married suddenly at the age of sixty-four, just before he retired. FDR, we heard, was really stunned but delighted, and congratulated Starling for putting one over on him.

Starling's wife was invited to one of the White House receptions, and she was quite terrified, telling me in the guest powder room, "Oh, I'd rather stay down here with you on ground floor than go up and pass that receiving line." I told her not to worry, to remember other guests were as stunned as she until they got used to the White House, and to remember the First Family were just people like everyone else.

After Starling retired, Mike Reilly, his successor, fell heir to the cat-and-mouse games.

The Roosevelt grandchildren with their nannies, or nurses, slept on the third floor. We had three or four rooms set aside for all the grandchildren that passed through.

Sistie and Buzzie spent the most time there. Sistie, who was named Anna Eleanor like her mother and her grandmother, the First Lady, was six when she came to the White House. And Curtis who grew up to hate his childhood nickname Buzzie, was only two. Their nannie was named Beebe.

I spent a lot of time there too, as did all the household staff, working or resting or checking the schedule that was posted there for all servants. The schedule told who was arriving as guest and any other pertinent information.

Most of the Roosevelt sons' wives did not want the children down on the second floor where they were, so the poor little tykes were kept captive upstairs with their nannies and us about all the time. A long table was set up in the hall for their activities. Children were not permitted to roam around the second and first floors of the White House and had to be accompanied when they left the third floor.

They were freed occasionally to go down and play with their grandfather—maybe romp on his bed while he ate breakfast. Or pay their respects to him before his Oval study got too full of cronies, before dinner. Or they came down to visit awhile with their grandmother, Eleanor, before she had lunch with her friends, or before she left the White House for some meeting. The rest of the time they played in the long wide hall in front of my sewing room. They played out there, and they ate at the table out there with their nannies. It was like a small town with shops and dwellings on either side and a sidewalk cafe for the kids.

It was busy and exciting and I loved it. Loved seeing the grandchildren, the maids, the butlers, the valets. Hearing the social secretary talking on the phone, the buzzers sounding. Out in the hall, you heard them loud and clear. Three bells for the President, two for the First Lady.

Loved all of it, and especially the bits of startling information that would be whispered. Stories of "Old Sara," FDR's mother, and life at Hyde Park. The inside stories of Roosevelt marriages on the rocks—another daughter-in-law on her way out of a marriage, a daughter-in-law screaming at her husband downstairs in their bedroom about some alleged infidelity.

And in the mid-30s there would be talk of how nervous Ethel Du Pont was and how she was talking to herself again. We really worried about Franklin Jr.'s marriage and wondered how it would end. She would come to the White House without her husband, and he would follow and make up. But we knew by her nervous pacing up and down, night and day, that she wasn't happy. Once a maid came into the sewing room saying she had answered Ethel, not realizing she was talking to herself, and Ethel had looked at her blankly and said, "What are you talking about?"

Hyde Park, with its all-white staff of butlers and maids and chauffeurs and cooks, provided many tidbits.

We would laugh about how Sara couldn't tell the White House black servants apart and was always asking, "Which one are you?" no matter how often she saw someone.

But when it came to her dogs, Sara had no problem with identity. She loved her dogs so much that she would send them post cards when she was vacationing in Europe, and the maids swore the cards were read to them.

And as we exchanged news that would not get beyond the White House walls—at least from our lips—along would come the tiredest men in the White House, dragging their feet, and we would revive them with humor or a sympathetic word. They were the valets, who lifted the weight of the President many times in the course of a day and forced themselves to stay awake long hours, just to get what the President wanted.

They were his legs, his arms, his nursemaids, and each was on duty twenty-four hours straight. They would take turns—Prettyman and Cesar. One would arrive at seven A.M. and stay until seven A.M. the next day, when the other would take over. They would run upstairs to rest when FDR fell off to sleep or wanted privacy, but one push of the button by the President and they would go flying down the stairs again, no matter what the time of day or night.

Sometimes they'd need a favor in a hurry. They always wanted me to fix the President's swim suits because the wheelchair ripped holes in them.

Before McDuffie's nervous breakdown, when he had been the sole valet, on duty night and day, week after week, year after year, without letup, we had shaken our heads, knowing he couldn't stand the strain forever. So when he snapped, we weren't surprised.

I started to say before, there were always three live-in male household staffers—valet, chef, and butler. Among butlers who lived-in were Armstead Barnett and Charles Ficklin.

Looking back at the chefs, the most colorful name from the standpoint of history was the live-in chef named Jimmy Carter. The first Jimmy Carter to live at the White House didn't come from Plains, Georgia, but from Baltimore, Maryland. It is amusing, looking back, to see how we were surrounded by Carters in the Roosevelt administration. A cook, an usher, a florist, and a storeroom man were all Carters. Messages for them were always getting hopelessly tangled. Also there was the bathroom maid, Lily Carter.

After Maggie left, Lily Carter the bath maid was inspired to retire as well. For twenty-five years she had been taking care of bathrooms at the White House and had been in charge of the linen. She had also set up the powder rooms for all the formal White House parties—I inherited that part of her job. And the job of keeping the linen inventory. Only once did I try to help by cleaning a White House tub. It was the one in the Lincoln room, so huge that I had to take off my shoes and climb into it to clean the sides.

I smile when I recall that Lillian Carter, presidential mother to the thirty-ninth President of the United States, Jimmy Carter, wasn't the first Lillian Carter to grace the Executive Mansion. Our humble bath maid was.

Now and then, the little ones shouting and screaming outside my open door were shooed into the solarium to play. It was a glass-enclosed porch that the Coolidges had added, and Mama and Mrs. Coolidge had sat out there many times sewing. Only one little child did not want to play there—Scoop Crawford, Faye Emerson's little boy. Unless his mother went with him, he would fuss until he was taken back downstairs to her.

Diana Hopkins, at five years of age, also had a room on the "Village Green" of the third floor. She enjoyed the other children, and was sad when they would go home. Once we worried because she had run away. She hadn't gotten too far. She had somehow escaped the grounds, but Secret Service found her only blocks from the White House. We sighed with relief. It would have been a black mark for everyone had something happened. Diana practically grew up at the White House and saw her father married there.

We were delighted to have a child around, especially when the family was away and there wasn't too much doing. Even when the family was there, we would have fun teaching the little child all the things she wanted to know—fun to her, work to us—like how to make cookies, set tables, make beds. When the Roosevelts were away, Diana would play hostess with the maids, serving lunch which she herself had put together, on the third floor. She played pranks on White House guards, painting a mustache on one.

After her daddy married Louise Macy, her stepmother brought a woman from New York to be her companion, but she didn't last long because Diana gave her a hard time. She would hide under beds and not answer. When the woman got ready to leave, Bluette noticed that she was collecting White House fruit knives for some reason. Bluette collected the knives right back for the White House. We were never surprised that many people wanted souvenirs.

Besides battling sons who roughhoused up and down the stairs, the Roosevelts arrived with biting dogs. Not Major and Minor, as one of the butlers suggested they be called, but Major and Meggie. Major was a black and buff police dog who took orders from the President—but not too well. Major had been trained to protect his master, and he did this by holding some part of a new visitor in his teeth until they satisfied some kind of taste test and Major was convinced they were safe.

Anyone who moved too soon did so at his own risk. A female senator moved too soon. A British prime minister did likewise. New members of the household staff sometimes failed to pass muster with Major, and threatened to leave.

Someone may have had more trouble with Major's teeth than he could bear, and simply kicked the dog back. Whatever happened remained a secret, but Major ended up at the veterinarian's with a broken leg. When he got back from several weeks at the pet hospital, the household staff hoped and prayed that Major had been cured. But no, he was still the same old tyrant. As long as he only bit intimates and household help, he got away with it. But finally he went too far.

He was out on the lawn surveying people through the White House fence, when some friendly soul reached his hand in to pat Major. That was a big mistake. End of Major's stay at the White House.

Which brings us to Meggie, who was Eleanor's dog and as intent on protecting the First Lady as Major had been on protecting the President. Not only did she bite famous people, but she drove us maids crazy by stretching out in dirty fireplaces for a nap. For some reason ashes felt good to her, and even if the fireplace had been swept out, enough of the odor and flakes of ash remained to please her. She got almost as much use out of the fireplaces as the presidential family, except they liked them hot and she liked them cold. Complaining about Meggie's fireplace fetish did no good, but what did Meggie in was having the effrontery to bite both presidential grandchildren, Sistie and Buzzie, in a frenzy of jealousy. Even Cinderella couldn't have gotten away with that, and indeed, Meggie's Cinderella story ended there. Immediately the dog's permanent residence was switched to the estate of the President's veterinarian, where she lived happily ever after, from all reports.

In fact Meggie was there to attend the funeral of a third

White House dog, a setter named Winks, who came to the White House from Warm Springs, Georgia, where the President went for treatment of his polio. Wink's life at the White House was almost as brief as a wink. He failed to get used to the idea of being shut in by an iron fence and ran smack into it before the summer was even over. Dr. Buckingham came but could not save Winks, so he and Meggie accompanied the body to Rosedale Dog Cemetery in Maryland where they made sure Winks had a proper burial with full honors.

Besides the Roosevelt dogs, grandchildren brought dogs. Aides parked their dogs at the White House while they worked. Loving strangers brought dogs or shipped dogs to the President. Visiting royalty sometimes brought a dog.

Sometimes the din inside and outside the White House was unbelievable. We used to say anyone working at the White House deserved double pay for functioning under combat conditions with danger on every hand.

Even the dogs couldn't stand it. One of them, a bulldog named Pal, cracked up and threw himself into the cement fountain, when any sane dog could have seen there was no water in it. Fortunately or unfortunately, Pal recovered and continued to add his voice to all the rest.

Jack and Jill couldn't stand it. They were Anna Dall's red setters and were sent to stay at the White House while she got her divorce. They thought the White House was some kind of kennel they were being parked in, and they objected loudly.

Then Anna Roosevelt Dall married again, becoming Mrs. Boettiger, and added a new child, Johnny—and a new dog, Ensign—to the White House hubbub. Ensign was a retriever, and he retrieved everything that wasn't nailed down.

But he was an angel compared to Blaze, a big ape of a mastiff, that Elliott brought home. Nobody could handle him. A houseman locked him in the Library on the ground floor, and he proceeded to chew up all the towels in the ladies room there.

FDR finally put it half-jokingly, "There's room for you, son, or for your dog. Which will it be?"

Soon both Elliott and dog departed.

II
THE PEOPLE AROUND FDR

The Men Around FDR

FDR had a lot of people around him, but only a very few really knew him and heard his innermost thoughts. You could almost tick them off on one hand. Only with them did he relax completely—let it all hang out, as a later president, Nixon, would do—cuss and complain and freely discuss his secrets. But five of FDR's confidants were valets.

The other was Louis Howe.

Only one of this crew, Howe, talked back at FDR, cursed him now and then, and dared treat him like a retarded child ("You goddam idiot, can't you get this through your thick Dutch head...").

No one else was so close to the President. Eleanor was always complaining to intimates that she didn't really know FDR because he didn't confide in her. His sons said they didn't get really close to their father, and it possibly was true, from what I heard, that FDR was afraid what he confided to them might get back somehow to Eleanor.

The names of the valets read like a litany—Cesar, Prettyman, McDuffie, Fields, Esperacilla. And they were names he lived by. As he once told McDuffie, "You are my lifeline, the keeper of my keys." He didn't mean real keys, but the keys to FDR's secrets. Their position of trust did not keep FDR from poking fun at his valets and enjoying them.

McDuffie had been FDR's valet at the Governor's mansion and came right along with him. He traveled with the President and spent every waking hour around him until his breakdown. The public had no way of knowing how often the President actually consulted McDuffie on New Deal projects and plans and got his thinking.

The People Around FDR

Eleanor gave people the idea that it was only she who was able to fill FDR in on what was going on in the outer world and how people really lived. But we, backstairs, knew what perhaps even she didn't know—that FDR's valet, McDuffie, and Gus Gennerich, his bodyguard, sneaked people into FDR's Oval study to talk with him about breadlines and life on poverty row.

After McDuffie broke down, never again would one valet have such a burden as he—six years of twenty-four-hour duty with only a half day off a week. FDR realized the job was too much for any one man, and two men had "divided custody," as FDR humorously put it—Arthur Prettyman of the Navy and George Fields of the butler's staff. Then Fields went into the service and Cesar took his place. Cesar loved the President like life itself, but the job was agony for him when he had to set foot on the *Sequoia*, the presidential yacht. Cesar was seasick from the moment he got on the boat until he got off. He would do anything to get out of sea duty.

But even with two men to do the work that McDuffie had done all by himself as FDR's first valet in the White House, the work was grueling and there was never a time a valet was free of pressure. There was so little that the President could do for himself physically that each valet almost had to be two persons. Everything connected with the bedroom involved the valet. Every telephone call. Much lifting of FDR's heavy body. And much running hither and yon to fetch and carry.

Prettyman tried to lighten his own load by simply picking out an outfit for the President to wear and that would be that. Cesar was too kindhearted to just fling something down on the bed and presume to tell the President what to wear. He would wheel FDR into the wardrobe closet and they would have a little closet consultation until FDR himself selected the clothes that suited his mood of the day.

All of the presidential confidences that Cesar carried around with him were almost as heavy a burden as the work. Eventually his health snapped, and Cesar, too, had a nervous breakdown.

Arthur Prettyman was the senior valet, and a Filipino steward from the President's yacht, the *Sequoia*, was assigned to assist him—Irinea Esperacilla, who had a lot of trouble getting anyone to pronounce his name right.

The Men Around FDR

He ended up as plain "Isaac," and that's what everyone called him, including the President.

Isaac remained until the President died, but he was not at Warm Springs on April 12, when death came to the Little White House. By sheer chance Isaac had accompanied the President on the trip before, so it was Prettyman's turn.

April 12th was something Prettyman had to live with the rest of his life. It continued to haunt him until his death of a heart attack in 1957 after serving President Truman. Prettyman had loved and almost worshipped FDR, and FDR was always making a fuss over Prettyman, kidding him about having a pretty face like his name. Prettyman wore a small, neat moustache and the President teased him about being a lady killer.

Prettyman retorted, "One does not refute the Chief Executive, Mr. President."

"You would," replied the President.

FDR came to the White House with two sets of invisible crutches. His son, Jimmy, was his physical crutch. Louis Howe was his political crutch. People did not realize how much he needed both of them—Jimmy to lean on in what passed for walking and Louis to help him with his strategy.

James was FDR's closest son. But the closest to him of his whole family in his last years, after Howe died, was daughter Anna, whom he trusted with his biggest secret of all—his desire to keep seeing Lucy Mercer Rutherfurd, even in the White House. Anna covered for him, serving as hostess sometimes when Lucy came. Still, that was just one phase of his life. Anna cooperated to make her father happy, but she did not hear all his innermost thoughts. Those were heard only by Howe and FDR's valets.

Howe was the man closest to FDR. In fact, FDR was the most important thing in Howe's whole life, and for a time Howe was the most important in FDR's—while he was getting him the presidency.

For love of FDR, Howe gave up his wife and family life in 1924 and moved in with the Roosevelts—first at East 65th Street in New York, then wherever Roosevelt's career led, all the way into the White House. The wife Howe left behind, Grace, took it stoically. She had cooperated fully during those years, moving to Poughkeepsie to be near their daughter, Mary, who was a student at Vassar. Through the years, Howe would visit his wife now and then, but most of the time he followed FDR around, even going to Hyde Park, where FDR's mother Sara would shudder at the sight of him and mutter about "that horrible little man."

He was no beauty. He was tiny and he dribbled cigarette ashes wherever he went. He never changed his style of talking and acting like a tough newspaper man out of "The Front Page." He could look menacing with his large eyes glaring out from behind big bushy eyebrows, and his tight turned-down lips that never smiled. He could look scary, but the women staffers and secretaries who got past his gruffness said he was really a pussycat.

Even Eleanor seemed a little scared of him until he became so sick that he was rendered harmless. She would ask his advice and take everything he said seriously. Some people have given Louis Howe credit for making Eleanor into the person she was, even giving her speech lessons. Backstairs we said that was a bunch of malarkey. He may have encouraged her a bit, but many women influenced and shaped Eleanor's life in her early days, getting her involved in causes.

And we knew the woman who gave her speech lessons. She came to the White House every week.

No, Howe was strictly FDR's man and FDR's "creator" and Eleanor knew it. The way we knew was an incident between FDR and Eleanor. FDR had voiced some resentment to Eleanor about the fact that his children were working for William Randolph Hearst, who was insulting FDR daily in the newspapers he published. Eleanor had stopped her husband in his harangue, reminding him that he himself had made his pact with the devil, and that he owed his presidency to the man he hated. FDR angrily retorted that Louis Howe had enlisted Hearst's aid, "It was his idea. I just went along."

The way the story was explained to me by McDuffie, FDR's valet in those pre-White House days, James Farley was rewarded for his campaign help by being made Postmaster General, but it was that little old hacking, coughing, chain-smoking, President-maker Louis Howe who deserved the credit for putting it all together.

The Men Around FDR

William Randolph Hearst was backing Texas Jack Garner for the presidency and Governor Roosevelt was the favorite of New York. However there was another candidate from New York who was sure he was going to make it—former governor Al Smith, who had lost four years before and considered it his right to have another try at the Presidency. FDR had backed Al Smith all the way in 1928, but in 1932, it was "no way, Jose" that the man in the leg braces was going to step aside for anyone. All three had been nominated.

So there they were in a three-way battle at the Democratic Convention in Chicago in the heat of July 1932. Except of course, FDR was not there in person. In those days candidates stayed home and tried not to look eager until they got the good news. The balloting had stagnated. FDR couldn't win.

Louis Howe, sick as he was, was leading the pack for FDR, and James Farley was helping him. Franklin Roosevelt was called the weakest of the presidential candidates until Louis Howe had gotten James Farley, a Democratic bigwig, to support him. And how had Howe enlisted Farley's aide? By making a deal to help Farley become head of the Democratic Committee.

That was Deal 1.

With Farley's help, FDR went ahead of the other two men, but he still fell short of the required number of delegate votes. So Howe's strategy of using Farley failed to work. The situation at the Convention had evolved into a deadlock, and they were getting ready to bring in a dark horse to stampede the election—so none of the three would get it. Not Jack Garner, not Al Smith, not Franklin Roosevelt.

That's when Howe came up with Deal 2. He conferred secretly with William Randolph Hearst, asking what he'd take to throw his Garner votes to FDR. The way Howe told it in the hearing of the valet, Hearst had been adamant against Roosevelt, at first, freely admitting he detested FDR for supporting the League of Nations and being an "internationalist." Hearst was a supporter of the America First Movement, as was Garner, and he wanted Jack Garner as president to keep the U.S. out of "foreign entanglements."

Howe soothed Hearst by saying they could work something out. What they worked out was that FDR, if he became president, would drop his support of the League of Nations. And furthermore, FDR would pass the word that he wanted the Convention to give him Garner as his vice-presidential running mate.

So that's how it happened that FDR got his chance to be president in the dark days of the Great Depression. McDuffie would laugh and say, "And it wasn't even done in a smoke-filled room, but just on the telephone."

Eleanor eventually learned about it, McDuffie said, and was very upset that her husband would no longer support the League of Nations, which was so important to her. But FDR had told her that was politics—to do some good in one direction, you had to compromise in another direction.

Howe never acknowledged that there was a door to FDR's office. Or that there was any time of the day or night that a phone call from him to the President wouldn't be welcome. And the President just put up with it as one of the prices he had to pay for having been made president.

As Howe got sicker and testier, however, and made his calls later and later, FDR connived with his valets to intercept and keep the calls away from him. When Howe was terminally ill in a hospital in 1936, Eleanor made daily visits and kept his wife, Grace, informed. After that, each year I would hear that Eleanor had sent flowers to Howe's widow on some anniversary.

Though until the end Howe was Number One, FDR had other cronies who came and went from his private study upstairs, down the hall from where Howe lived. With them, FDR could relax and tell jokes and have a few drinks. And with them, he would also pick brains and discuss how the New Deal was going.

Some of his cronies were on his personal staff—like bodyguard Gus Gennerich, and the military aide who was famed for his wit, Edwin Watson. Some were outside the White House, cabinet officers and advisers. All those he truly liked, he teased and dubbed with nicknames. Two important lawyers of the New Deal, Thomas Corcoran and Ben Cohen, were called "the Gold Dust Twins." FDR hadn't made up that name, but had borrowed it from a columnist. When he spoke of or to Corcoran alone, he called him, "Tommy the Cork."

FDR liked Gus Gennerich, his bodyguard, enough to play tricks on him. Once, the story was, FDR pretended there was someone hiding on the roof at Hyde Park and insisted Gus go up there to check it out for security. Then he had someone remove the ladder. Another time he pretended he was drowning in the pool so Gus would jump in with all his clothes on—and he did. FDR didn't give his longtime friend and bodyguard another name. He thought the name Gus was funny enough.

Steve Early was "Steve the Earl."

"Steve the Earl," FDR's press secretary, kept the press at bay and properly respectful of the President. He did this by keeping all the reporters standing almost at attention, cramped together as they made their notes, often using each others' backs.

Nor did Early encourage reporters to assume a familiar air with the President. FDR sharpened his wit on reporter's battered egos to the extent that some were afraid to ask questions at all for fear FDR would laugh at their "stupidity," or as he once did, tell one bluntly, "Go stand in a corner." No matter how abused they felt, reporters still deferentially sought permission to open a subject, asking, "Mr. President, would you entertain a question my editor has given me concerning the reason for your wife's trip to England?" Or, "Would the President care to answer a question on the subject of youth camps?"

A few reporters were pets and were always up close to the throne, FDR's desk. In fact, two could be found actually seated on each side of the President—radio man Earl Godwin, and a saucy female reporter famed for her hats, May Craig. We would see them around the White House and we knew they were the envy of their colleagues.

FDR must have turned over in his grave years later when all reporters were provided with seats for presidential press conferences and courted for their good will by later press secretaries, such as Pierre Salinger and James Hagerty.

Colonel Edwin Watson, whom FDR eventually promoted to General, was always called "Pa" Watson. Some of us thought that was his real name. He was frequently the butt of FDR's jokes, but he also was a presidential social buddy. Once we thought Pa had evened the score. He invited FDR to come to dinner at his lovely home in Charlottesville, Virginia, promising him great mint juleps. FDR promptly came down with food poisoning.

FDR proved how close he felt to his son James, who was his aide for a while, by giving him the name of "Jay, the Rose." FDR's own half brother James had been nicknamed "Rosie." Jay the Rose sat in on many of FDR's personal meetings and knew more secrets about his father than any of the younger brothers. Backstairs we thought part of Eleanor's objection to James working for his father was that she wanted to spare him too much knowledge of the more unsavory side of the family's life.

Every Monday Henry Morgenthau would walk over from the Treasury Department, which he headed, and join the President for lunch, bravely eating whatever came out of that giant aluminum thermos-on-wheels that had been rolled over from the White House kitchen.

There was a special relationship between FDR and his old neighbor from Hyde Park. They genuinely liked each other. But FDR could not resist playing little pranks on the secretary of the treasury. Sometimes Henry would get so angry he would threaten to quit his job and sometimes FDR halfway believed him. The President felt a certain amused attachment to Henry because he'd been in some wild schemes and made some money with Henry's father, Henry Morgenthau, Sr. They had invested, for example, in a new gadget that took pictures of people after they put a coin in a slot. It was ahead of its time. People couldn't afford the luxury, and the company was soon going broke. Henry, Sr., saved FDR's hide and got him out in time with a small profit on the sale of his stock. FDR and Henry, Jr., would reminisce about the old days over lunch, and about how FDR and his father could have made millions had they been born a little later.

But FDR wasn't content with talking about the good old days. He couldn't resist making the most of every rumor he heard about Henry. He had heard, he told him, that Morgenthau had been leaving his Treasury Department unmanned, to investigate conditions at the Interior Department, and had discovered Interior

Secretary Harold Ickes in the act of checking the amount of time each lady spent in the toilet. According to the servant who served the food, FDR really had a field day with that one, suggesting that since Henry seemed to have a lot of spare time, he'd like him to come over to the White House and run a time check on how long the female employees there stayed in the toilets.

Morgenthau, Jr., was furious, but there had been a grain of truth to the story. He had happened to mention to Eleanor that he had heard this bit of gossip about Ickes ordering a time check done surreptiously on his female employees. Whether Ickes really did or not I never did find out, but it was perfectly natural for Henry Morgenthau, Jr., to gossip with Eleanor because they were old friends, and Henry's wife, Elinor, was one of Eleanor's best chums. The two couples, in old days, often picnicked together at their neighboring estates in the Hyde Park area. The Morgenthaus lived at Fishkill Farms.

According to my source, Henry said if the President thought that was all he had to do with his time, then it was time to hand in his resignation.

Another time he was about to hand in his resignation was when the President took advantage of him in a poker game. We thought it was uproariously funny when we heard about it the next day. There had been a poker party in the President's study on the night Congress was adjourning for a holiday, and everyone had agreed to play until Congress called the White House to say they were adjourning. Morgenthau was way ahead, so FDR had someone intercept the message from the Hill and kept the game going until poor Henry lost every penny. *Then* the message came.

We got a further bulletin on it when Morgenthau proved he wasn't as dumb as some people seemed to think. He read the morning paper, learned when Congress had really adjourned, and went storming into the President's office.

But we had to really respect Henry Morgenthau, because he had such integrity that he didn't care who was involved in some suspected illegality—he went after him. Once one of FDR's sons tried to help a Hollywood friend who was accused of income tax evasion. Morgenthau threatened to resign if FDR got involved, or if anyone tried to influence the IRS or use their influence in any way. This time FDR stepped away and let justice proceed. The man was tried and convicted and did serve some time in prison.

It was just this stiff-necked righteousness that made FDR respect and retain Morgenthau in the post where integrity was so important. But it also made him the perfect foil for FDR's deviltry.

We really were shocked when we heard of the most embarrassing trick the President played on Morgenthau. It happened right next door to the White House, on the steps of the Treasury Department, where a war bond drive was going on. Morgenthau rose to say a few words, and just as he was getting warmed up, a messenger sent by the President hurried up the platform with a note, which he handed Morgenthau. As Morgenthau paused for a moment to receive it, the messenger said softly that the President wanted him to add the message to his speech. Morgenthau looked at it and turned five colors. It was an obscene joke.

Morgenthau was not the first treasury secretary with whom FDR had his fun. FDR loved home entertainment, since it was difficult for him to get out of the White House very often, and fortunately, his first treasury chief, William Woodin, was talented. The housemen and valets would hear FDR say on the phone, "Will, bring your zither or your violin and if you behave yourself, you can even play some of your own compositions."

The President loved to hear Woodin play classical pieces on the violin. The treasury secretary was said to be very musically gifted. Unfortunately, after only one year, Woodin had to resign because of poor health. He had found the late hours very hard and hadn't been able to keep up. Sometimes it had been one o'clock in the morning before FDR paused in some poker game or strategy conference in his bedroom study to call for music.

FDR and his cronies loved to bet. We would hear about pool slips left around the morning after FDR would have his gang in— men like Harry the Hop, and Steve the Earl—for drinks and congeniality.

They would, I heard, bet on just about anything. They had a pool going on whether King Edward VIII would marry Wallis Simpson or live in sin. And if he married, when the nuptials would take place, and under what circumstances. After the King gave up his throne for his American true love, the gang got together over drinks, and the slips with the individually written bets were removed from a locked drawer and read aloud for comic value. But FDR had obviously gotten rid of his own slip. It was understood he would rather lose his money quietly than have the news slip out of the scandalous thing he had predicted the King and Wallis would do.

They bet on baseball games and elections. They bet on horses. They would always use their nicknames for their bets.

Harry Hopkins—Harry the Hop—was one of the inner circle, though he had started out in the Eleanor camp. She acted annoyed when FDR won him over to his "wicked" ways of drinking and partying.

Ickes was another special case in which Eleanor was involved, due to a pet project of hers called Arthurdale, which was unfortunately in his province—of which more later.

The point here is that as a result of her many quarrels with Ickes over the treatment of the people at Arthurdale, Eleanor carefully avoided inviting him to White House parties. FDR, however, except in the case of Lucy Mercer in his youth, never gave up his friends even temporarily to please his wife. So, all by himself, FDR would go to Ickes' home, make himself comfortable, and spend the evening joking, eating, drinking, and occasionally playing poker with Ickes and his young, very attractive wife. It was the kind of evening that would have bored Eleanor.

Secretary of Interior Harold Ickes was always "Harold the Ick," and FDR would be heard saying on the phone, "Ick, I have a problem I'd rather not talk about on the phone, so would you mind coming over here?" If FDR were having cocktails and Ickes had not shown up yet, he would call out at the sound of someone approaching, "Is that you, Ick?"

Unfortunately, the Ick was not one of Eleanor's boosters. Though Ickes and Eleanor saw eye to eye on such things as the correctness of letting Marian Anderson sing on public property—the Lincoln Memorial—he felt she was infringing on his territory. It was a little feud that the public didn't know about. Nor are too many people aware that Ickes was the token Republican FDR appointed to his cabinet.

Vice-President John Nance Garner was never at the gatherings of the President's cronies. FDR did like Texas Jack's sense of humor, however, except for the one statement he made about the vice-presidency. It's about the only thing Garner is remembered for, and it is often quoted incorrectly. The way they quote it, Garner said, "It isn't worth a pitcher of warm spit." But it wasn't spit he said originally, it was another body fluid.

6

The People Around Eleanor

It was said that Eleanor Roosevelt surrounded herself with women who looked like herself, rather serviceable looking and not long on glamour. One day the joke around the White House was that a little old man, a guest at a White House reception, had been confronted with the sight of Eleanor and her two secretaries— Tommy, her private secretary, and Edith, her social secretary— towering over him. He looked up at them and said with great chivalry, "Which of you lovely ladies is Mrs. Roosevelt?" The servant who heard this had only to tell it once, and it spread backstairs like wildfire.

I asked, "Which one looked insulted?"

He said, "None. They all looked flattered." Soon my comment was making the rounds.

Tommy and Edith may not have been beauties—Tommy had a look that said *no* before you asked, and Edith entered a room like a steamship under a full head of steam—but I loved them both. Edith Helm's White House Social Office was right next to my sewing room. This made life very exciting because I could not help hearing what was doing in the White House social life, or what new, outrageous letter had been received.

Sometimes there would be a roar and I would be treated to some funny thing that had happened concerning the Roosevelt family. Usually Edith would call Tommy Thompson downstairs and tell her the unusual happening right away, and if she still needed an audience, she would stand in the doorway of my sewing room and tell me.

I remember once Mrs. Helm told me that she had been called in the middle of the night by a girl who was entertaining one of the Roosevelt sons. The girl said there was something wrong with the bathroom, and water was spreading on her floor. She wanted Edith to call the White House and have them send their plumber right away. I asked her what she told the gal. She said she told her she was not in charge of the plumbing of the White House or any other place a Roosevelt happened to be, and she was certainly not in charge of any plumbers.

Once Edith was not amused to intercept a gift that had arrived for the First Lady—a pair of worn-out shoes. The accompanying letter complained that the sender had worn out these shoes campaigning for FDR and had not gotten any gift or show of appreciation. She thought if the First Lady knew, she would be sure to send her something.

As I recall, all she got were her shoes back. But Edith always said that Eleanor was so tenderhearted that she had to be careful not to show her some of the truly phony appeals for help or Eleanor would have sent money anyway. With all the checks that Eleanor sent for personal charities, there may be some valuable autographs around. But probably not. Eleanor Roosevelt was so unpopular in her day that I doubt many people would have saved a check for her autograph or paid someone else for one in order to keep the check from being cashed.

I think the letter that made Edith laugh the most was one asking her to cut off one of the President's shirttails so the writer could make it into an apron and auction it off at a charity bazaar her club was having. The woman added that she would also need a letter telling about all the shirttail's adventures, the meetings it had attended, and the history it had seen. I seem to recall that I did cut off the shirttail of one of FDR's castoff shirts, but I don't believe the lady got a run-down of the shirt's adventures.

Edith Helm was a sweet woman, and I could go to her if I needed something. The only trouble was that she would go to Tommy. Tommy Thompson was really the boss and much closer to Eleanor, so I usually approached Tommy directly with my questions. Next to Eleanor, Tommy was the real boss at the White House. Even Henrietta Nesbitt listened carefully when Tommy Thompson spoke.

Malvina "Tommy" Thompson had come into Eleanor's life by way of the Red Cross and the Democratic Committee in New York.

Eleanor had stolen her away to work for her. It was Malvina who introduced Eleanor to Lorena Hickok when FDR was running for governor of New York, and Lorena had come into the Democratic Committee offices to get information on a story for the Associated Press. That meeting did not seem to kindle sparks, but four years later, when Lorena and Eleanor met again during FDR's presidential campaign, they became inseparable.

Malvina "Tommy" Thompson wore the very plainest of clothes and hats, but Edith Helm spent a small fortune on her more feminine clothes and had a fabulous collection of hats. When some famous personality was due at the White House, Edith would rush home unexpectedly and come back in a fancy hat, which she'd wear when she greeted the caller. Then, just before tea time, she would take off her hat in her office, pat her hair, and come to the tea table. Tommy never served tea with her hat on.

Being closer to Eleanor, Tommy usually ate lunch with her, although there would usually be another guest or two as well. Edith Helm was not invited to these intimate luncheons. She went home to eat.

One of the most important persons in Eleanor's life at the White House was Henrietta Nesbitt. Much has been said about the bad food at the Roosevelt White House, and all of it is true. Almost all of it could be traced to Henrietta, the housekeeper, whom Eleanor had hand-picked. Following Eleanor's lead, Henrietta had a great contempt for the desires of the President. If he ordered something special, she just ignored it. She served what she wanted or what had been planned by the First Lady, in conference with her.

Of course, Henrietta did not personally do the cooking, but she stood over the cooks, making sure that each dish was overcooked or undercooked or ruined one way or another.

It wasn't only the President who suffered. It was anyone who had the bad luck to share his lunch at the office or be invited to dinner at the White House. Some brave people even refused a dinner invitation and suggested they come after the meal, although a White House invitation in those days was pretty much considered a command performance.

Every now and then we would get a chuckle out of hearing that someone had conspired with the staff to smuggle the President something he liked to eat. Usually it would be something that needed no cooking or just warming up.

It was hard to find anyone backstairs at the White House who had a really kind word to say about Henrietta Nesbitt. Each had some little atrocity to relate about "Fluffy," as we called her.

I'll never forget the time Wendell Willkie was coming to the White House to have a secret dinner with FDR. Willkie had lost the election, but somehow the President was fascinated with his ideas and wanted to get better acquainted with the unusual Republican. The word was that FDR was probably sizing him up for a possible Cabinet post to show how broadminded he was.

The word trickled out of the Oval Office that FDR did not want to ruin his reputation with Willkie by subjecting him to one of Mrs. Nesbitt's meals. We laughed heartily when we heard how the President solved his dilemma. He hired an outside cook to help the White House cook, much to the annoyance of our Fluffy.

Wendell Willkie did not live long after that dinner—though that isn't what did him in to the best of our knowledge. The point is that we never did find out whether FDR would have given him a Cabinet post.

Another thing I'll never forget is that during the fourth-term furor, word went around the domestic staff that the President said he had to get reelected, if only to fire Mrs. Nesbitt. He told this to his daughter, Anna, who passed it along to a very appreciative audience of maids.

Mrs. Nesbitt sometimes tried to defend her cooking by blaming FDR or the First Lady for adding more guests than had been cooked for. "How can the food taste good when I have to keep watering it down?" she once said bitterly.

Once Mrs. Roosevelt complained to her husband about all the requests she was getting for things from all over the country, and mentioned that among them were hundreds of requests for White House recipes. Laughing, FDR said she ought to send some of Henrietta Nesbitt's recipes for brains and sweetbreads—that would certainly dry up requests for recipes in a hurry.

I don't believe the public knew that Mrs. Roosevelt had a speech teacher who came to the White House once a week and stayed as an overnight guest. She was very exuberant and never could get used to the idea that she was really there. She once startled us by taking along the flowers from her room as a souvenir when she left. The only person who seemed a little put out was the florist in the bouquet room, Redmond, who had to make up a new bouquet for the room.

The flowers were a fringe benefit. We understood she got a fee for each overnight visit. For a day or two after she was gone, Eleanor would be very careful and precise in saying each word. We were told the voice teacher had given the First Lady special exercises to make her voice deeper, but we hardly noticed a difference. Maybe Eleanor was too busy to do the exercises.

One of the persons around Eleanor who helped shape her life and activities in the White House was a black educator. Mary McLeod Bethune came to visit many times. She was so black that she made many of us backstairs look ghostly white by comparison. Mary was famous for having founded the Bethune-Cookman College, but she was then stationed in Washington, in charge of Negro activities of the National Youth Administration.

Eleanor and Mary would sit by the hour talking about the needs of blacks all over the country, especially housing, health care, and jobs. She was always bringing Eleanor the name of some worthy and well-educated black person who deserved a higher-level job.

Mrs. Roosevelt hated to sit still that long. She would jump up and take care of other things and then run back to talk with Mary Bethune some more. Once Eleanor told someone she was grateful to Mary for having freed her of the bondage of racial prejudice and she had proven it to herself by giving Mary a kiss. Another time the White House bouquet room was in an uproar because Eleanor had ordered that flowers be sent to her black friend on a regular basis, until she recovered from an illness.

Most people don't know that Eleanor and Mary Bethune were among the first to fight segregation, way back in 1939. The way it came about was that Eleanor and Mary had gone to Birmingham to help set up the Southern Conference on Human Welfare. Both blacks and whites were at the meeting—one group on each side of the aisle—and Eleanor wanted to sit with Mary Bethune. A policeman told the First Lady that she was guilty of breaking the law by sitting in the black area. Eleanor got up and took her chair to the aisle between the blacks and whites and sat there.

Also under the influence of Mary Bethune, Eleanor did a great deal of scouting around to make sure the black servicemen had places to go for recreation during World War II, when segregation was still in force. I remember she went to a little house run by blacks for black servicemen, and she came back saying it had been immaculate.

Later I heard that the Secret Service worried about her when she went to places where she was the only white woman. She peeped into every corner as if *she* were running the country.

Now and then Eleanor locked horns with someone very important to her. As we saw it backstairs, it was just too bad that Eleanor's special interests and pet projects happened to fall in Ickes' domain of the Interior Department. Ickes' department controlled PWA—Public Works Administration—which is not to be confused with Harry Hopkins' WPA, and he had a finger in Hopkins' WPA—Works Progress Administration—which paid a living wage to artists and writers and painters whose work can still be seen in many government buildings.

Like it or not, Eleanor had to work through Ickes if she wanted to help certain people. FDR, we were told, secretly enjoyed Eleanor wrestling with "the old curmudgeon," as he was called. It took the heat off FDR. He didn't have to wrestle with the Ick or with his wife—he just let them fight it out.

Many times, so I was told, Harold the Ick would come storming over to FDR's office saying that Eleanor had claimed the President wanted Ickes to do this or that. Almost always it would turn out that the President knew nothing about it. Or was he just trying to stay out of it? We wondered. Once, a valet admitted to us he almost laughed out loud when he heard Ickes tell FDR irritably that any day now he expected a call from Sistie and Buzzie telling him what to do.

The worst clash that Eleanor and the Secretary of Interior had was over her project called Arthurdale. It had been Eleanor's dream to supply low-cost housing for the very poor, and she had finally gotten FDR, through Ickes and his Public Works Administration, to build a model community with houses that people could afford, a good school, and factories to provide jobs and medical aid. Eleanor had seen the poverty in West Virginia mining communities. It was her dream to lift the hungry, out-of-work miners from their miserable surroundings and give them a fresh start.

The new town got its name from the farm bought to build it on—the Arthur estate. This was early in the Roosevelt administration. From what I heard, Lorena Hickok had her finger in the project, being the first to interest Eleanor in the plight of the area's poor. As I recall, Hickok investigated the area first in her job of reporting conditions to Hopkins, and Eleanor had gone down to join Hicky and see for herself. Together they had interviewed families living in rotting shacks and had seen how they barely survived in spite of husbands who hadn't worked for years. Eleanor had come back with a dream. It was a model community that would be an inspiration to the nation and would solve the problem of poverty because it would be copied across the land.

Eleanor pressed FDR until he got Congress to appropriate $25 million to resettle destitute families on farms. Each new house was to cost only $1,000. Families would have thirty years to pay. Since the homeowners would work in factories brought to the community, this would also be the answer to urban sprawl.

Ickes wanted to proceed slowly and cautiously, but Eleanor combined forces with Louis Howe and forced the project to go faster than Ickes could get each suggestion researched. Somehow, Louis went ahead on his own and ordered the first batch of houses. Only later did they discover that they might come in under the $1,000 price limit, but they were like cardboard against the cold. A little later, they discovered that everything was wrong with them and that they would cost a lot more than the $1,000. Eleanor was shocked that the houses were going to have nice fireplaces but no indoor toilets. *No bathrooms.* The male attendants to FDR were amused to report how everyone had gotten into the toilet hassle—Ickes, Howe, Hopkins, Eleanor, and some housing experts whose names they didn't know. FDR sided against indoor plumbing and drew a perfect outdoor privy to show what a homesteader would be happy to have. Eleanor was hurt and shocked that the homes would have no indoor bathrooms. There went her dream.

The project proceeded and Eleanor did her best to help the families and the school—donating a lot of her own earnings—but industry did not rush to Arthurdale, and eventually the project was written off as a government loss.

Eleanor was a little chagrined that Ickes had been proven right and had gotten the last word. But at least she felt she had tried to do something constructive for the poor. She had fond memories of becoming just another warm human being, another face in the crowd during her visits there.

At Arthurdale, Eleanor had enjoyed the kind of evenings she liked—square dancing, without a drink in sight. We heard that she started an annual contest that featured country music singing, jig competition, and even a mouth harp contest.

I grew to love Eleanor Roosevelt for the many kind things she did for those around her. When Harry Hopkins' wife Barbara died in 1937, Eleanor insisted that his five-year-old daughter come to live with her at the White House. Hopkins stayed in Georgetown, where Eleanor went to visit him a great deal.

Eleanor felt so close to him that she told Hopkins, we heard, if anything happened to him, she wanted to be the legal guardian of Diana. Later we learned that Hopkins had indeed changed his will to provide this.

Diana wasn't happy to be torn from her father this way. She led a lonely life among us, having friends catch as catch can when the Roosevelt grandchildren were around. She lived on the third floor, and since my sewing room was there, I tried to watch over her—as did all the rest of the maids. She was our pet.

Eleanor wanted to spend more time with her but couldn't—she was just too involved. Poor child. *Everyone* was too involved. I remember once Diana was excited because she was going to meet Winston Churchill. But *he* was too involved. He just gave her a gruff hello and went on his way, ignoring her. He didn't even bother to ask her a single question like what she wanted to be when she grew up or what she was learning in school.

Around the White House there was some little talk that Eleanor was romantically inclined toward the gaunt Harry

Hopkins. It was hard to imagine because whenever we saw him he always looked like death warmed over, but in his earlier days, when Eleanor first met him, he had been a firebrand interested in social reforms, an ambitious social worker. Eleanor had taken him under her wing in New York and had gradually gotten him her husband's acceptance. When Hopkins lost his wife in 1937, he clung to Eleanor for comfort, making her feel important to him.

For three years, until he moved into the White House, everything was just great. It was obvious that Eleanor was even pushing Roosevelt on his behalf, trying to get FDR to commit himself so that Harry Hopkins would be the one he would back for president after his own second term was over.

But then, as we heard it, a terrible thing happened, from Eleanor's point of view. The word backstairs was that high society had gone to Hopkins' head, and he was out nightclubbing and courting society women. The old social worker no longer was there. Even worse, Hopkins started ingratiating himself with the President. Soon he had little time for Eleanor and was part of FDR's intimate circle.

Eleanor was really hurt at the change in Hopkins and jealous of her husband for stealing him away. Every now and then, we backstairs were aware of some tug of war between the President and First Lady. And it was never so evident as in the case of Harry Hopkins. Eleanor was only sick in bed at the White House two times in twelve years, and once it was over Harry Hopkins.

It happened right after Hopkins moved into the White House, and the way we understood it backstairs, Eleanor had thought she had a new, exciting relationship right in the White House. But she quickly got the picture that Hopkins was now dancing attendance on FDR. Eleanor felt betrayed. She took to her bed. But finally she reminded herself that "life is life," and that she was used to disappointments. She climbed back out and got busy with other things. Suddenly she became very critical of Hopkins, and no longer did we hear that she was singing his praises to her husband or pushing him for the presidency.

It was in May of 1940 that Hopkins moved in, and the word backstairs was that Eleanor liked him less and less the more she had him under the same roof. Now she was learning his faults, which were the kind she could not tolerate. He was dazzled by attention, accepting invitations from glamorous people. Eleanor was not impressed with people who were merely social or glamorous. She only respected doers. She discovered that Harry Hopkins liked to gamble and went to race tracks. She hated gambling. He went to night clubs. She did not like night clubs.

More and more Harry spent his time in FDR's study having drinks and lively chatter, and she expressed a certain bitterness that Franklin had changed Hopkins—and not for the better. There would be a roar of laughter from FDR's study, and it would be "Harry the Hop," as FDR called him, telling him some story. If Harry was missing at happy hour, FDR would tell his valet, "Go get Harry the Hop. If he's in conference, tell him the President needs him."

His health was almost as bad as Howe's had been, but still he was an incurable romantic. First we heard he was courting the movie actress Paulette Goddard. Then it was suddenly announced that he was marrying a New York fashion editor, Louise Macy, and bringing her to live at the White House.

She was a mere thirty-six to his fifty-one. Harry had most of his career behind him—the position as head of WPA and his Cabinet post as secretary of commerce. Yet he was able to convince a younger woman to marry him during a courtship of only four months. What is more, they were married in the White House—something even the Roosevelt sons had not done.

I was at the White House when the wedding took place in July of 1942. A reporter from the *New Yorker* had given Harry the Hop a new nickname, and so on his wedding day it was said that this was the first time "an animated piece of shredded wheat" had ever gotten married.

Because of the size of the room, only three backstairs members were invited to the wedding. Lizzie was one of them.

After Harry Hopkins got married in the White House, a lot of people wrote to ask why the Roosevelts couldn't provide the same service for them or for their daughter or son. And some assured the First Lady that they would bring their own refreshments.

When Harry Hopkins married Louise Macy, and Eleanor arranged everything for the ceremony at the White House, we maids were so happy for Diana's sake, saying, "At last the poor child will have a home and a mother." We couldn't have been more wrong. All that happened was that Louise Macy moved into the White House too, and Diana was still the lonely child on the third floor.

It's important to note that the Roosevelts didn't stage a big wedding for the Hopkins. Nothing fancy in the East Room. Eleanor staged a simple wedding in FDR's own White House study where only a small group could fit. Some of us felt that as long as FDR insisted on having his friend married in the White House, he could have insisted on a better room.

One would think that Eleanor would be happy that Harry Hopkins had found someone to look after him. The fact that he married in the White House certainly would indicate it. But the word backstairs was that it had been FDR who insisted that Harry and his fiancée be married in the White House.

Then the plot thickened. Eleanor did not seem at all happy, and we maids were shocked that Eleanor continued to hang around. She was supposed to leave immediately after the wedding and had told everyone she was going. But she didn't. She just stayed around like a watchdog.

The way the help figured it, and from what we heard, Mrs. Roosevelt wanted to establish that she—Eleanor—was the hostess, and just because Louise Macy had moved in, she must not get the idea she was the "hostess of the White House." As one butler put it, "The Lady has had all the hostesses she can put up with—Old Sara, Young Missy, Daughter Anna, and now this."

Eleanor hung around for ten long days before she finally decided to leave and go about her business. But there was still an explosion when she got back, a little later than scheduled. The First Lady rushed in and said she needed the place cards to arrange the seating for a luncheon immediately. The ushers told her that Mrs. Hopkins had taken care of it. The First Lady really flipped her lid this time, reminding one and all that she was the hostess and made such decisions.

We knew word had reached poor Louise from FDR, via her husband Harry, to stay out of Eleanor's way for a bit. She stayed in her room most of the time, except when she passed by on her way out of the building, and was not a part of Eleanor's White House life. Only FDR's.

I recall Harry Hopkins didn't even take time off for a honeymoon because FDR needed him. Louise graciously told reporters, "What other bride could say she had had her honeymoon at the White House?" But actually, it was a boring time for her, with nothing to do.

It wasn't considered right for a White House occupant to do her own housework, so what little there was to do was done by us as well as a maid named Margaret Jones, whom Louise brought from her New York apartment. Margaret didn't live at the White House, but came to take care of Louise and her husband on the second floor.

The character who did live in was Susie, Louise's French poodle, who slept in her room. Fala, who seldom left the President's side, took a fancy to Susie.

The little fellow would trot from the President's room the length of the center hall, about half a city block, and scratch on the door of the Hopkins room for Susie to come out and play.

The President said sternly, "What is going on here?"

I told him and added, "Who would have thought Fala would start chasing girls?" FDR laughed and laughed.

We were not surprised when Louise Macy Hopkins told us that she was taking a volunteer job as nurse's aide at Columbia Hospital for Women. She said she could not look at four walls all day. Every day she would get out and ride a bicycle to "work." Some maids said it was like a red flag to Mrs. Roosevelt, who wanted to be the only colorful one around the White House wearing her riding habits.

Someone overheard Eleanor telling Tommy she hoped the newspapers would not make a big thing of Louise's riding out into the world each day on bicycle to fight pain and suffering. We were amused that it sounded like a little jealousy.

I remember one day when Louise Macy Hopkins was thrilled that she had been at the hospital when Gene Tierney, the movie star, had her baby. Afterwards she talked with Gene and rejoiced over the baby.

The happy event turned into a tragedy. Gene Tierney, who was married to dress designer Oleg Cassini, accidentally came in contact with a woman who had German measles during a crucial time in Gene's pregnancy. The baby eventually was found to be mentally retarded.

It was a fortunate thing that Louise decided to become a nurse's aide and do volunteer work. Louise told one maid that getting out and working at the hospital saved her sanity. As it turned out, she stayed at the White House a full year, and it was a rough year for her.

When Louise and Harry Hopkins moved to Georgetown, Mrs. Hopkins gave her bicycle to Wilma Holness to give to her little sister. We knew then Louise Hopkins was going to concentrate on being a fashionable hostess—and we hoped a full-time mother to her husband's child.

The only character who couldn't bear to see the Hopkins family go was Fala. When Susie moved bag and baggage and dogfood to Georgetown with the Hopkins family, I thought for a while the President would hold her hostage for Fala. But no, he let her go on her way, making Louise promise she would not stand in the way of young love.

At Home With FDR and Fala

To say that Fala was a smart dog would be to insult him. Fala hadn't only a mind but a sensitivity that kept him from hurting anyone's feelings. He was a gentleman. A scholar. A keeper of secrets. A dog that could sit around endlessly listening to bad jokes and pretending he liked them.

He was, in other words, the indispensable dog.

By the time Fala entered FDR's life, the President had already served two terms in office and was fairly fed up with dogs. He neither wanted nor needed another dog, and he had just given away a beautiful English sheep dog, appropriately named Tiny, because he did not want any more dogs no matter how large and wonderful.

Then along came the President's distant cousin, Daisy Suckley, with the gift of a little black puppy, a Scottie named Big Boy. The dog had been given to her by friends, and she didn't want him.

FDR took one look at Big Boy and *did* want him. Laughing at the funny quizzical look of the little creature, he said Big Boy reminded him of one of his Scottish ancestors who was recorded in history as "Murray, the Outlaw of Fala Hill."

From that moment Big Boy never heard his name again— only the name Fala. Backstairs we considered the story of Fala almost biblical.

He was so sweet and gentle that all the mean dogs around him hated him and wanted to do him in. They never lost a chance to nip at him or steal his possessions, and had he had a coat of many colors they would have undoubtedly taken that. But he was a humble dog. All he had was a simple Army blanket near the President's bed to sleep on and the little, inexpensive doll Missy or

FDR talked a grandchild into contributing to keep Fala company. These two things he defended. Defending himself wasn't always easy, though.

Once Blaze, Elliott's mastiff, attacked Fala in a fit of jealousy at all the attention Fala was getting. Fala ended up at the vet's, getting a few stitches and still more attention.

And not all the indignities to Fala came from dogs. During one conference trip with FDR, Fala had to stay on the battleship because *his* presence would reveal the presence of the *President*. When FDR returned, he could hardly recognize Fala. The crew had been snipping him for souvenirs and he looked like a half-plucked chicken.

The President was furious. Who had perpetrated this dreadful deed? Nobody would tell.

After Fala came, the hired help would comment that although the Roosevelts had the worst animals who had ever come to the White House—the most undisciplined—that one little gentleman, Fala, made up for the rest of them.

Fala was respectful of the First Lady, but he took his orders from Missy. He was FDR's dog first and Missy's second. After her stroke, in 1941, Missy talked about how FDR said they were "the Second Family—Missy, FDR, and Fala."

Fala made such an impression on the nation that some people think he came to the White House with the Roosevelts in 1933. Not true. Fala did not arrive until the spring of 1940, in time to help the President through the dark days of World War II.

Fala had feelings, and he could be hurt. But more than hurt, he was insulted the morning of January 20, 1941, when it was obvious that FDR was trying to give him the slip. Fala took a flying leap and landed on the limousine seat beside the President, where he always sat. The Scottie's worst suspicions were confirmed when it became evident that he was being booted out of the car. "Not this time, Old Man," FDR said.

Fala could take a hint. He leaped from the car and ran all the way into the White House to the elevator, where Prettyman opened the doors and let him in. And haughtily, he stalked out onto the second floor where I was standing.

And that's how it happened that Fala literally *sat out* the historic third-term inaugural ceremony—sitting on his personal Army blanket, in the President's bedroom, sulking.

Various other dogs gave the White House that lived-in look before the arrival of Fala—staying on to vent their jealousy at the poor little Scottie who had stolen their master's heart.

For example, when the King and Queen came to visit in 1939, it was a Great Dane who greeted them. Its name was "President." President was the gift of the ten-year-old son of Congresswoman Isabel Greenway of Arizona. The royal couple were a little startled to hear a dog addressed as "President," but since it was their first visit on American soil, they were prepared to accept anything.

Fala was probably the best traveled dog of his time. He crisscrossed the world, usually by ship. Once the President was accused of wasting $15,000 of the taxpayers' money by sending a destroyer back to get Fala when he supposedly had been left behind in the Aleutians after a conference. This accusation was made by the Republicans just before an election and the President protested, while never admitting or denying that it had happened, that Fala was most insulted at this accusation.

I don't know whether it happened or not, but I do know that if the President left Fala behind, he would have sent *something* for him. It's hard to believe FDR would have started off without him because Fala was with him almost every minute.

As for sending a *destroyer,* FDR even refused to send a destroyer for his own aunt once. His mother had insisted he could do it if he wanted to. Wasn't it *his* Navy and wasn't he the commander in chief? And after all, it was only to England. But FDR said, "No, Mother, England is just a little too far out of the way."

FDR longed to see what Fala's offspring would look like, but he didn't have time to become a matchmaker. However, so beloved was FDR by all his aunts and cousins that he had only to whisper a desire and forces were at work.

Daisy Suckley heard and answered the call, arranging a meeting with a suitable female of his own class named Buttons.

There was to be a short courtship before the honeymoon took place at Hyde Park. FDR later swore that Daisy must have picked out a female from the Oyster Bay branch of the family because she was bitchy from the start, greeting Fala with growls and snarls instead of a wagging tail. When Fala tried to get cozy and romantic, she gave him such a bite that he ended up at the vet's, swearing off women completely. Thereafter, Fala refused to even look at the little Scotch dog. The veterinarian resorted to artificial insemination, and Buttons gave birth to twins who were immediately named Peggy and Meggy. (This was a second Meggy, the first having been banished from the White House for conduct unbecoming a dog in high office—biting a guest's nose).

One day Eleanor returned from a trip to find an urgent message waiting for her at the White House to come to see the President in his bedroom. She had been worried about her husband's health and rushed there. The President looked very concerned. "I'm so glad you're here," he said.

"I came right away. What's wrong, Franklin? Have you seen Dr. McIntire?"

"No," he said, "I've seen Fala's vet. He left this special diet and says it's very important. So will you please give this to the cooks and see that this special medicine is added to it?"

Nor did FDR hesitate to have his fun and play to an audience at Eleanor's expense. In fact, Fala and other imbibers of food and drink at the presidential happy hour were treated to occasional samples of the President's more acid humor when the subject of Eleanor came up.

Once the President asked his valet where Eleanor was. The valet said, "She's in prison, Boss." What he meant to convey was that the First Lady was on one of her fact-finding trips.

FDR shot back, "I know she is but what the hell has she done this time?"

It's a good thing Fala didn't drink. A lot of martinis swirled overhead as he listened to the Boss tell his cronies about the latest insults the newspapers had heaped upon his presidential person.

Or had sent through the mail. When the President got too many letters to reply to all the insults, he would sometimes return them to the sender with a comment in the margin. On one such letter, he wrote simply, "Ho hum."

FDR was forever having minor fusses with the Oyster Bay Roosevelts because they couldn't resist needling him. We decided it was because he had two strikes against him. He was a Democrat, and even worse he was worshipped by the public—even more so than their hero Teddy had been.

One story that made the rounds of kitchens and sewing room concerned a letter FDR received from an Oyster Bay female cousin telling him she regretted she would be unable to vote for him. We loved FDR's answer—a very sweet note thanking her for writing. The kicker came at the end: "It had never occurred to me that you would vote for me."

Over a martini, FDR would also reminisce about how another Republican member of the Roosevelt clan felt about him. Even after FDR was safely in office, FDR said, Teddy Roosevelt., Jr., the son of the other Roosevelt president, couldn't reconcile himself to having "this bastard Roosevelt in the White House." Teddy Jr. had gotten his perfect opening when someone asked exactly what his family relationship was to "*that* man in the White House." According to FDR, Teddy Jr. had snapped, "He's a fifth cousin, soon to be removed." FDR acted as if he would forgive an enemy anything if he just made him laugh.

One thing that made the President laugh was crazy names. He spent hours finding just the name that suited the victim, and some of the names remain a part of New Deal history. But getting a nickname from FDR was a stamp of approval—you were IN. Even if it was a horrible name like the one he gave one of his top New Dealers—Harry Hopkins—"Harry the Hop."

And you were IN if Fala accepted a tidbit from your hand. Everyone fed Fala hors d'oeuvres, and sometimes there was nothing left for the late guests. No matter. Fala's approval was the important thing.

FDR tested Fala's I.Q. now and then, saying, "Go to Harry the Hop," or someone else. And if Fala felt like it, he would. He would amble over and gravely give a sniff at the cuff of the right person, no matter how nonsensical the name.

The People Around FDR

Nicknames were certainly an important part of FDR's humor and the game of nicknames brightened his day.

Louis Howe was called "Felix the Cat" dating back to the 20s, when there was a tough little cartoon character named Felix, who was indeed a scrawny cat. Even sick as he was when he moved into the White House, Louis was still a scrawny, tough cat.

Poor Henry Morgenthau could only be "Henry the Morgue," but he was so strait-laced he didn't use nicknames in return.

One of FDR's special men, who was involved in wartime security to check goods coming in for the President, was named Richard Tracy. What else could FDR call him but "Dick Tracy"? He kept the name from then on through other administrations.

Bill Hassett, FDR's trusted correspondence secretary, was called "Bishop" because he knew all FDR's secrets and was a Catholic. FDR kidded that Bishop Hassett received his confession. Missy was not amused at this because she was a good Catholic and didn't like clowning around about her religion.

Even FDR's mother, Sara Delano Roosevelt, had a nickname within the family. She was called "Sally."

Everyone whom the President was extremely fond of had a nickname. Even Lizzie had a nickname given to her by the President and used only by three people—FDR, her husband, Mac (another presidentially-bestowed nickname), and Gus Gennerich, the President's bodyguard. Her nickname was "Doll." None of us dared call her that backstairs for fear she would kill us for ruining her exclusiveness.

I was known by three nicknames, thanks to my size—"Little Lillian," "Little Girl," and "Little Maggie." The latter labeled me a chip off the block, since I was Maggie's daughter.

Franklin D. Roosevelt, Jr., had a lot of nicknames, none of which were "Junior"—except backstairs, where we had to let some servant know in a hurry which FDR wanted service. In his family he was sometimes called "Brud," sometimes "the Sunshine Boy," and sometimes "Rosie," by outsiders.

But the real Rosie of the family was James, who was called that after his uncle James Roosevelt Roosevelt. FDR, as I've said, called his son James, "Jay, the Rose."

At Home With FDR and Fala

FDR Sr. learned of FDR Jr.'s purloined nickname Rosie when he opened a love letter addressed to "Franklin Delano Roosevelt" and began reading, "Dearest Rosie." It didn't take long to realize it was meant for the "Sunshine Boy," who was home from Harvard. FDR teased Brud about it at the dinner table, and Brud was not at all amused. It was a definite invasion of privacy even if the sender had failed to put "Jr." after the name. The President said he probably should have known it wasn't meant for him when he couldn't recognize the brand of perfume that emanated from the stationery.

FDR claimed he didn't know the exact formula of his martinis because they had been worked out by a family committee. Son Jimmy, he said, liked a mild martini, but not as mild as Anna's. Then son Franklin got old enough to speak up and argue for a still stronger martini. Then Johnny shot up so tall, he demanded to be heard and insisted on a martini so dry it could be mistaken for sand—a formula of seven-to-one.

All this time the President would be mysteriously mixing vermouth and gin so that no one could see what his formula was. When he was finished he would say that as chairman of the committee, he had the power to decide the ultimate taste of a martini, and he would ostentatiously add Pernod to his concoction. At this point, some people—aghast at this addition—weren't sure they wanted a martini after all.

When he had time on his hands, FDR also enjoyed amazing his friends with something he called a Haitian Libation, a frothy, frosty drink he whipped up using special strong, dark rum that came from Haiti, chilled orange juice, dash of lemon juice, egg whites, and brown sugar. The valets, who helped make it, said it tasted sweet and powerful. The proportion was half and half of fruit juice to rum; orange slices and cherries made a nice decoration.

Anna, the firstborn child, was called "Sis." It was just one little step, then, to call her child "Sistie." When Anna's first son was born, there was already a "Brother," in the family, which had been twisted to "Brud" by young mouths, and made official by FDR, so Anna's son was called "Buzzie." Elliott's nickname was "Bunny."

The People Around FDR

When the sons grew up, they acquired still more nicknames. FDR Jr. was called "Big Moose" by his men in the Navy when he was executive officer on a destroyer.

John was only called Johnny, except when his father talked to his mother about him. FDR would say, "Did our Chick get back safely to school?" He did not call his youngest son "Chick" to his face, but only in speaking about him.

I was told that all the Roosevelt brood were referred to as Chick when they were little. In the happier days before Lucy Mercer, I understand FDR would tease his wife by referring to her as the mother hen with all her little chicks around her.

FDR was incorrigible when it came to nicknames. He had a nickname for everything, including the first presidential airplane in history, which he insisted on naming "the Sacred Cow." I remember some of his aides said that the President should have given it a more respectful name, and if he wanted to be funny about the very serious matter of aviation, he should have named it for one of his grandchildren, "Sistie" or "Buzzie." But "Sacred Cow"? Never.

Later presidents would name their planes sentimentally for people or places—Kennedy with his "Caroline," named for his daughter, and Truman with his "Independence," named for his home town. But I truly regret that no president since has had the provocative sense of humor that the thirty-second President of the United States had.

Incidentally, FDR was the first presidential nominee to use an airplane to fly to the convention to give his acceptance speech. And the first to go to the convention hall and give it in person. It was considered by some to be a flashy thing to do and in very poor taste. But the Roosevelt charm made everything seem right and fitting to the public.

Even the subject of death inspired a nickname. FDR called the Episcopal Bishop the "Body Snatcher" because the churchman had wanted FDR to agree to be buried in the National Cathedral. FDR did not like to be reminded of death, we were told. He hated enclosed places and wanted to be buried under the blue skies and natural trees of Hyde Park. The Right Reverend James Freeman might be his bishop, but nothing was sacred when it came to the President dreaming up nicknames.

Sometimes the joke was on FDR, but the wily President always managed to make a graceful recovery, even when he was caught with his foot in his mouth.

I'm thinking of the first luncheon that Madame Chiang Kai-shek ate at the White House. She came to visit without her husband and brought along a very thin, young, crewcut female relative to serve as her attendant. FDR was trying to be friendly to the relative, who was also at the table, and he said, "My boy, I hear you've been out seeing Washington today." Somebody whispered to the President that this was a girl. Proving himself a perfect politician, FDR immediately added, "I hope you won't mind that I call every youngster 'My boy,' whether boy or girl."

FDR was a great winker. He was always saying some outrageous thing about one person while winking at another to show that he was only joking. He would also wink at me now and then as he was wheeled by in the hall. He would say, "I'll have to see why the Little Girl never has any work to do around here."

The joke was that I would be carrying a stack of linens up to my chin to be sewn or mended while using the other arm for my crutch.

FDR was not one to go out shopping for presents for relatives or even to send anyone else out shopping. His generosity consisted of giving away the things that had come to him in droves—and he gave them all to his beloved grandchildren as well as to his offspring.

Someone had given him a fancy lemon squeezer for his drink tray, and he remembered that Sistie liked lemonade. He gave it to her so she could make her own. He received a silver decanter, which he promptly sent to daughter Anna. Dozens of pairs of wool socks were distributed among his sons. He also gave each son one of his many gold watches. He always wore the watch awhile so that each son would be able to say it had been worn by his father.

When it came to Anna he was stumped, but rather than waste a man's watch on her, or order a dainty one sent from a store, he gave the watch to Buzzie, her firstborn son.

FDR was wary of gifts that might make it look as if someone were getting a concession or special treatment from the government. One day one of the valets was telling with pride how FDR had managed to accept an expensive gift and yet make it look right. Some cattle breeders wanted to give him some fine stock to improve his herd. He thought about it awhile and said he couldn't accept more than a bull or two, and he would only accept those if he could make it a community affair, with all the farmers of the area free to use the bulls to improve their herds as well. It tickled his fancy to be involved in the love lives of vast numbers of cows.

But next to Fala and other fauna, FDR got the greatest kick out of the species known as the Secret Service. With his perverse sense of humor, their grim guarding of him took on a humorous aspect. A favorite story involved the Secret Service and his predecessor, Herbert Hoover, however.

The way that particular story went, President Hoover was going to be arriving in Miami from a trip to South America, and Secret Service Chief William Moran sent a message to one of his men based in Texas to proceed to Miami for the emergency assignment. The agent wired back that he had just had all his teeth pulled and his new plates weren't ready, so he didn't think it advisable to take the assignment. Back came the order from Chief Moran: "REPORT TO MIAMI IMMEDIATELY. YOU ARE THERE TO PROTECT THE PRESIDENT, NOT BITE HIM."

8

A Royal Mess

Eleanor Roosevelt certainly deserves credit for bringing the protocol of entertaining out of the Dark Ages.

When she arrived at the White House, all invitations were delivered by hand. She thought it was silly not to use the mails. And that was that.

Often there wouldn't have been time for invitations. She thought it silly not to invite people off the street to visit her at the White House if she wanted to, and she did that more than once. Usually they were young men who caught her fancy. Sometimes they were angry young men. More often, they had interesting ideas about how to solve the world's problems. Some ended up talking half the night or staying the night. Some she met at meetings and just brought along home with her.

Once there wasn't enough room at the White House for an entire war protest group she had invited to stay the night. She spent hours on the phone finding sleeping quarters for the overflow.

That was Eleanor.

One guest became such a favorite that he courted his future wife at the White House. That was Joseph Lash, who was head of the Youth Congress. Eleanor invited him and his girlfriend Trude Pratt, and her two children, to visit the White House often.

We servants would see the love birds, Trude and Joe, happily wandering around the White House together. We knew how guests rated by how motherly Eleanor became toward them.

Joe Lash was one such person. Eleanor mothered him and went shopping for him. Once she shopped for a watch he wanted to give to his fiancée, Trude. And once it was a whole supply of underwear that Eleanor brought from a shopping trip and asked one of the maids to put in Joe's room.

As it turned out, Joe Lash's White House visits were to be of utmost importance. Years later he wrote a best-selling book, *Eleanor and Franklin.*

Another pair of lovers came from Hollywood. Carole Lombard was a guest with Clark Gable shortly before the plane crash that took her life and shocked the nation. I believe they were the most romantic couple we had at the White House—walking down the halls hand in hand, staring into each other's eyes, and stopping to kiss. After the tragedy, I read that Lombard was the only woman Clark Gable had ever loved, and I could believe it.

A different kind of loving pair was Gertrude Stein, who came to tea with Eleanor Roosevelt, bringing along her beloved Alice Toklas. I don't recall if any other guests were at the tea, but I do remember that afterwards, the talk backstairs was about how deaf Gertrude Stein was—and how rude. And how even Lorena Hickok looked feminine by comparison! Miss Stein was so proud of her own cleverness, she didn't let Eleanor get a word in edgewise.

Eleanor knew just about everyone in the literary and theatrical world. She mentioned once that she had known Hemingway's wife, Martha Gellhorn, before she met Ernest, and she had let them use her beloved Val-Kill cottage before they were married.

Eleanor liked writers. Fanny Hurst was an overnight guest, not once but several times, telling the maids how thrilled she was to find herself in the White House. Many guests said that, but the famous writer was more eloquent about it. She didn't win any applause from the help, however, when she announced that she didn't know of any living American woman who had the stuff of which presidents and vice-presidents were made. At the time, she was looking right at Eleanor, who we thought could handle any job—including the presidency.

Then there were Eleanor's personal friends from pre-White House days, such as cigar-smoking Nancy Cook, who had run the Val-Kill handcrafted furniture business with Eleanor, and Marion Dickerman, who, with Eleanor, had been involved in running Todhunter Private School for Girls. In fact, they joined her in setting up the Val-Kill cottage industry, whereby the local indigent could earn a living making furniture.

A Royal Mess

Around the White House, the old-timers among the help wondered about the relationship of Eleanor and these women with whom she had spent most of her time as early as the twenties—Nancy and Marion. In the years after she learned of FDR's affair with Lucy, they were the ones who kept her interested in living and enjoying and rising above painful memories. At times they were inseparable, even traveling abroad together.

They grew so close that Eleanor had all the towels embroidered with a combination of their initials—EMN—at Val-Kill. Nancy Cook, I recall, would come to the parties Eleanor gave for "Gridiron Widows" (wives of reporters) and would take part in the skits kidding Eleanor. Once Nancy dressed in overalls and kerchief as a trainman flagging Eleanor down.

Nancy was short and Marion was tall. Both were involved in early women's lib. Both were in and out of the White House a good deal at first. Then they seemed to grow apart from Eleanor.

Once Marion Dickerman caused a ruckus. FDR's valet Cesar reported in alarm that someone had been in FDR's sitting room during the night, and things were amiss. The Secret Service was all over the place questioning everyone, taking fingerprints.

It was mystifying. Later we learned that the President's desk drawer had been left ajar. It had various top secret papers in it. Burnt matches were found in the wastebasket. The fingerprints matched none of ours.

Even after they solved the mystery, it didn't make sense. It seems that Marion remembered that she had promised her students that she would copy the plaque that told about FDR's desk having been made from the ship *Resolute*. It was late at night and she was about ready to go to the train station when she remembered the inscription. She hurried to the President's Oval sitting room, rummaged around in the President's top drawer and found matches, lighting quite a few of them to read and copy the inscription. As a result of this episode, the President ordered that Marion be fingerprinted and her prints kept on file.

But what we never could figure out was why Marion didn't turn on the light. Had she been afraid light would show under the door of the President's bedroom and he would know someone was in his sitting room? His bedroom door was always closed at night.

All in all, we thought it rather cheeky that anyone would dare sneak into the President's suite in the dead of night without his permission.

Marion Dickerman was not the most popular visitor with the White House maids. She seemed to think she was still teaching. Once, as if to let the maids know the dresser mirror needed washing, she made a long streak on it from side to side with soap. It was not appreciated.

And then there was Earl Miller.

I was told by servants who saw them together that around Earl, Eleanor would radiate happiness and carry herself like a beautiful woman.

Maids had many jobs, not the least of which was looking after guests. To keep from having too much contact between males and females, housemen acted as valets to male guests. They pressed the clothes for the male guests only.

Whenever Earl Miller, the ex-New York patrolman, visited Eleanor at the White House, the housemen were ordered by Mrs. Roosevelt to take good care of him. He seemed to be her pet.

We, the hidden family backstairs at the White House, used to wonder why Eleanor didn't use her influence to have Earl Miller named a Secret Serviceman so he could be with her as he had been in New York. Some decided it was because she had a new interest—Lorena Hickok. She had her life neatly compartmentalized.

When she was at Val-Kill, Earl might be there. And the White House help saw with their own eyes that Earl kept some of his clothes in her half of the cottage.

I saw Earl Miller at the White House, He was a very handsome man. Sort of a muscle man. As a matter of fact, he had been an amateur boxer. It was easy to see why Eleanor was smitten with him. They had much in common. Earl taught Eleanor to ride a horse. This meant a lot to her as it was her only outdoor sport. Earl had been an exceptional horseman, even performing tricks on horseback at fairgrounds.

Earl gave Eleanor a horse when she was the Governor's wife, and she brought it to Washington. Its name was Dot, and it threw her not once but three times. Still she was sentimental about that horse because Earl had given it to her. She wouldn't ride any other.

FDR'S GOOD RIGHT ARM was his own son, James, his eldest and the apple of his eye. Through four inaugurations and on countless other occasions, FDR chose his son to lean on as he made the few shuffling steps that kept the public from knowing the President was really a wheelchair case.

DOING THEIR OWN THING. Eleanor would start knitting wherever she found herself—not well but prodigiously. FDR loved to read. The scene is the Hyde Park estate in New York, and the little scene stealer to the right is Fala. At Christmas 1941, the President and First Lady autographed a similar picture, minus Fala, for my Christmas present. (*National Archives*)

A RARE PORTRAIT of Eleanor in a formal gown.

MAMA—MAGGIE ROGERS, head maid at the White House under the Roosevelts until she retired in 1939. But she didn't stay retired. She returned in 1941, at Eleanor Roosevelt's request, to take care of Missy LeHand, after the President's live-in private secretary had a stroke.

VALET TO A PRESIDENT.
Cesar Carrara was one of several who worked so hard in the service of the polio-crippled President that their health broke. Cesar loved the President, and FDR returned his affection, letting him choose any place in the country he wanted to work after he could no longer serve as valet. I now share a home with Cesar's widow, Louise.

MISSY LEHAND was the mystery woman of the White House. She lived on the third floor, where my sewing room was, and divided her time between her suite and the President's suite on the second floor. No picture could do her justice. Missy was sunshine and laughter, and all the maids loved her dearly. We were devastated when she suffered a stroke just months before Pearl Harbor. She was FDR's private secretary, and he was the center of her life—so much so, that she never married.

FIRST MOTHER SARA DELANO ROOSEVELT. FDR's beloved mother
reads some of the congratulatory telegrams her son has just received upon
his election to a second term in 1936. Some of the wires back him in his
plea for a stronger Army and Navy in view of dictator Adolf Hitler's
military buildup in Germany. (*National Archives*)

MADAME CHIANG KAI-SHEK did not want this picture to be taken. It
wasn't the only thing she balked at. She was difficult on every point, and
the First Lady was hard pressed to continue to be a good hostess. After
pleadings, Madame Chiang agreed to have her picture taken with Eleanor
on the South Lawn, but everything had to be done her way—they had
to sit on chairs, with her to the cameraman's right. Even then,
she refused the cameraman's repeated request for a smile.

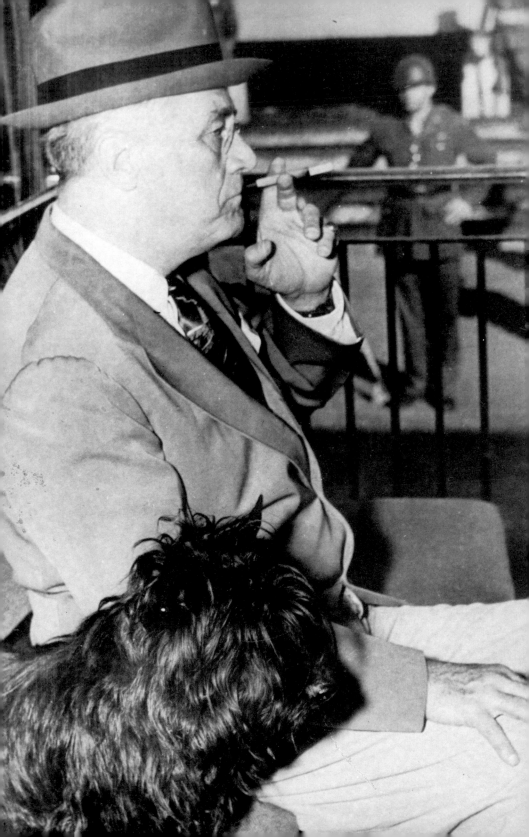

ANOTHER PAIR OF INSEPARABLES. British Prime Minister Winston
Churchill and FDR spent much time together. In fact, Churchill acted as if
he belonged in the White House during the war years, he felt so much at
home. Here they are in the President's Oval Office, with the presidential
flag behind Churchill, and one of FDR's sailing prints behind the President.
(*National Archives*)

THE INSEPARABLES, FDR and Fala, his Scottish friend. They were
together in life and are together in death at the Roosevelts' Hyde Park
estate in New York. Fala is buried close by, beside the sundial in the rose
garden. In the presidential library is Fala's corner, with all the things the
little dog used in life—his collar, his dog tags, and even his
personal dinner bowl. (*National Archives*)

FDR VISITS THE ELLIOTT ROOSEVELTS. FDR thoroughly enjoyed kidding around with his daughters-in-law, and here, Ruth Chandler Googins, Elliott's second wife, takes liberties with the presidential hat, as Elliott Jr. and Chandler egg her on. Behind them is Elliott's home in Fort Worth, Texas. (*National Archives*)

CHRISTMAS 1939. What a happy time for the Roosevelts. Disaster was around the corner, but it hadn't struck yet. FDR's mother, Sara Delano, was still alive, and World War II hadn't started yet. Here, baby John Boettiger, son of Anna, forges ahead on his own, while others watch him indulgently. A bit of the Christmas tree can be seen twinkling behind John Roosevelt, youngest presidential son. To his left is FDR Jr., acknowledged to be the handsomest of the sons and the spitting image of his father.

In the middle row, seated, are (left to right): Eleanor Roosevelt, Sara Delano Roosevelt, FDR Jr.'s wife Ethel du Pont holding their son Christopher, President Franklin Delano Roosevelt, and his eldest offspring Anna. Cross-legged on the floor, Anna's Sistie and Buzzie Dall flank little Diana Hopkins, who made her home at the White House, full time.
(*National Archives*)

THE FOURTH INAUGURAL, January 20, 1945, was a cold and bleak affair, held on the South Portico of the White House because it was wartime. We knew the President didn't feel up to making the traditional trek to the Capitol, followed by the parade down Pennsylvania Avenue. He was truly exhausted, though he rallied now and then, feeling like his old self. A covering was placed on the frozen ground to protect the soldier's feet. It scarcely helped. Hidden to the right are all of us— the household staff. (*National Archives*)

THE LAST HURRAH! This historic picture is the last taken of President Roosevelt and his grandchildren. As if he had a premonition, or maybe just because it was an historic occasion, FDR insisted that all the grandchildren gather in Washington for his fourth-term Inauguration. He even paid for the transportation for some of them. Thirteen came. It proved to be an unlucky number, because he died before the year was well underway, on April 12, 1945. The date of the picture is January 20, 1945. First Lady Eleanor sits at extreme left, and the President sits at right with two grandchildren on his lap—David Boynton Roosevelt (Elliott and Ruth Chandler Googin's son) and Franklin Delano Roosevelt III (FDR Jr. and Ethel du Pont's son). Ethel always dressed her sons alike—her other child, Christopher, sits at the extreme left in the first row. Sitting with Chris on the floor are Anne Sturgess Roosevelt, and behind her, Haven Clark

Roosevelt (children of John and Anne Sturgess Clark), John Boettiger (son of Anna Roosevelt and John Boettiger, half brother of Sistie and Buzzie), Elliott Roosevelt, Jr. (Elliott and Ruth Chandler Googin's son), and Kate Roosevelt (James and Betsey Cushing's daughter). Sitting on the chair at extreme right is Sara Delano Roosevelt, Kate's big sister. In the middle row, with his grandmother's hand on his arm, is Curtis "Buzzie" Dall (son of Anna Roosevelt and Curtis Dall), who made his own decision to change his name legally to Roosevelt. Behind Buzzie is his sister, Anna Eleanor "Sistie" Dall. Also seated on the couch with their grandfather are William Donner Roosevelt (Elliott's son with Betty Donner, his first wife) and Ruth Chandler Roosevelt, whom everyone called Chandler to distinguish her from her mother, Elliott's second wife, Ruth Chandler Googins.
(*National Archives*)

THIS IS WHAT IT LOOKED LIKE IN 1921 AT CAMPOBELLO, an island off the coast of Maine where Franklin Delano Roosevelt contracted polio at the age of thirty-nine. Here FDR and Eleanor picnic with friends. (*National Archives*)

FDR DID NOT WANT STATUES TO HIMSELF cluttering up the American landscape but that didn't stop the British. This is one of only three statues of FDR that I know of—all outside the U.S.—and it stands in Grosvenor Square, London. It was erected after FDR's death, and Eleanor attended the unveiling on April 12, 1948, the third anniversary of that fatal day in Warm Springs. (*National Archives*)

THAT DRATTED HAIRNET. Eleanor Roosevelt wore a hairnet for the longest time to keep her hairdo intact. Even in the photograph here, taken at a fancy dinner in London, Eleanor has a hairnet. All the people closest to her tried to get her to stop—Hicky, Anna, and Earl Miller. Finally she did. But in the hairnet days, if she wasn't wearing a hairnet, she loved to wear a ribbon around her head, especially outdoors. (*National Archives*)

CHEESECAKE. Faye Emerson, third wife of Elliott Roosevelt and a Hollywood star of the day, poses for leg art considered bold at the time of their marriage in 1944. She became very prim and proper and always wore her hair in a bun at the White House. (*National Archives*)

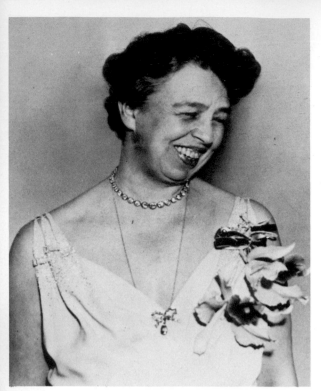

ELEANOR HAD LOVELY SHOULDERS.
Everyone said they were one of her best
features. In certain gowns and poses, Eleanor
could look almost sexy. (*National Archives*)

ELEANOR ON DOT, the
horse her dear friend Earl
Miller gave her. Eleanor
brought Dot from Albany and
kept her stabled at Fort Myer.
Though Dottie didn't return
Eleanor's loyalty, throwing her
now and then, the First Lady
would ride no other horse.
When Dottie died, Eleanor
simply gave up riding. Here
she is on the bridle path of
Potomac Park, along the
famous river, accompanied by
Captain John Reybold, her
husband's military aide.
(*National Archives*)

ELEANOR ROOSEVELT WAS NEVER MORE HAPPY than when surrounded by bright young female faces. She taught for years at the private girls school Todhunter in New York City. Here, early in 1945, she visits Navy government girls who are furthering their college educations through night school. (*National Archives*)

"I'M PUTTING ON MY TOP HAT ... " FDR loved the pageantry of royalty, and one of the highlights of his life occurred in June of 1939, when he donned his top hat and paraded down Pennsylvania Avenue with King George VI, who arrived for a goodwill visit. Their wives, riding in a separate limousine behind them—Queen Elizabeth and Eleanor Roosevelt —didn't fare as well, but smiled through their agony. The Queen had a headache from the unaccustomed heat, and Eleanor was miserable because of a wool dress she was wearing. (*National Archives*)

FORMER FIRST LADY ELEANOR ROOSEVELT WITH THE MAN WHO FIRED HER from the United Nations, President Dwight D. Eisenhower. It is ironic that she, who didn't drink at all, was fired because of something she said about drinking, and that the man who fired her in a moment of pique had been her husband's top general. (*National Archives*)

FDR JR. LEARNED what it was like for his late father, President Roosevelt, when he suffered a leg injury in 1950 and had to hobble on crutches. Behind him and his wife, Suzanne Perrin, is the Capitol, where Junior served as a Congressman from New York from 1949 to 1955. The leg injury, incidentally, occurred when he fell from a horse on his farm near Hopewell Junction, New York, while trying to calm a neighbor's horse. Thirty years later FDR Jr. would make news again when he was married on horseback. (*National Archives*)

A SECOND ROOSEVELT CONGRESSMAN was James, FDR's eldest son, who served the state of California from 1955 to 1965. In this picture, taken August 12, 1948, he wasn't yet in office, but was a Delegate to the Democratic National Convention. Here he confers with Congresswoman Helen Gahagan Douglas just before he announced his support of President Harry Truman. (*National Archives*)

HERE'S HOW THEY CAMPAIGNED IN THE OLD DAYS. FDR speaks
into a battery of mikes as he rides around in his open car in 1940 hustling
votes for his third term. (*National Archives*)

STARTING TO LOOK
FRAIL already in the autumn
of 1944, FDR addresses a
crowd of 100,000 at Soldier
Field, Chicago, campaigning
for a fourth term on October
28. (*National Archives*)

HERE THEY SHARE A LAUGH, Vice-President "Cactus Jack" Garner and FDR in John Nance Garner's hometown of Uvalde, Texas. But it wasn't a happy relationship, and in 1940 FDR ended up feeling Garner was the enemy. (*National Archives*)

ELEANOR LOVED TO HOBNOB WITH HOLLYWOOD STARS, just as FDR preferred royalty. Here the First Lady is the center star among many luminaries including Brian Donlevy, Brian Aherne, Joan Fontaine, Walter Pidgeon, Jinx Falkenburg, Red Skelton, John Garfield, and Yvonne deCarlo. In profile at right is Justice William O. Douglas, a New Deal supporter, whom FDR appointed to the Supreme Court in 1939. (*National Archives*)

INAUGURATION DAY 1941 finds Franklin D. Roosevelt again tophatted and again leaning on his favorite right arm, James, the son he doted on, dressed in Marine Captain's uniform.
(*National Archives*)

THE MAN WHO MISSED HIS DATE WITH DESTINY BY A NARROW MARGIN. Had FDR died just a few months earlier, Henry Wallace would have gone down in history as the thirty-third President. Few people, especially the young, even know that there was a vice-president named Wallace. This was Henry Wallace's greatest hour—Inauguration Day 1941.
(*National Archives*)

WARM SPRINGS—THE LITTLE WHITE HOUSE where the President
died on April 12, 1945. There is a lower level on the back of the house.
The front, however, is a picturebook cottage, with vines twining round the
pillars of the romantic little front porch. Inside, it was a sailor's delight,
with a huge living room–dining room filled with all things nautical,
including a model of a Nantucket whaler on the mantel of a large stone
fireplace. (*National Archives*)

ELEANOR ROOSEVELT AND THE MAN WHO SUCCEEDED HER
HUSBAND. When Eleanor was informed of her husband's death, there
were two things she did before sending for the Vice-President—she
composed the telegram that was to be sent to each of her four sons, and
she ordered Mabel, her maid, to pack a bag. When Harry Truman arrived
at the White House from Capitol Hill, he still had no idea of why Eleanor
had summoned him. "Harry," she said abruptly, "the President is dead."
Truman was too stunned to speak. Finally he asked if there was anything
he could do. Her answer haunted him, "*You* are the one in trouble now ... "
and needing help. (*National Archives*)

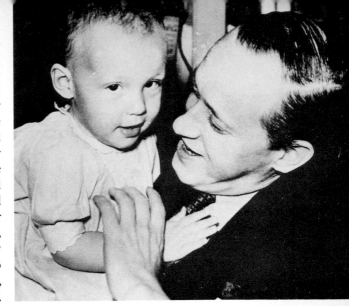

HARRY HOPKINS WITH BABY DIANA, whom Eleanor practically adopted. Diana came all alone, after her mother died, to live at the White House when she was just five. Eleanor was her substitute mother and we observed how attached Eleanor was to Federal Relief Administrator Hopkins. However, later, when Harry Hopkins moved into the White House, Eleanor was not happy.

THREE DEAR FRIENDS OF MINE WHO SHARED ONE NAME but didn't use it: Anna Eleanor. First Lady Anna Eleanor Roosevelt didn't like her first name and never used it. Her daughter didn't like her middle name and used only Anna. Little Anna Eleanor Boettiger, Jr., never got a chance to say what she wanted as a child because everyone called her Sistie. This picture was taken July 7, 1948, when Sistie married Van H. Seagraves of Oregon City, Oregon. Mother Anna Boettiger is placing the bridal veil on Sistie's head at their home in Phoenix. (*National Archives*)

MAKING UP FOR LOST TIME. Backstairs we felt so sorry for Eleanor because she forever regretted that she didn't know how to enjoy children until she became a grandmother, and that she had let nannies and maids raise her own children and act as substitute mothers. Here she holds baby John Boettiger aloft. Johnny, who was daughter Anna's child, was acknowledged to be the prettiest baby to set bootie in the White House. We all joined Eleanor in doting on him. It's a good thing he got away from us, or he would have been irrevocably spoiled. (*National Archives*)

THE VALET WHO WAS WITH FDR WHEN HE DIED, Arthur Prettyman, is seated on the right. Prettyman helped carry the stricken President to his bed at Warm Springs and was haunted by the memory of that fatal day for the rest of his life. In this picture, taken on an earlier day, he and Armstead Barnett are happily exchanging wartime adventures during Barnett's visit home on leave from the Navy. Barnett was a White House butler who now has his own catering service in Washington, D.C.

THE "VILLAIN" IN THE CASE was Housekeeper Henrietta Nesbitt, as far as FDR was concerned. He had a running battle with her over the food he was served, and though he campaigned to get her fired for not serving the food he liked, Eleanor stood fast by her Hyde Park friend, and the Roosevelt administration saw only one housekeeper. Here Mrs. Nesbitt, at left, shows a pledge against wasting food that she has just signed, November 4, 1941—the month before Pearl Harbor—to Eleanor Roosevelt, who also took the pledge, which stated, "I will waste nothing." FDR didn't mind their not wasting, but he was sure *he* was getting the wastes. At right is Harriet Elliott, Associate Administrator in charge of the Consumer Division, Office of Price Administration (OPA), who wrote the pledge for housewives that also states, "As a consumer, in the total defense of democracy, I will do my part to make my home, my community, my country, ready, efficient, and strong...."

ELEANOR AND HICKY, typical view: Lorena, with a cigarette dangling from her lip, listening to Eleanor. This is one of the nicest outfits Lorena Hickok had. Eleanor had a few outfits made from imported materials as a gift for Hicky. (*Credit: UPI*)

THE WAY THEY WERE. These were the intimates on the presidential staff who closed rank around the Boss, as they looked in March of 1943. Most important, they kept the secret of Lucy Mercer Rutherfurd's reentry into FDR's life, her visits to the White House—and they kept the secret even after he was laid in his grave. Left to right are Marvin McIntyre, appointments secretary; Grace Tully, the private secretary who succeeded Missy LeHand; Steve Early, Press Secretary; and Major General Edwin Watson, the Military aide whom FDR always called "Pa" Watson. (*Credit: UPI*)

AND THE WAY *THEY* WERE. Eleanor Roosevelt had someone on her staff who kept her secrets too—Malvina "Tommy" Thompson, her private secretary. They even shared a cottage, each leading her own life. Louis Howe, accompanying the ladies on a 1933 trip to New York, also kept the First Lady's secrets. The only trouble was that he also kept the President's secrets, and his first loyalty was not to Eleanor, but to FDR. (*Credit: UPI*)

JOHN ROOSEVELT, THE
YOUNGEST and the tallest of
the Roosevelt sons, shown here
in June of 1938 with Anne
Lindsay Clark at their wedding
in Nahant, Massachusetts,
bragged for years that he was
the only Roosevelt son who
could stay married to one
woman. But eventually, even
he got a divorce, making it
unanimous. John, however,
continued to be unique among
the four Roosevelt sons—he is
the only Republican.
(*Credit: UPI*)

IT'S HARD TO BELIEVE this is still John. He has changed the most of all
the Roosevelt children that I watched through a dozen years at the White
House. Here he is on his second honeymoon aboard the *Queen Mary*, en
route to London and Paris. His bride is Irene Boyd McAlpine, and the
time is November 1965, twenty-seven years after the first wedding picture
was taken. (*Credit: UPI*)

LUCY MERCER NEVER LOST the lovely, vulnerable look she has in this photograph, which shows the President's "lost love" at about the time FDR contemplated giving up his marriage for her in 1918, when he was assistant secretary of the Navy. Even at the White House, when she would be secretly slipped in to visit FDR, she sometimes wore a seductive ribbon around her neck. The valet who smuggled Lucy— then Mrs. Winthrop Rutherfurd— into the President's study called her "the beautiful lady," and all who were lucky enough to see her agreed. She, not Eleanor, was with the President when he died at Warm Springs, April 12, 1945. (*Credit: Wide World*)

THE LAST TIME I SAW ELEANOR ROOSEVELT, February 27, 1961. How happy and busy she was, bustling about her apartment in New York City and telling me, "Lillian, I'm so glad you finally wrote the book." She had her arm around me, pulling me close to her. I had given her the first copy to come off the presses of *My Thirty Years Backstairs at the White House*, which combined my White House adventures with those of my mother. She had said she could hardly wait to start reading it, telling me it would go down in history. How could either of us know that before the following year would be over, she would be dead. (*Credit: George Mathieu*)

A Royal Mess

At the White House, she would call the stables to have the horse made ready and would drive out to go riding very early in the morning. Once she came back all muddy, but happy that Dot had chosen a soft spot to dump her.

Guest Earl Miller was so much a part of the family that Elliott Roosevelt acted as his best man and Anna was bridesmaid at his second wedding, which Eleanor arranged for him at the Roosevelt Hyde Park estate. He had divorced his first wife, and there had been gossip about Earl and Eleanor.

His second wife was the cousin of his first wife. His new marriage stopped the gossip more or less, but he divorced again in 1934 and continued to be Eleanor's guest, usually at Val-Kill. The White House gang was not surprised by his second divorce in 1934. Or that he married again in 1941 and divorced a third time. One of the wives, incidentally, named Eleanor as corespondent.

What was the attraction in each case? The household staff had it figured out better than any psychiatrist. Earl needed to be mothered, tough as he was, and that meant Eleanor.

Eleanor, in turn, was flattered that a man so handsome and strong, desired by many women, enjoyed her company. Being married to FDR, her ego needed flattery, and Earl gave her lovely compliments that he seemed to mean.

It seemed nothing could break up this friendship. From what I heard, Eleanor and Earl continued to have a close relationship until the end of Eleanor's life in 1962, during which time Earl remained single. As a matter of fact, Miller lived eleven years longer and never remarried.

We always had small emergencies—protocol problems. Once when Amelia Earhart visited the White House, she brought her husband. This threw the social office into a tizzy. As Tommy Thompson, Mrs. Roosevelt's secretary, put it, "In New York he's Mr. Bigshot Publisher. But in Washington, what's a publisher?"

The question was where he would sit at the table at a state dinner. Tommy and the social secretary, Edith Helm, hated to do it, but she was famous and he wasn't. G. P. Putnam was end man at one side of the horseshoe table, while the first woman to fly the Atlantic sat with the President.

Once a prominent Congressman's wife wrote complaining that she hadn't been invited to a certain White House party and angrily demanded to know why. Her husband had received an invitation, she said, but she had been left out. She threatened to "investigate." Furthermore, she had checked other Congressional wives and they had been at the party. The social office did a little discreet investigating of its own and discovered that the Congressman had simply taken his secretary-sweetie to the party instead of his wife.

As Edith Helm pondered how to avoid a scandal, be diplomatic, keep from outright lying, and smooth the woman's ruffled feathers, she muttered over and over, "This is a royal mess—a royal mess!" How Edith solved this royal mess, I don't know. And there was always another one.

We had so many royal visitors during the war years that someone suggested the President should call himself King Franklin, or at least Prince Franklin, so he wouldn't be upstaged all the time. Before the war, Missy used to teasingly call him "Your Majesty."

We entertained Grand Duchess Charlotte and Prince Felix of Luxembourg and their son, Grand Duke Jean. We hosted Crown Prince Frederick and Princess Ingrid of Denmark, and Queen Wilhelmina of the Netherlands, as well as her daughter, Crown Princess Juliana, and Prince Bernhard of the Netherlands.

And King Peter of Yugoslavia. And King George II of Greece. And Crown Prince Gustavus Adolphus of Sweden. And, of course, the President's all-time favorite, Crown Princess Martha of Norway, who came often, and her husband, Crown Prince Olaf, who came occasionally. Princess Martha was the most flirtatious of the royal crowd. Eleanor did not take kindly to it.

Madame Chiang Kai-shek was another woman who knew how to play up to the President, but for some reason, the word was Eleanor was egging her on, instead of acting irritated or hurt. Then Madame Chiang went one step too far and started going to the President's Oval study—where Eleanor was sometimes not a welcome guest—and talking with him far into the night.

A few times, Eleanor even acted against her self-imposed rule of leaving FDR alone, and went busting in to break it up. Her excuse, which did not impress the valet too much, was that Madame Chiang needed her sleep.

We didn't worry about Madame Chiang. She got her rest in the morning, between the silken sheets that she had brought and I

A Royal Mess

sewed together each day to make a luxurious sleeping bag for her super-sensitive person.

Everyone sighed with relief—even Eleanor—when Madame Chiang finally left. We agreed with Tommy Thompson, who told several of us maids in an exhausted voice. "There goes one of the most spoiled guests in the annals of White House history."

She didn't want to go lay a wreath at the Tomb of the Unknown Soldier. She had to be coaxed. She didn't want to have her picture taken with Eleanor on the White House lawn. Chairs had to be provided and all kinds of things done before she would simmer down and let the photographers do their work. And even then, she looked grimly at the photographers and resisted their efforts to make her smile.

Madame Chiang was a sweet little headache to everyone at the White House and even to the leaders of Congress when she came to visit in 1943, not as a State visitor but as a guest of Eleanor Roosevelt.

Although she wasn't even a chief of state, she made a grand pronouncement that she would make but one speech to the members of Congress, meaning that they would have to hold a joint session. But Congress had not even invited her to speak, and the leaders were most annoyed.

The word trickled around the backstairs household that Madame Chiang was jealous of Queen Wilhelmina, one of the few women in the world to have addressed a joint session, so she was using regal tactics to get the same treatment for herself. We who waited on Madame Chiang knew that she considered herself royalty—or better.

Anyway, poor Eleanor got involved in trying to help "the Dragon Lady"—as some servants called her behind her back —fulfill her dream. But she fared no better. The best that could be worked out was an invitation from the Senate to speak to them and a separate invitation from the House to speak to them. And when she said she would only speak once, both houses said okay, she could choose the chamber and they would make available to the other body the remarks she had made!

When Madame Chiang saw that she couldn't lead the Congress around by the nose, she simmered down, and docile as a declawed tiger, went to each chamber to speak.

The People Around FDR

We guessed Madame Chiang didn't want to blow her chance to ask Congress for money and munitions to fight the Japanese.

I'll never forget the special tea Mrs. Roosevelt had set up to greet Madame Chiang upon her arrival at the White House. It was such a special event that FDR joined his wife. But Madame Chiang turned it into a disaster by her disregard for Eleanor's feelings. Mrs. Roosevelt proudly told her Chinese guest that she had gotten this special tea from the Chinese Embassy for the event, and that it was a hundred years old. Instead of exclaiming at how thoughtful her hostess had been, or making polite noises on how good the tea was, Madame Chiang said, "Humpf, in my country we only use this tea for medicine."

But that was only the beginning of Eleanor's troubles with the grand dame. Madame Chiang not only brought two nurses, but she also brought along two relatives—a nephew-bodyguard and a reed-slim young niece to act as her companion. The niece immediately informed our backstairs crowd that she considered herself superior to the white race—she claimed the family was descended from Confucius—and started to act her conviction out by treating Eleanor Roosevelt like some kind of servant.

This creature would go barging into Eleanor's room to tell her what she needed. Finally Eleanor had to explain to her that she must go through the proper channels, and if someone else, such as her social secretary, was unable to get what Madame Chiang wanted, the social secretary would talk to Eleanor about it.

But the worst was to come when Eleanor Roosevelt realized Madame Chiang had no intention of leaving and did not mention any departure date. Eleanor thought it would be the standard three-day visit.

The farthest Eleanor dared to go was to have Edith suggest to the haughty young Chiang relative that they might like to move to the Blair House, the President's official guest house. Without even consulting Madame Chiang, the girl said no indeed, they intended to stay at the White House.

So they stayed until they were good and ready to leave— about twelve days later.

The most famous White House drop-in guest was Winston Churchill, who acted as if he belonged there. A lot of people around the White House were half-afraid of Churchill—including

A Royal Mess

Eleanor. She admitted to intimates that she had trouble talking with him, that he intimidated her by his loudness and abruptness. Also, he gave his opinion and didn't seem to care what she thought.

Early in the morning when I arrived at the White House, Churchill would be stalking the halls of the second floor shouting, "Where is my man?" He wanted his valet. Although he was up and around, he told me he was not officially out of bed until eleven o'clock, and that I shouldn't tell anyone he was up.

It was ridiculous because he was so noisy, everyone knew when he was up, but he wanted to be ignored until eleven o'clock. This kind of thing made the help back off, but it didn't bother me. I knew he was just a jolly old soul acting gruff. With me, he would laugh and kid a little. And because the President called me, "Little Girl," so did he.

Socialites remarked what a pity it was that poor Mr. Churchill had no female companionship at the White House. We backstairs knew that wasn't completely true. He didn't have girlfriends or other companionship at the White House, but he did have various friends *away* from the White House. When he had been in residence for more than a week, he would get stir-crazy and send his trusted aide to notify his friends that soon he would be paying them a call—under strict security.

Then for a few days he would be calm and serene.

Eleanor said she hated to see all the trays of liquor around when he was there, and FDR was once quoted as saying after Churchill left that he hoped he wouldn't have to look at another drink for a week. For a day or so, he didn't.

Eleanor once dared to tell FDR that she worried about Churchill's influence on him because of all the drinking. FDR retorted that she needn't worry because it wasn't *his* side of the family that had a drinking problem.

Poor Eleanor had seen what liquor did to the two dearest persons of her youth—her father and her brother, Hall. FDR enjoyed his martinis and old-fashioned, but we never saw him intoxicated.

Churchill was not the ideal guest from the servants' viewpoint. Some White House guests gave generous tips for the slightest help, or even in appreciation for how well their rooms were kept. All Churchill came up with was a bunch of cheap little photos of himself, which he didn't even bother to autograph. Adding insult to injury, the word "souvenir" was printed on them.

At least one person that I know of did eventually get a little gift from the British Prime Minister. On one of his visits, following what I heard was a little hint from FDR, he brought a doll from England for little Diana Hopkins. It helped make up for the time he had ignored her. And he warmed up enough to have a gag picture made with Diana wearing an identical "siren suit" which someone had made for her. Both were grinning from ear to ear as they modeled the famous suits the Prime Minister had designed for himself.

Much has been made of the 1939 royal visit of the King and Queen of England—George VI and Elizabeth—and reams have been written in glowing terms, making the visit seem all sweetness and light. Well, now let me tell you the rest of the story.

To begin with, the real purpose of the visit was never really told, to my knowledge, outside the President's office. It was to jolly the American people into developing an affection for the British.

Within hearing of the White House help, FDR told aides that we might have to enter a great world war in Britain's rescue. At this point in history—the spring of 1939—war clouds were heavy overhead. In fact, several months after the royal visit, Hitler fired the opening gun and marched into Poland.

All kinds of peace movements and organizations were bent on avoiding foreign entanglements and letting Europe settle its own problems. Many called FDR a warmonger for preparing for war by getting shipbuilding and ammunition plants going.

Almost every man in Congress hated FDR and was determined to keep from spending tax money on armament. Youth groups marched against Roosevelt. They weren't thrilled that FDR had said in his second-term renomination acceptance speech, "This generation of Americans has a rendezvous with destiny!" Youth did not care for that rendezvous. Nor did Congress.

The talk around the White House was that this was a visit to sway the emotions of the public, and thus sway Congress. In fact, before the visit was over, the King went to Congress and did a little swaying of his own.

A Royal Mess

The game plan was that the royal couple would go to Canada and then casually come to the U.S. Bit by bit the public, through stories about the upcoming visit, got all steamed up and welcomed the Britishers with open arms.

George VI and Elizabeth arrived from Canada by private train at Washington's Union Station on the morning of June 8. The President and Eleanor went to greet them as they arrived with their entourage in their own royal train made up of a dozen luxurious blue- and silver-streaked cars. A reception was held in a special room of Union Station, which had been redecorated for the event. The price was no object.

It was an event of pomp and ceremony—the King and Queen marched through a military guard of honor to where the President and Mrs. Roosevelt stood with the Secretary of State, and British Ambassador Sir Ronald Lindsay, and Lady Lindsay. Half the Embassy turned out, as well as our cabinet members.

We were very amused at some of the orders given by the royal couple, but the protocol people who had to explain all this silly business had a royal headache. For example, the King and Queen decreed that no flashbulbs could be used closer than fifty feet from their royal bodies. Even for ordinary photos outside in the sunlight, no photographer was permitted closer than twenty feet from King George VI and Queen Elizabeth. The messengers to the President reported that photographers were furious and muttering, "Who the hell do they think they are—the President?"

It was a weak joke to emphasize that even FDR, who could make such bans, didn't. FDR was much loved by the photographers for always cooperating and flashing his famous grin.

After that *great* beginning, everything else developed some sort of fatal flaw, beginning with the procession through the streets of Washington to the White House, where the whole diplomatic corps was waiting. The day—June 8—was exceedingly hot, and the Queen was used to the cool of England and Canada. Her delicate skin immediately developed a painful sunburn, and worse than that, she arrived at the White House with a blazing headache.

She didn't dare tell this to Eleanor Roosevelt, her hostess, who sat beside her also suffering in silence in a hot wool dress in the heat. I only learned of it later from the royal maids in the entourage. Miserable as she felt, the Queen had to smile fixedly as she made a grand circle with the King in the East Room, being greeted by more than seventy diplomatic personages.

Then, sick as she was, the Queen had to eat her first meal, which I was told, was nothing to help a queasy stomach. Green turtle soup, sweetbreads, and pineapple shortcake. It would have been small comfort to her, I'm sure, had she known that the President had been eating a lot of sweetbreads lately—thanks to Mrs. Nesbitt's pigheadedness—and was not in the mood for them either.

At 2 P.M. the household staff had been ordered to be outside the White House in best bib and tucker to see the King and Queen off on a sightseeing tour. Again the heat and the hubbub. The streets were filled with happy Americans, except for the hundredplus who, in the course of the day, suffered heat prostration and had to be taken to hospitals by ambulance—one dead on arrival. Even Girl Scouts fainted on the White House lawn.

After this ordeal came something worse for the poor Queen's headache—a garden party at the British Embassy. The British subjects bowed, and she held her aching head high as she again made a grand circle while someone from the Ambassador's staff brought special people over to her.

The British staff told us later that the royal couple had gotten precious little sleep as they traveled from Canada in their train, all through the night of the 7th, to arrive at ten A.M. on the 8th.

So the garden party was no treat. But the worst still lay ahead—the torture of the State dinner that night, after only a small rest from the garden party.

Although the queen had held a parasol above her white hat and white, wide-skirted gown as she rode in the open car and stood on the Embassy lawns, her sunburn was considerably worse.

Now she had other problems, such as walking with the President, who was scarcely able to walk the few steps to his chair, and charmingly telling the President what had impressed her most about his city, through the haze of heat, crowds, and general malaise.

And the meal wasn't the kind one welcomed if one's stomach was already slightly distressed: clam cocktail, calf's head soup, terrapin, corn bread, boned capon, cranberry sauce, and a variety of vegetables, including sweet potato cones, beets, and peas, frozen cheese and cress salad, and a heavy dessert of maple and almond ice cream with white pound cake.

FDR didn't seem to notice that the Queen, seated on his right, only toyed with her food. He had a job to do and he did it, giving a message to the world, via his toast to the King, that England and the United States were as one: "It is because each nation has no fear of the other that we have unfortified borders [Canada-U.S.] between us. And it is because neither of us fears aggression on the part of the other that we have entered into no race of armaments, the one against the other."

Then the King of England did his part, drawing the union of the two nations closer together: "I pray that our great nations may ever in the future walk together in a path of friendship in a world of peace."

As I heard it later, the Queen would have been grateful to escape to the first comfortable bedroom in several days—she had been unable to sleep well in the train from Canada—but that was not to be. First she had to sit smiling through a strange musicale. The East Room—not air-conditioned at the time—was crowded and hot beyond belief.

She didn't know the drama she had missed. First of all, the President had insisted that his special friend, Missy LeHand, be at the most coveted royal dinner party, which would make her the only "secretary" there. Eleanor had countered by inviting her *two* secretaries—Tommy Thompson, her personal secretary, and Edith Helm, her social secretary.

Then there was the drama that went on unnoticed involving the special entertainers. Marian Anderson, the controversial black singer was there as a sort of punishment for the DAR—the Daughters of the American Revolution—who had not permitted her to sing in Constitution Hall because of her color. As we black servants at the White House chortled, "The DAR may not think Marian Anderson is good enough to sing in their Hall, but the First Lady thinks she is good enough to sing for a king and queen."

But we felt Anderson let us down a bit that night when she refused to sing the songs that had been scheduled for her, and which she had agreed to do. Suddenly Negro spirituals were beneath her. She said she was going to sing opera. Fortunately she was dissuaded.

Then Kate Smith said she had to sing her song first because she had an appointment elsewhere and couldn't let singing for a king and queen interfere with her schedule. The White House was so miffed with her that had the King himself not sent word in advance that he would like to hear her sing "When the Moon Comes Over the Mountain," she would have been excused from singing altogether.

Fortunately, one part of the musicale soothed the royal brow.

For a touch of class, Eleanor had invited opera's Lawrence Tibbett. But unfortunately, for a touch of novelty, she invited the Coon Creek Girls from Coon Creek, Kentucky, to sing their country music special, "How Many Biscuits Can You Eat."

The biscuits did not go down too well.

Then, adding to the Queen's already royal headache was heard the clomping of the hard shoes of eight pairs of square dancers that Eleanor had recruited from the mountains of North Carolina—farmers, teachers, and mechanics. They called themselves the Soco Gap Square Dancers, and they brought special shoes along to give an added whack to the wooden floor as they danced. The combined sound of thirty-two feet stomping the stage in the hot, crowded East Room to the wild hooting of a song called "Dive and Shoot the Owl," gave the Queen a throbbing pain as each foot met the floor.

Then the third entertainer couldn't be found because someone had played a nasty trick on him, warning the White House police and Secret Service that a suspicious looking character was trying to enter the White House to get to the royal couple. Just because the folk singer, Alan Lomax, was long of hair and short of socks in a day long before hippies were fashionable, he was searched, frisked, and third-degreed until he was all shook up.

He got into the room and on stage just in time and managed to muddle through, which was more than the Queen managed. The wife of the British Ambassador and another guest had to lead her out into the cooler night air for fear she would faint.

Meanwhile, life had been no happier for us upstairs with the royal entourage. The royal couple had brought so many retainers that we couldn't begin to accommodate them. Many had to return to the train station and sleep on the train. A few of the top staff members fared better and were sent to the British Embassy.

I think an American reader would get a kick out of seeing what royalty thought they had to take along for even a short trip. They made American presidents and first ladies look like hillbillies in comparison. The Queen brought a lady-in-waiting and an assistant lady-in-waiting, each with her own maid. The King brought a lord-in-waiting who had his own manservant. The King also had two equerries to look after the horses he must have forgotten to bring. And a king's page and a male secretary. Her Majesty had two personal maids and a queen's footman. His Majesty countered with a king's footman and four spare footmen, plus two valets. The Queen trumped with a lord chamberlain to the queen.

All the King could summon for the great finale to his game of status symbols was one clerk, a press officer, two Scotland Yard inspectors and a troop of Canadian mounted police.

When Queen Elizabeth went to her room, she suffered a new shock. Our irrepressible Lizzie had slipped a hand-drawn caricature of the Queen into her room.

The British guards were horrified. They viewed it as a terrible breach of security and put it in the category of a voodoo doll that signaled a death wish.

But there was nothing sinister about it. Lizzie was simply trying to help a struggling artist among the backstairs staff, who hoped the Queen would sign his work of art to increase its value. He was not trying to put the hex on her.

There was a big hullaballoo about it and Lizzie was in deep trouble. But not for long. Being the dear, sweet apple of FDR's eye, she got away with a little scolding.

The Queen also found heavy blankets in an already stifling bedroom. She had forgotten that, thinking the month of June could be cold, she herself had ordered them. The White House had followed blindly the requests for "coverlets."

The next day was also a killer. As the King and Queen charged around Washington, sped on by Eleanor, we pitied the poor monarchs and said, "Eleanor seems to think others can keep up with her."

That second day the "schedule" included a visit with both

houses of Congress, lunch on the Potomac, a tour of Mt. Vernon, the laying of a wreath at George Washington's Tomb, a tour of CCC—Civilian Conservation Corps—work in Virginia, the laying of a second wreath at the Tomb of the Unknown Soldier at Arlington Cemetery, an afternoon tea on the White House lawn, and in the evening, the traditional return dinner at the British Embassy with the King and Queen playing host to FDR and Eleanor.

Thus endeth the second day.

The second phase of the royal visit consisted of a trip to the President's estate at Hyde Park, which, as every school child in the nation learned from extensive press coverage, involved a picnic at which royalty learned about hot dogs.

Those of us who didn't have to go with the First Family to Hyde Park were certainly relieved. Mama, who had stayed long enough to help on the Washington end of the visit, now officially retired from the White House. I kept busy putting the pieces back together at the Mansion for the return of the First Lady.

I remember one last laugh Mama and I had in reviewing the royal stay at the White House concerned a last minute check by Tommy and Edith of the rooms the King and Queen would be staying in. They found an etching in the King's bedroom that would certainly have been insulting—the surrender of the British General Cornwallis to the Americans at Yorktown!

The Queen had been given six orchid corsages on the trip to Hyde Park, and she could, of course, only honor one benefactor by wearing his corsage. Not so for our Lizzie McDuffie, who got off the train at Hyde Park with five orchid corsages across her bosom, gaily calling out to the other White House servants, "I am Queen Elizabeth. Now where is my lady-in-waiting?"

Only Lizzie would get away with such deviltry. Later, when a valet told this story to FDR out of earshot of royalty, the President laughed and said, "Damned if she isn't."

When the backstairs crew came back from Hyde Park, I soon learned that the bad luck streak hadn't changed. Everything that could go wrong at Sara Roosevelt's fancy dinner for the English monarch had.

The President's mother hadn't had enough chinaware to set the table for such a crowd and had borrowed from her widowed

A Royal Mess

step-daughter-in-law, Mrs. James R. Roosevelt, who lived at a nearby estate. A stack of these fine dishes fell to the floor during the meal, and the thoughtless relative said loudly, "I certainly hope those weren't *my* dishes that were broken." The President's mother was mortified to have the Queen know she had to *borrow* chinaware.

And yes, they were broken. Followed by a butler breaking a bunch of glasses and almost breaking his leg.

That was the formal dinner at Hyde Park. But the only part of the Queen's visit that people still talk about is the good old American picnic at which Eleanor served the royal couple hot dogs.

I have heard people blame Eleanor for having done something so gauche as to serve cheap hot dogs to a king and queen. These people don't know that other standard meals were also served. They only remember those hot dogs.

So I'd like to set the record straight. In the first place, the idea had originated with the President himself, not Eleanor, although she liked the idea. Many neighbors in the Hyde Park area pitched in and brought other specialties for the picnic.

For example, Henry Morgenthau and his wife, Elinor, who lived nearby at Hopewell Junction, brought strawberries from their estate for strawberry shortcake. Another guest brought smoked turkey. There were also hot sausages, Virginia ham, and baked beans. And beer, as well as soft drinks and coffee.

Some of the guests were invited BYOL—Bring Your Own Lunch. They ate on the lawns. The royal guests didn't sit on blankets on the ground, eating with the ants. They sat at tables for four on the porch of Hilltop Cottage, the little hideaway that FDR was then constructing for himself.

After the King supped on hot dogs and pronounced them good, and stuffed himself with smoked turkey and strawberry shortcake, he turned to the Queen and asked what she would like to do. She had a one-word answer: "Rest."

But FDR and the King were not in a resting mood. The President asked George VI how he would like a dip in the pool. Soon they were both on their way in FDR's special car with FDR at the wheel. FDR had no pool at his cottage, but Eleanor had one at her cottage, Val-Kill, so they headed there.

The People Around FDR

The King, I heard, looked absolutely ridiculous in a mid-Victorian bathing suit with little sleeves and pant legs. FDR had a modern suit. The King was so shy and conservative that when they ran into a gang of newspaper photographers lurking around in wait for them, FDR had to send word that there would be no swimming unless they got lost or made a gentleman's agreement to take no pictures.

They promised not to take pictures and stayed. And history is the poorer.

While they were swimming, Tommy and Edith realized that the King and President would want to change into dry clothes at Val-Kill cottage so they rushed there and threw into drawers and closets all the stuff that had been left out by guests. One thing they were very careful about was the bathroom the King would use to shower and change clothes.

Only later did they realize they had been so careful they had blown it. They had taken off the shower curtain to change it for a new one and had forgotten to hang it. Tommy said, "Oh well, everything else fell apart during this visit, it's a fitting end to disaster."

But it wasn't quite. The parting shot was when Sara Roosevelt crushed what was left of the butlers' spirits by labeling them all clumsy and uncoordinated. They heard her.

We looked at the poor bedraggled butlers when they arrived back at the White House, so tired they were almost falling over their feet—and one hobbling with a sprained ankle. These same poor men had worked so hard in Washington that they had no juice left for Hyde Park.

We wanted to tell them we understood—so we sang a line from an old song: "Nobody knows the trouble I've seen..."

III
GROWING UP ROOSEVELT

9

Long Ago and Far Away

I often wonder how different Eleanor and Franklin's life would have been had they not been related to Theodore Roosevelt. Rough rider Teddy with his "Bully, bully," had made life in the Governor's Mansion and the White House seem like sheer fun.

FDR had not had too much fun in his youth, being an only child and saddled to a smothering and doting mother. As a boy he determined to go into politics and become Governor of the State of New York. When Teddy became President, that became young Franklin's goal, too.

Even before that, Teddy was Franklin's hero. FDR used to tell his cronies at the cocktail hour that when his fifth cousin was storming up hills in the Spanish-American War, he almost enlisted at the age of sixteen. The only thing that stopped him was a siege of scarlet fever.

According to the valets, FDR would slap his useless legs after telling this story, and comment sadly that some drastic health problem had always arrived at every important time of decision. Polio had almost nipped his political career in the bud. We didn't know then that a cerebral hemorrhage would interfere at the very time FDR was deciding to use the atomic bomb to bring a war to its end—and that Truman would have the honor of "winning" World War II.

FDR was proud that the hero of San Juan Hill was his fifth cousin. But actually Eleanor was a much closer relative of the twenty-sixth President. Theodore Roosevelt was her uncle. President Teddy Roosevelt was actually Theodore Roosevelt, Jr. Eleanor's father, Elliott, Teddy's brother, was only two years younger, having been born in 1860. There were two girls in the family as well, an older sister, Anna—called "Auntie Bye" by Eleanor—and a younger sister, Corinne—called "Auntie Pussie."

Eleanor's father, Elliott, was the black sheep of the family because he drank. According to Eleanor and other members of the family, he turned to drink to ease the pain in his head. It turned out that he had a brain tumor.

Yet, he had crowded a lifetime of adventure in a short thirty-one years. He was a swashbuckling adventurer when he captivated and married Eleanor's mother, Anna, one of the reigning debutante beauties of her day. He had just returned from a hunting expedition in India, where he had stalked tigers and elephants.

• Already a wealthy young man when he married Eleanor's mother, at the age of twenty-one, Elliott had financed his safari from what was then a sizeable inheritance from his mother's family—around $150,000.

The two brothers certainly had a different slant on life—Teddy spent his time and wealth furthering his career, while Elliott spent his avoiding pain and trying to get some fun and excitement out of life. He drank and played polo and became famous for both.

Eleanor's father took drugs as well as drank—a bad combination. Laudanum was the addictive drug of the day, and the disasterous result was that he eventually became suicidal. Fortunately total disaster was averted by placing him under doctors' care.

Eleanor avoided talking about her father's ailment. I heard from others, and later read, that it had been thought to be epilepsy before it was found to be a tumor.

We thought one reason Eleanor was so health conscious was that both her parents had died at an early age. Her mother was just under thirty when she died of diptheria. Eleanor was only eight years old. Her father died two years later in 1894, when he was only thirty-one, of alcoholism, or the tumor, or both. Or of injuries brought on by drinking. Actually, he fell off a horse in a collision with a lamp post—"A lamp post did him in."

The way I heard the story from the staff who frequented Hyde Park, as a child Eleanor's greatest love was her father, who had made her feel pretty and important to him. She resented her beautiful mother who had insulted her by nicknaming her "Granny" and told her what a pity it was that she was ugly.

Long Ago and Far Away

When her mother died, Eleanor hadn't been too upset, thinking that she and her father would have a wonderful time together. Instead, her maternal grandmother, Grandma Hall, took her and her brother Hall, and told Elliott he must stay away, or she might have him committed to a mental institution. Eleanor's mother had earned little Eleanor's undying hostility by having had Elliott committed to an insane asylum once before, in Paris, so it was no idle threat. Eleanor's mother then tried to gain control of the purse strings by having the American courts declare Eleanor's father legally insane.

While the courts were still debating the insanity case, Teddy Roosevelt rushed to Paris and offered his brother a compromise. If he put the money in a trust fund to protect his wife and children and went to a clinic to dry out, the court case would be dropped and he could come back to America.

He agreed, but after he had done what his wife wanted, she still wouldn't allow him to come home, and he went back to the bottle, with moments now and then of trying to fight alcoholism.

At the White House, we household helpers wondered what the public would think if they knew Eleanor's history. They saw only the cool, efficient dynamo who dashed around the country— the arms and legs of her polio-impaired husband. They did not know she was also a haunted woman, still mourning for her father.

She also mourned for her little brother Elliott Jr. who died when he was four. Both he and Hall, who was three, contracted scarlet fever; only Hall survived.

We would sometimes hear Eleanor Roosevelt telling someone in her high-pitched voice about how dark and dismal her grandmother's house had been to an eight-year-old girl, and how the only sunny thing had been her little brother Hall, who had made her feel important.

We were glad to know that something had helped make up for the constant disappointments of her relationship with her father. He would promise to come and then not show up. When he did come and take her for an outing, he would stash her somewhere and forget about her while he went for a few drinks.

Poor Eleanor would put up with anything if only she could be with the father she loved. She pleaded to live with her father, but of course it was hopeless. She learned to live for the wonderful letters he sent her, which made everything he wrote about seem a happy adventure that someday she would be a part of.

Then even the letters stopped. As we heard it, within several weeks, he had suffered two falls from horses while drunk, and the second killed him. He died without his adoring Eleanor at his side, and she was very bitter.

We wondered if Eleanor was so abnormally intent on taking care of Hall because of some feeling, young as she had been, of not having taken care of her father. Eleanor was that kind—always seeming to feel guilty if she didn't take care of the hurt or downtrodden.

It may sound a little harsh, but we used to wonder if FDR would have married Eleanor if she hadn't been so closely related to his hero, Teddy Roosevelt. They waited to set their wedding date until President Teddy found a date on which he could give the bride away.

Eleanor would laugh a little ruefully as she told guests how unwise it was to have a president at a wedding because he steals the show, and the party becomes his and not the bride and groom's. Before they went to one of their sons' weddings, she warned FDR not to do the same thing Uncle Teddy had done.

Teddy had been like the pied piper. All the guests followed him and Eleanor had been most embarrassed to stand alongside her bridegroom with nobody paying them any attention.

FDR laughed at Eleanor's warning because it hadn't bothered him a bit that he had shared his big day with her uncle. Someone once asked FDR what Teddy had told him at his wedding, and FDR had said Teddy Roosevelt had boomed out two important statements—"Where are the refreshments?" and "It's just bully keeping the name in the family."

There was wealth on both sides of the Roosevelt family—the Oyster Bay side, to which Eleanor and Teddy Roosevelt belonged, and the Hyde Park side, to which FDR and his mother, Sara Delano Roosevelt, belonged.

When they were children, Eleanor had tried to befriend Alice Roosevelt, Uncle Teddy's daughter and her first cousin. The friendship ran hot and cold. First Alice would be friendly, then she would be snooty.

Eleanor was treated as a disposable friend.

Long Ago and Far Away

They corresponded on and off, but Eleanor said she was always aware that Alice wrote clever, witty things that she could not think of while writing a letter. Both were close to the same Auntie Bye, their fathers' sister. At various times, both lived with her.

Another link between Alice and Eleanor was that early in life they both had lost parents. Eleanor felt sorry that Alice had known death even earlier than she. Alice's mother, Alice Lee, for whom she was named died two days after giving birth to her. Her paternal grandmother, Mittie Roosevelt, also died that day.

It was on this terrible day, we heard at the White House, that Eleanor's father ran out of Teddy Roosevelt's house declaring that the Roosevelt family was cursed.

Alice and Eleanor were only months apart in age—Alice born in February 1884, and Eleanor on October 11 of the same year.

Eleanor once said within Lizzie's hearing that from the first she had been aware that her cousin Alice was prettier than she, and that there had been family talk of what a beautiful baby Princess Alice—the "title" bestowed by the newspapers—had been.

Since I was on crutches, it was an interesting point to me that the Roosevelt family seemed to have a bone weakness on the Oyster Bay side of the family. Eleanor Roosevelt wore a back brace when she was just a few years old to correct a spine curvature. Teddy Roosevelt's sister, Auntie Bye, had a curved spine all her life and could not straighten up. Alice had to wear braces on both her legs as a child, and as a tot, Eleanor's son Elliott had to wear leg braces, too.

It was ironic that Eleanor married a man who, for a different reason, ended up in a leg brace that he had to wear for the rest of his life.

One of the stories told around the White House when I went there to work was how Alice, as a White House brat, had been a most difficult child to raise—always defying her father. When he forbade her to smoke, she spent a lot of time on the White House roof, smoking.

He also didn't want her to drive, but he gave in, and she tooled around in her own car at an early age. Eleanor did not learn to drive until she was middle-aged.

Alice certainly was not reticent when it came to talking about her private life. She bragged that while her husband was in Congress, they had happily broken Prohibition with the help of a very efficient butler, making wine and gin at home.

That was the kind of thing Eleanor didn't think was funny. Even after Prohibition was repealed, she served only beer at her private dinner parties, and hated to do that. FDR served drinks of every kind to his guest, but that was his business, and she didn't interfere.

I don't think the importance of two FDR relatives—Aunt Polly and Daisy—has ever been realized. They were the only two relatives, outside of daughter Anna, whom FDR trusted in the last days of his life concerning his love affair with Lucy Mercer Rutherfurd.

Both were spinster relatives. Polly was actually named Laura Delano. She was the youngest sister of his mother Sara. I don't know exactly what FDR's relationship was to Daisy, but it was a remote one. She was Polly's cousin, and when you saw one, you saw the other. They were inseparable.

Daisy's name was Margaret Suckley. History knows her as the lady who gave FDR his famous dog Fala. Both ladies hovered over FDR and relished every detail about him because they had no public lives of their own.

Laura was tiny and beautiful, and the inside story was that when she had been very young, a young Japanese man had fallen in love with her and she with him. She had gone to China to visit her father, who was living there. He quickly sent her home and broke up the budding affair.

Since her love had gone unfulfilled, she determined that the same thing wouldn't happen to others—especially not to her beloved FDR. We figured this was why she cooperated with FDR to make it possible for him to see Lucy Mercer, even after she became a Rutherfurd. And anything Aunt Polly—as everyone called Laura—wanted, Daisy went along with.

I would see both of them at the White House—thicker than thieves with FDR, but not with Eleanor. They were truly *his* friends and lined up in his camp.

Aunt Polly was still lovely. Although some kidded her about dyeing her hair "blue," I thought it was a lovely blue tint. She was very dainty but Daisy Suckley was plain and looked like an old-fashioned school marm. They both were a lot of fun, and we enjoyed having them there.

We could see that Eleanor bristled whenever Aunt Polly was around, so we helped keep her out of Eleanor's way. That was part of life at the White House—knowing which Roosevelt a guest was loyal to.

The first Roosevelt to come to America was Claes Martenszen Van Rosenvelt. He arrived in 1640. That gave rise to the rumor that the Roosevelts had Jewish blood. This was something Sara Delano Roosevelt bitterly resented because she was quite prejudiced against both blacks and Jews.

From what we heard at the White House, Eleanor had been bigoted at first but had grown to admire both Jews and blacks and became good friends with them after she became acquainted with people such as Bernard Baruch and Mary McLeod Bethune. As a matter of fact, we heard that Eleanor overcame her prejudices first and had to gently lead FDR into open-mindedness.

To return to old Claes, his two sons started the lines that produced Eleanor and Franklin. Eleanor was descended from Johannes and Franklin from Jacobus, or, as he called himself, James.

Eleanor also had an illustrious ancestry on her mother's side—the Livingstons. Robert Livingston was the man who administered the oath of office to George Washington, and Philip Livingston was one of the men who signed the Declaration of Independence.

On the darker side, Eleanor also had some slightly weird relatives. One aunt was famous for dying her hair purple in a day one didn't dye one's hair at all. One uncle was downright dangerous. That was Uncle Vallie, who used people for target practice and shot at them with a rifle from his upstairs window if they came too near. Now and then he had to be restrained for his own good—and everyone else's.

On FDR's side, about the most peculiar thing anyone did was to name his child James Roosevelt Roosevelt. He was called "Rosy." FDR's half brother was twenty-eight years older than he and peculiar enough to balance everything out. After being married to an Astor, he turned his back on money and married a barmaid. His son, also an eccentric, eventually ended up a recluse living in a garage.

Outside of that, FDR's side of the family seemed very stable.

Eleanor grew up fearing and dreading Old Barleycorn. Her father had been institutionalized because of drink. Her uncles drank. Then, after a bad marriage, her brother Hall turned to the bottle.

Eleanor was powerless to stop his self-destruction. Once Hall almost destroyed his own son. As we heard it, it happened at Val-Kill, a mile or so from the big mansion. Hall and his young son Danny were visiting Eleanor. Under the influence of liquor and while Eleanor was away, Hall became so enraged when Danny didn't jump to do something, he knocked him down.

Danny fell in such a way that he had to be taken to a hospital. The story, as we heard it from the servants who knew Hyde Park well, got more complicated. Instead of calling immediately for an ambulance, Hall drove his son to the hospital himself—or tried to. He was so drunk that he drove off the road and was apprehended by the police.

When Eleanor first heard of the incident, she understood only that her nephew had wound up in a ditch with a broken collarbone. At the time, Marion Dickerman was also a guest at Val-Kill, and Eleanor immediately assumed Marion had been driving. She tongue-lashed her. Poor Marion didn't know what she was talking about.

The way we heard it, Eleanor never apologized to Marion. She just said no more about it. Marion, understanding Eleanor's emotional hang-ups about her brother, forgave her and said nothing either.

I wish I could say that Hall quit drinking and Danny grew up to be a great success. But it didn't happen. Hall continued his self-destruction, and Danny was killed in an airplane crash in Mexico in 1937.

Hall was divorced from his wife Margaret Cutter at the time, and, as usual, Eleanor was the one to take care of everything and keep Hall going through this terrible time, including accompanying Hall and his son's body to the burial.

Long Ago and Far Away

Eleanor had seen too much of death too soon in life, we said of her, and we felt sorry. Once, when someone backstairs received news from a relative of a child's death, she told Lizzie and me that her first awareness of death had come when she was on a ship at about the age of three.

She and her parents were sailing for a vacation in Europe aboard the *Britannic*. In the fog they were rammed by another ship, and a child was beheaded. Other passengers were also killed. Eleanor ended up in a lifeboat. She never got over it or learned to like water.

Eleanor helped support her brother, we understood, and got FDR to help find him jobs with nice titles. In the thirties, for example, Hall was named assistant to the mayor of Detroit, Frank Murphy, an FDR crony.

Although the First Lady was only six years older than her brother, she acted as if she were solely responsible for him. It began when her mother died. Eleanor was eight and Hall was two. She took charge of him when they went to live with their strict Grandmother Hall. Like a little mother she petted and pampered him and would let no one discipline him but she, herself.

Hall laughed about it at the White House, where he was the life of the party whenever he was in residence. He always said Eleanor was too serious, and he tried to make her laugh. Of course, we knew he was drinking heavily, even at the White House.

On FDR's side, we decided *he* deserved sympathy because soon after he married Eleanor in 1905, she insisted that Hall be invited to live with them so he would feel he had a family. Some said it was the worst thing she could have done because it kept FDR and her from having a normal, carefree early marriage.

Poor FDR, we said. He got away from his mother only to be saddled with another heavy family situation.

Everything we heard of Eleanor's early married days showed that she didn't enjoy sex, and in later years, when I read Elliott Roosevelt's book, *An Untold Story; The Roosevelts of Hyde Park,* I noticed he said that, to his mother "Sex was a wife's duty, never a source of joy."

No wonder FDR sought his satisfactions elsewhere. And so did Eleanor.

But to return to Hall, he was no angel. Though divorced, he had plenty of female companionship and was attractive to women. Even on his deathbed, Zena Raset, a woman friend of some years, was at Walter Reed Hospital with Eleanor, holding his hand and crying silent tears.

We heard the report that until the very end Zena was sure there would be a miracle and Hall would somehow recover. Eleanor accepted the fact that his liver had been destroyed beyond repair.

When Eleanor lost her dear brother at first she seemed rudderless but then quickly jumped into high gear, building up the Office of Civilian Defense.

There was one other Roosevelt who seemed to have a stranglehold on her life—as if they could not get away from each other—Alice Roosevelt Longworth. I don't believe the public knows the importance of the relationship between Alice and Eleanor.

It was a deep and complicated situation with almost sinister overtones. It was as if Alice was bent on destroying Eleanor's happiness and peace of mind.

Alice Longworth, the daughter of President Teddy Roosevelt, was the thorn in Eleanor's side all her life. It's hard to understand how Eleanor kept being nice to her at the White House, and inviting her when Alice only used her visits to get more ammunition for her slams against her first cousin.

Backstairs we said there was only one explanation for why Alice was out to get Eleanor, and that had to be *jealousy.* There were many signs of it, and those who had been with the Roosevelt family longer knew many things that had happened between them in their youth.

At a White House party, while I stood with the water pitcher, or took care of the guests' rest room, I heard Alice imitating Eleanor's voice as some of the other guests laughed nervously. And I was told of other times she had done it.

Once, in fact, I heard Alice had done her imitation of Eleanor at Eleanor's own request and during the party Eleanor controlled herself and laughed as if she enjoyed it. But afterwards Eleanor, a young bride, had fallen apart.

As we saw it, Alice Longworth had always been a trouble-maker. Back in the Hoover administration, Alice started out with her nose out of joint. She thought her husband should have been president instead of Hoover. Nick Longworth, whom Alice married soon after Eleanor had married, was the Republican Speaker of the House and considered to be presidential timber.

Hoover got the Republican nomination on the first ballot at the 1928 Convention and eliminated Longworth. Thereafter, Alice Longworth acted the spoilsport, trying to muddy the waters for the Hoovers and succeeding in making a "tempest in a teapot."

The issue was whether Alice, as the wife of the Speaker, should sit at a higher place at table than the hostess of Charles Curtis, the Vice President. The hostess was not Curtis' wife, but his sister.

Alice started the ruckus herself, claiming she should not have to sit lower than the sister of a part-Indian Vice President. Mother, who was the top maid at the White House in Hoover's time, and I used to laugh about this silly business and say that had Alice called the Protocol office at the State Department, she would have learned that whomever the Vice President designated his hostess had precedence over the wife of the Speaker of the House, who is number *three* in succession to the President.

But Alice, as daughter of a president, and having much greater social clout than Dolly Gann, was able to convince a lot of people that she had a case.

Poor Lou Hoover, the First Lady, didn't know how to handle the situation gracefully. So she avoided the issue by increasing the number of parties so the Vice President would be the ranking guest one time, and the Speaker of the House another. Looking back, what a bore it seems.

At the White House in the Roosevelt Administration, Alice proudly admitted she had started the whole business "out of meanness." She could afford to laugh because by then Dolly Gann's name was a thing of the past.

It seemed to us that Alice Longworth hoped she could draw blood again in the Roosevelt administration, but Eleanor was too much a lady. The public didn't know that even Franklin Roosevelt himself got hot under the collar when he heard of some of Alice's nastiness and her unfair treatment of his wife. He finally told Eleanor *he* did not want Alice invited to a particular party. Eleanor was relieved. The help said Eleanor had been afraid *not* to invite Alice. It was continuing problem.

Growing Up Roosevelt

It seemed that Eleanor had always been a little afraid of Alice Roosevelt since Alice had come to play with her when they were little girls. Even then, Alice had tormented her and acted superior. Eleanor refused to compete.

Later when Alice was dancing at the White House and the belle of the ball, Eleanor was already submerging herself in social work for the East Side tenements in New York. Eleanor had been a guest at the White House with Franklin at a New Year's Eve party and Alice had gone out of her way once to barge in on a party where she knew Eleanor and her boyfriend Franklin would be.

We heard that Alice had tried to take Franklin away from Eleanor at one point and had been amazed that he simply dropped her after several dates. We said Alice's bossiness must have reminded him of his mother. And we heard some of the Roosevelt clan say that Alice had really wanted FDR for herself.

When she couldn't get the man she could love, she settled for the man with the most power, even though he was much older. Years later, Alice Longworth would admit she had felt very little for her husband.

Once Eleanor commented that in her youth she had wished she could be more like her cousin Alice and say bright and witty things, but that everything she said came out sounding so serious. She said that even the President had once commented that she sounded "grandmotherly."

Alice sounded like a perpetual teenager, we thought, and she played pranks as if she were. For example, as a married woman, she had tried to make a social comment in a most peculiar way about a household in her neighborhood where a Catholic cardinal had been entertained. She thought it was very smart to slip over in the dark of night and hang a sign on the front door saying: IRISH EMBASSY.

This was back in Mama's day at the White House, before I had become a member of the staff. Mama said that even then a little mean streak was noticeable in Alice.

We had the theory that what Alice couldn't have she tried to destroy, and in a way she did help destroy Eleanor's marriage. She did this when she entertained Lucy Mercer and FDR together, without Eleanor, encouraging their romance.

And then, to make sure she succeeded, she went to Eleanor and told her in a smug, amused way that she'd better be careful or she would lose her husband. The word was that this made Eleanor so apprehensive she played detective until she had proof of his straying.

Incidentally, Alice had gone to Eleanor's wedding as bridesmaid and had been given her bouquet. When Alice got married the following year, Eleanor couldn't go because she was too large with her first child, and at that time obviously pregnant women stayed out of the public eye.

But FDR did go to her wedding and took his mother.

Eleanor, remembering how Uncle Teddy had stolen the show at her own wedding, grudgingly admired the way Alice had kept the whole spotlight on herself at her own wedding by having no bridesmaids. Eleanor heard afterwards how cleverly Alice shoved her father, the President, aside, keeping him out of camera range.

I don't know when Alice first said it, but one of her famous quotes about President Teddy Roosevelt was, "He always wants to be the corpse at every funeral, the bride at every wedding, and the baby at every christening."

As part of Alice's competition with Eleanor, as soon as it was announced that Eleanor was going to write a column, Alice announced that she too was going to write a column. The difference was that Alice's column was as vitriolic as she, and she did not have the staying power to stick with it until it had been thoroughly established. She soon gave up.

Eleanor Roosevelt now and then talked about her popular cousin but seemed afraid to be outright critical: "Alice always said the clever thing—the thing everyone wished they had said, or at least thought. But sometimes she went too far and hurt people."

She certainly hurt Eleanor when the report reached the White House that Alice had said, "FDR is one-third mush and one-third Eleanor." Alice just couldn't think of enough insults for him. She insisted Eleanor had married a lightweight, a birdbrain, (even if he was president), and once called him a "feather duster" to show how lightweight he was.

Eleanor didn't feel she had to defend her husband's brain.

Alice didn't dare attack Eleanor's brain, so she dismissed her as "the Great White Mother in the White House."

Once, during a White House reception, when someone was telling Alice all the good things Eleanor was doing for the women of the nation, Alice was overheard to retort, "Spare me. Do-gooders are so boring."

I don't know how many of these insults about Eleanor got back to the First Lady, but I'm sure a lot of them got back to FDR. I know that he knew what Alice said about him when she heard of his engagement to Eleanor. A valet heard him tell with amusement the typically sour grapes comment with which Alice met the news: "Franklin is the kind of boy you might invite to the dance afterwards—but not to the dinner."

What we did know hurt FDR was that President Teddy Roosevelt's widow, Eleanor's Aunt Edith, and Alice Longworth, whom he had once mildly romanced and who had been an attendant at his wedding, had come out publicly against him and had campaigned for his opponent, Herbert Hoover.

As FDR so nicely put it, over cocktails in his office, "If they didn't like me, they could have kept a discreet silence." He added that Eleanor was a more forgiving type and had sent Alice a letter saying she would be welcome in the White House any time.

Backstairs we muttered that Eleanor was more forgiving than we would have been. As far as we could see Alice never buried the hatchet. Sometimes we heard that Alice was barred from the White House. Later she'd be back in.

Eleanor felt life had made Alice bitter. She said she couldn't be too angry with her no matter what she did because she knew her tragedies—past and present—too well. When Eleanor came to the White House in 1933, she was feeling especially sorry for Alice because Nicholas Longworth had died not too long before—in 1931—leaving Alice to raise their six-year-old child Paulina.

Eleanor was entering a whole new phase of life and Alice was ending one.

The whole family had rejoiced when after many years of marriage, Alice and Nick Longworth finally produced a child on Valentine's Day of 1925.

There is a sad footnote to the story. Paulina eventually committed suicide at thirty-one by taking an overdose of sleeping pills. Destiny seemed to be fulfilling Eleanor's father's statement, repeated now and then by Eleanor when she was suffering over her personal problems: "The Oyster Bay clan is cursed. There is a curse hanging over it."

I remember the talk of Washington was that Alice didn't seem to want to spend a minute's time with her daughter and was very sharp with her. Paulina was raised by nannies. All the ladies agreed that forty-one was a difficult age to start a family, and when her friends commented on the fact that she had waited a long time, she retorted with her usual irreverence, "I'll try anything once."

As we compared them, Eleanor and Alice were completely different. Alice smoked, Eleanor didn't. Alice drank. Eleanor didn't. Alice gambled. Eleanor didn't. Alice bragged, in fact, that one year she had made over $10,000 at poker. Alice once stood on her head at a party to get attention. Eleanor never would.

Eleanor was interested in politics but shunned the limelight. Alice loved the limelight and made the most of her one little political role—delegate from Ohio to the 1936 Republican Convention.

Eleanor was always working toward a better society for all people. Alice was always looking for a good time and put all her energies into dreaming up amusing activities so she wouldn't be bored. She admitted she was a "hedonist," and added, "What's wrong with that? At least when I die, I'll have lived."

When Alice finally died, long after Eleanor, at age 96, people around Washington joked that although the obituary said pneumonia, Alice had died of meanness.

So the last laugh was on her.

10

Growing Up Roosevelt

At first all Roosevelt boys looked alike to us but quickly we sorted them out.

James was the dependable one.

Elliott was the wild one.

FDR Jr. was the handsome one.

And John was the tall one. John was also the one with Republican leanings. But since he didn't go into politics, the family didn't feel it mattered too much.

He didn't come out of the political closet and declare his Republicanism until after FDR died, however, and backstairs we commented that for sure FDR must be turning over in his grave.

The Roosevelt sons looked so handsome and well-behaved it was hard to associate them with the outrageous stories we heard. Their fame preceded them, and we heard tidbits about life with the Roosevelt kids before they even reached the White House. How Eleanor had survived, we didn't know. We heard Eleanor laughingly tell someone during inaugural time how her son Franklin Jr. had something in common with George Washington.

George Washington had chopped down a tree, she said, and discovered he couldn't tell a lie. And Franklin Jr. had chopped down a tree and discovered he couldn't tell a tree from his leg. He ended up wearing a bandage for weeks.

Eleanor also cautioned some of the household help not to be concerned if her two youngest, Johnny and Franklin Jr., seemed to be at each other's throats. It didn't mean a thing, she said, they had always been very competitive with each other. Once, she added, Franklin Jr. had hung his little brother out the window by his heels.

When they were home at the White House during school vacations, they would go zooming down halls with pillows and have terrible pillow fights. FDR would hear them from his study and shake his head. When Eleanor's brother, Hall, was at the White House during vacations, he would behave just like the kids and join their pillow fights.

The President and First Lady, we heard, didn't approve of the special treatment their sons received when stopped for careless driving.

In one case the magistrate he appeared before ended up taking the Roosevelt boy home to dinner. The son made the mistake of bragging about it at the White House. Instead of being complimented for his charm, his parents scolded him for his lack of civic-mindedness.

There was another kind of special treatment the First Couple didn't like either—and that was the way classmates of the younger boys had fun using the Roosevelt name to get special privileges or play tricks. If you said a Roosevelt son would be along later, you could crash any party. The White House didn't hear about this kind of thing until the boys themselves reminisced about what was happening back at school. Once the White House did find out, though, because a foreign government became involved. One of FDR Jr.'s college mates had gotten the bright idea of calling Paris to speak to French Prime Minister Daladier, using the name of Franklin Delano Roosevelt. The prime minister didn't find it funny and complained to the State Department, which called the White House.

FDR was always cautioning his younger sons not to spread their impish ideas too much—especially when Johnny advised his father in a letter from Harvard to tell Congress to go home and the Supreme Court to go to hell. FDR flashed that letter among cronies. He laughed and said he'd written John that he would have to find some other way to get around the Supreme Court which was finding some of his New Deal unconstitutional, but to keep the ideas coming.

John seemed to be the quiet one in the family, but when he broke loose it made news around the world. It was right after FDR was starting his second term that Johnny took a trip to Cannes to see the summer film festival in 1937.

Growing Up Roosevelt

Having just come of age, at twenty-one he was trying out his new-found powers and freedom. This involved pretty girls and a lot of champagne, some of which, the story went, he proceeded to pour into the hat of the mayor of Cannes, who was officiating. FDR was chortling with amusement at his boy, but Eleanor was calm because she did not believe it had happened. She said he wasn't that kind of boy. John said it was grossly exaggerated. The housemen and butlers backstairs wanted to believe it was so; they had nicknamed him the "Old Lady" for being so dignified.

As the story came back to us in bits and pieces it seemed it was even worse—and now FDR was not so sure it was a good thing. The mayor was quoted in the newspapers as charging that John had been drunk and had also used a bouquet of roses to hit him over the head repeatedly. Ambassador Bullitt said it wasn't true.

One of the best stories around the Roosevelt White House was Jimmy Roosevelt's adventure with a horse while on a college vacation trip to Europe, when he was twenty years old or so. He used his travel money to buy the horse and cabled his father for money to get home, explaining about his wonderful investment. This was years before the White House, but FDR's acid wit was already there. He cabled his son his congratulations on the investment, adding: "Suggest you both swim home." There was no money with the cable. As FDR told the story amidst much laughter from his cronies gathered at his study for happy hour, it was at that moment that his son grew up. James quickly sold the horse and caught the boat home.

For a time, it seemed that the First Lady was destined to spend every Christmas at a hospital, looking after one of her children. In 1936, it was a Boston hospital were she spent Christmas comforting FDR Jr. who had had a sinus operation. In 1937, Anna was in the hospital for Christmas, having an operation of some sort.

Eleanor's traveling was not always appreciated. Anna, we heard, had complained that "Mother has her own husband and I have mine. She didn't have to come here to look after me." The thought left in the air was that Eleanor might do a little looking after her own husband.

Every family has one child whom the others think was favored. In the Roosevelt family, Elliott was considered the spoiled one. Anna said they all knew their mother favored Elliott, dating back from the time he was a little boy and had to wear leg braces. Elliott was the one who got out of going to college, and the one who always seemed to be able to get the most financial help from both his mother and father.

Anna explained that her mother probably loved Elliott the most because he seemed least able to take care of himself, and it brought out the maternal instinct in her. As Anna put it, "Even an old bum in hobo clothes brought out the maternal in her."

Probably mother and daughter did not get along so well because both were equally independent. But to return to Elliott, Eleanor's special treatment of him continued after his father's death.

Eleanor did many things to help him. She made him producer of her radio and TV appearances, and he acted as the sales agent as well. But that didn't bother the other children, from what I understand, as much as what happened with the Hyde Park estate.

The mansion was turned over to the government as a national shrine, the birthplace of a president. But Eleanor helped Elliott get Hilltop Cottage, FDR's hideaway, and some of the precious Hyde Park land. Instead of cherishing these places dear to his father, Elliott sold his Hyde Park holdings. Members of the family confessed that Elliott's action had saddened them and made them feel a little bitter.

Anna thought Elliott was his mother's favorite because he was the next child born after the death of the first FDR Jr.—in fact, just ten months later. Eleanor had blamed herself for not personally being there and taking care of baby Franklin—as if she could have prevented his death. So, according to Anna, Elliott was doubly precious. And there was something else.

Once, as a little tot, Elliott fell into a campfire at Campobello because of the carelessness of a nanny, and was badly burned.

Eleanor once told someone she was at least partly to blame for the fact that her children had married very early and had gotten away from home. She didn't believe herself to be an ideal mother or homemaker.

Growing Up Roosevelt

According to what the Roosevelt children said, in childhood they had felt closer to their grandmother Sara than to their mother, who seemed a little remote. They loved their mother, but were a little shy with her. If they saw their mother crying, they didn't dare go up and put their arms around her. Instead they pretended they didn't notice and left the room to protect her privacy.

The First Lady more than once commented on how she hadn't understood, until she had grandchildren, how to show love. And once, after I hugged my mother, Maggie, for a moment because she was so exhausted from looking after Missy, the First Lady happened to be hurrying in and saw this display of tender affection. She said, "Oh Maggie and Lillian, you don't know how lucky you are to have such a close relationship. So many families get estranged."

Later, comparing notes, Mama and I thought Mrs. Roosevelt might have been referring to her own relationship with her daughter, Anna, which waxed hot and cold.

In the early days, whenever her mother-in-law had been around, Eleanor had tended to be shy and let Grandmother Sara speak up and tell the grandchildren what to do. Sara called the shots and Eleanor seldom disagreed. But she herself admitted, in servants' hearing, that this had tended to make her take it out on FDR. She wanted *him* to stand up to his mother, but he couldn't either. His excuse was that he couldn't hurt her, and he knew how much she loved the children.

Much has been said about the relationship of Eleanor and her mother-in-law, Sara Delano Roosevelt, and Sara usually comes out the villain. Because of my crutches, I didn't go to look after the family when they went to Hyde Park, but I would listen to everything the staff would have to say when they returned to the White House.

I feel that poor Sara hasn't been given the credit she deserves and that a lot of the criticism is unjustified. Yet I can understand why some people criticized her so much. It was because they were on Eleanor's side. Through the years, Eleanor grew to be more and more hostile toward her husband's mother.

There were so many reasons for the hostility. As I was told by the servants who saw them both together at Hyde Park, Eleanor resented Sara's attempts to find out what was going on at Val-Kill Cottage. Sara couldn't understand why Eleanor had to stay in such a tiny hovel when she could be in the big mansion, which rivaled the size of the White House and even had eight rooms for servants. Eleanor would annoy Sara by coming to the big house only when she was specifically invited, or if there was some public affair where her absence would be noted by the press.

As a bride, Eleanor had tried to win the love of her mother-in-law, who actually had opposed the marriage of cousins, practically to the altar. She had dared send Franklin on a sea voyage and a grand tour of Europe to see if he wouldn't change his mind. He didn't.

Eleanor set about wooing her new mother-in-law and bent over backwards to please her. Eleanor's daughters-in-law thought that Eleanor tried so hard that eventually she just gave up and turned against the elegant lady.

And by the time she was in the White House, Eleanor was no longer grateful for all her benefactor had done for her. We servants thought Eleanor was lucky indeed that Sara had provided houses for them to live in and paid for part of their servant staff.

In our hearing, Eleanor ran down the houses she had been forced to live in, as if they were prisons. She particularly resented the dual house Sara had built so that they could all be together in New York—a duplex with one entry door, at 49 East 76th Street. Eleanor said she never felt that the house was hers but that she was more like a guest, especially when Sara would come popping through the connecting doors. And Eleanor bitterly resented what Sara would say whenever she wanted to put her daughter-in-law down. She would look down her elegant nose and say, "My son is a Delano and not a Roosevelt."

Eleanor said she got used to putdowns. When FDR went to Washington, D.C., to be assistant secretary of the Navy, and Sara came for her first visit there, the very first thing she did was complain about the appearance of the room and start rearranging all the furniture. And before that, as soon as Eleanor and Franklin got back from their honeymoon, Sara had a rented house ready for them, decorated to suit herself, with servants of her own choosing.

But that early in the game, from what I heard, Eleanor dared say nothing more than, "Thank you, Mother dear. You are an angel."

Eventually, Eleanor found her tongue and started arguing with her mother-in-law, but always ended up apologizing to her to keep the peace with FDR. According to those who knew, FDR had a fear of having to live on his own inheritance and would rather keep his mother happy than try.

FDR received $25,000 a year from his inheritance trust when they married, and Eleanor did a little better with an inheritance trust that gave her $27,000 a year. Even so, it was hard sledding in New York and then Washington, D.C., for a young couple who entertained and were trying to get ahead socially and politically. The maids who went to Hyde Park said they were told it cost more than $25,000 to maintain Hyde Park, even without mortgages over it.

Eleanor, the servants noticed, was a little jealous of how much her children clung to their grandmother, and seemed to feel they were slighting her. And sometimes they seemed to be.

It was well known among the servants that Sara had done everything for the children that most mothers do—indulge their love for sweets, give them extra spending money, sit with them through minor childhood illnesses and bumps and bruises, kiss the hurt away.

The funniest thing I ever heard about how Eleanor raised her children was that she invented a child-airing box for hanging babies out of the window of their New York home to get sunshine. It was supposed to have been banged together, at her instructions, out of strips of wood and chicken wire. "Mother's chicken cage" was frequently referred to amid much laughter when the whole clan got together at the White House for reunions. But one of the nannies who came with the Roosevelt grandchildren told me that one of the Roosevelt babies had howled so loud and long at being stranded out the window in the cage that a neighbor came and threatened to call the SPCC—Society for the Prevention of Cruelty to Children—if the child wasn't brought in the window immediately.

I always wanted to ask the First Lady how she had handled the situation, but I never did. I wondered, did she defy the neighbor or comply? Anna and I once talked about it. She thought she was the child in the chicken cage that day. At least, she was teased about it by her brothers.

Eleanor did not start kissing children until they were her grandchildren. She had been more of a tomboy and comrade with her sons, learning to fish and boat and play other water sports to be closer to them as they were growing up.

But even at the White House, we heard various Roosevelt children or their spouses telling of Eleanor's remoteness when they were little tots. In fact, Eleanor had hardly been in the picture at all. They each had a nanny who was in charge of them.

Sometimes this worked and sometimes it didn't. One nanny locked little children in a closet. Others gave vicious spankings. Anna claimed to have a nanny who once pushed her down and got on top of her, her knee digging into the child's stomach. What bothered Anna most, even after all those years, was that her mother refused to fire the cruel woman until later, when she staged a surprise inspection visit in the nanny's room and found a collection of empty whiskey bottles. *Then* she fired her. Anna also commented that her mother's idea of being a good parent was to get home each afternoon in time to read to them at reading hour. It was nice, but she wanted hugs and kisses and so did her brothers.

Of course the little Roosevelt boys didn't take the child abuse—real or imagined—sitting down, and if their mother would not defend them, they would do it themselves. Elliott once threw a knife at one female tutor. Fortunately, he missed. And the boys subconsciously, I believe, punished their mother for her lack of attention several times by throwing stink bombs into the midst of her guests when she was entertaining. It was FDR, a chip off the old block of Sara, who tucked the children into bed each night and kissed them good night.

Years later, at the White House, Eleanor was reported to have told someone, in a servant's hearing, that she was sorry she had had all those nursemaids for her children and felt she had missed the joy of bringing them up herself, as she saw other women do.

Now her daughters-in-law were bringing nannies to take care of her grandchildren, but Eleanor, suddenly a lot like Sara, would get down on the floor and play with them, or kiss them and give them anything they wanted.

Eleanor may have felt more than she let on. She had learned to hide her emotions. James' wife Ethel told some of us that once, when James was about twelve, an attempt had been made on the life of a cabinet member who lived in their neighborhood. At this time FDR was assistant secretary of the Navy. A bomb had been thrown at the other man's house, and it had blown out some of the windows in the Roosevelt residence at 1733 N Street. FDR and Eleanor returned from a party they had attended to find police in the street and little Jimmy looking out a jagged broken window.

According to Ethel, FDR rushed in and hugged and kissed his son and told him how happy he was to see him safe. Eleanor, on the other hand, had simply scolded Jimmy for having gotten out of bed and sent him right back.

Granny Sara became the children's refuge and protector and happiness. She called them pet names and hugged them, and any time Eleanor said no, they would go to Sara and ask her. She got them what they wanted and helped hide it from their parents. Eleanor might object when she found out eventually, but it was mighty handy to have Sara around when she didn't want *them* around. Once, when they all had some childhood disease— measles or whooping cough—Eleanor packed them off for Granny to take care of. And Granny did, happily.

It was Granny Sara, too, who would sit at the piano leading song fests for the kids.

At the White House, we used to say no wonder the old lady felt the children belonged to her—hadn't she paid every doctor bill for them, including their birth? We knew that, even from the White House, medical bills were being sent to her.

The daughters-in-law didn't mind repeating what Sara had told their husbands: "I've been all the things to you children that your mother should have been."

As the children grew older, Sara took various ones with her to Europe. Eleanor sometimes resented that and objected on the grounds that they weren't learning to respect money. What had bothered her most was that Granny had taken Anna abroad several times and had spoiled her thoroughly, according to

Eleanor. But Anna, looking back, loved her grandmother for having given her a great educational experience.

Even when they were young men, the Roosevelt boys would put the touch on Grandma. And sometimes they didn't even have to actually say anything.

Grandmother Sara was the tenderhearted one when Franklin Jr. wrecked the automobile Eleanor and FDR had given him for getting through Groton. Eleanor was bent on teaching Junior a lesson and said he would have to get around on foot power and buses. FDR Jr. took his long face to his grandmother and soon he was tooling around in a new and better car. The way we heard it, only then did Eleanor discover her mother-in-law had played lady bountiful without her permission. She was furious and sputtered at Sara, but when she tried to get FDR to take the car away and give it back to his mother, he refused to get involved or let her interfere.

Even before the White House years, Sara was taking a lot of responsibility for the support of the sons when they married. In 1930, when James married Betsey Cushing, Grandmother Sara gave the couple a $2,000 wedding present to get them started, and the offer of a big loan so that James could get his life organized or get a law degree.

He didn't accept the loan. Instead, he determined to go it alone, but he adored his grandmother for being there when he needed her. And she continued to be generous.

One of his bitter memories, which was part of the family folklore, went back to the days when he was the governor's son and explained why he was the only member of the family who had lost his hair. It happened while he was at Harvard. He got so sick that he went to see the campus doctor and was ordered to bed immediately. But all he could think of was going home, where he would get some tender loving care. He barely survived the agony of a six-hour train ride to the Governor's Mansion at Albany and stood at the door trying to get in—a poor bedraggled cat, too seedy looking for the new butler to let in, or even recognize from pictures.

Only when James pleaded with him to call the Governor's wife did Eleanor appear and ask why on earth he had come home.

"I'm sick," he said.

Eleanor helped him to bed and disappeared for the night, and neither she nor his father, the Governor, checked his condition for the rest of the night.

All night he suffered and waited feverishly.

By the next day he was in terrible shape with double pneumonia, and of course doctors were summoned. Before his fever had run its course, he had become prematurely bald. It was weeks before he was strong enough to go back to college. His mistake had been that he had arrived when his parents were in the middle of a dinner party.

At the White House, when FDR would kid Jimmy about his baldness, he was once heard to retort, "Yes, but if I'd stayed at school and gone to the hospital, I'd still have hair." At least FDR did try to make it up to his son, years later, for that act of neglect. When James had serious ulcer problems in 1938 and had to have part of his stomach removed, the President flew to the Mayo Clinic and stayed with him until the doctor pronounced him safely on the road to recovery.

This time, however, James was getting good care and comfort from another source, a nurse named Romelle Schneider. I don't know whether FDR dreamed that the nurse he was meeting would become a part of his family. When Jimmy left the hospital and went home to California, he took Romelle along to nurse him further.

At the White House we said, "No wonder he married her."

Vows Are Made to Be Broken

I had thought that this would be a family of happy marriages, but almost as soon as the Roosevelts moved in I had my first shock. I was passing down the third floor hall on my way to the elevator when I happened upon a scene I was sorry to witness. Anna Dall, the eldest Roosevelt child, was standing in the hall informing her husband, Curtis, that she was going away in a few days to get a divorce. I pretended I didn't hear. I just continued on my way to supper and kept the news to myself until it started to leak out from FDR's office.

Anna and Curtis had come with FDR on March 4th and Anna had stayed on after the inauguration. It was spring and everything had seemed so happy—then this.

Sistie and Buzzy were adorable children and I loved having them around. I felt very sorry that they were to be deprived of their father.

But it was Elliott who actually got the first divorce during the Roosevelt administration. Eventually divorces came so thick and fast that we got a little dizzy trying to keep up with all the names and faces. Even now, I have trouble remembering Elliott's first wife, Elizabeth Donner of Philadelphia, a name that spelled money.

Actually, all the Roosevelts married wealthy mates, the first time around at least, and many of their mates were members of the Social Register. But that didn't save the marriages. In fact, we wondered if their spouses resented knowing the sons received subsidies from their father and grandmother.

Anna was married first, to a very wealthy stockbroker, Curtis Dall. James married Betsey Cushing, daughter of a famous brain surgeon, Dr. Harvey Cushing of Brookline, Massachusetts. FDR

Jr. married a Du Pont, daughter of Pierre, the patriarch of the clan, and Elliott married Betty Donner, of Donner steel money. Even Baby John didn't do too badly for himself when he married Anne Clark, a North Shore debutante, whose father was a partner in a financial firm that bore his name.

Eleanor once said over her knitting that she probably should scold her sons more and try to get them to stay with their young wives, once they had made their bed. But, she said, having felt pressure from a mother-in-law, she didn't want to inflict pressure on anyone else. "I don't know," she said, "whether it improves a person's character to force himself to live with someone he can no longer tolerate." We wondered if she was also speaking of herself.

Actually, she did try now and then to keep the marriages around her from cracking up, but it didn't take her sons long to win her over to their side. She believed anything they told her about their reasons for wanting a divorce.

But that didn't stop her from being upset when one son had his next wife picked out before he was even divorced. And FDR, we knew, was very hurt when one son had divorced and remarried, and his new wife was pregnant, before she had even been brought to meet the President.

Even a president could have his feelings hurt by being ignored!

Eleanor once said that she grew up with the idea that one lived with one's mistakes.

As we knew, backstairs, her own marriage to the President was not a romantic thing, but more of a business–friendship. We servants put it into words the first time a divorce came to the White House, "Why can't they wait until their father is out of the White House and not disgrace the family?"

Looking back, that seems awfully amusing. Divorces are no longer a novelty even in the White House. And, it would have been a mighty long wait—FDR occupied the White House for twelve long years.

Why didn't any of the Roosevelt children marry at the White House? After all, Harry Hopkins married there. Why didn't the five children, in any of their marriages during the time their father was president, take advantage of that happy circumstance?

Vows Are Made To Be Broken

Some of the daughters-in-law themselves wondered. We heard there were two reasons: the kids felt their parents were too preoccupied with other things, and they, themselves, didn't want to be part of a publicity circus.

FDR Jr. had the reputation around the White House of hating publicity the most. We were always hearing, when Junior was in a scrape, that his mother had to soothe his ruffled feathers while he complained that if he had any other name than Roosevelt, nobody would notice or care what he did, and a mere traffic ticket wouldn't make the papers. Once his mother got tired of his complaints about his high visibility name and said, "If it troubled me that much, I would be especially careful to obey every traffic law and avoid getting tickets."

But getting back to marriages, Elliott had a much finer wedding in Hollywood than Harry Hopkins had in the White House, when Elliott married the movie star Faye Emerson. The multimillionaire Howard Hughes had the wedding in his own home and lent Elliott his private plane for their honeymoon.

At the White House there was some whispering about whether tycoon Hughes would be expecting favors from the President, and there was talk that FDR had used a few choice cuss words to indicate he wasn't going to be influenced by anyone currying favor with his sons. I don't know whether it was in FDR's time or later, but Howard Hughes was called before a Senate committee investigating aircraft contracts, and Elliott was involved in helping with his testimony.

Elliott's marriage to Faye Emerson was the most publicized of the Roosevelt marriages. But as I said, it wasn't his first marriage. Elliott first married Betty Donner, and he was married to her when his father came to the White House.

We thought he was very lucky to have a father-in-law who owned a steel company, Donner Steel. And we heard that FDR had said that Betty's father wanted to take Elliott into the steel business, but that Elliott was bored with steel and bored with his marriage.

Elliott had a darling little boy named Billy with Betty, and we at the White House oo-ed and ah-ed over him. But the little boy wasn't enough to hold the marriage together, and first thing we knew, there was a secret around the White House: Elliott had left Betty and headed west. He simply dumped her at the White House. Mama had caught her crying in her bedroom and knew she was unhappy. Soon after, Elliott left her. We heard Elliott had told his mother he needed to think things through and clear his mind and he would be back to patch up his marriage.

But it didn't happen that way. Elliott never came back for her. Eventually we heard that he had fallen in love with another girl. But first there had been a long silence.

We knew that Eleanor and Franklin were concerned about Elliott, and especially that, with the name of Roosevelt, he might be kidnapped. This was in the days before children of presidents were protected by the Secret Service. Elliott wasn't good about informing his parents of his whereabouts, and it was only later that they heard where he had been. In fact, when he decided to get a divorce, we were told he informed his wife Betty of his decision by phone.

Both Eleanor and Anna made trips out West to try to stop Elliott from remarrying so soon. They couldn't stop him from getting a divorce, but they pointed out that it just didn't look right to rush into a new marriage when the old marriage had hardly cooled off. They told him how hurt his father was.

The First Lady returned quite dejected. Eleanor was heard to comment, "I cannot live Elliott's life for him."

So Elliott became the first Roosevelt child to get a divorce in July 1933, going to Reno to get it. The White House was solemn when a letter came that Elliott had married his new love, Ruth Chandler Googins.

I remember when Elliott eventually came to the White House to make peace with his parents. Eleanor brought little Billy to the White House so he could see his daddy. As I recall, nobody from the White House had gone to Elliott's second wedding—not even Eleanor, who traveled at the drop of a hat.

But to return to Elliott's visit to the White House, it broke our hearts because we didn't see Elliott paying attention to his little child, Billy. They met on the stairs and Elliott didn't pick him up or hug or kiss him. The word got to Eleanor and she was heard dictating a note to Tommy to remind herself to tell Elliott he should spend more time with his son.

FDR was quoted by the servants as saying here he was with a pregnant daughter-in-law and he hadn't even met the girl yet. Ruth didn't come until the baby was born, and then she and Elliott brought the President his new grandchild, knowing he couldn't resist a baby. And of course FDR embraced the little peacemaker.

We didn't hear much about Ruth Googins, except that she and Elliott were involved in getting some new radio stations in Texas. Ruth was small and very pretty, with a beautiful complexion and dark hair. We always enjoyed having Ruth in the White House. She was cheerful and friendly and tipped the girls well who did her rooms. When she brought her first child, Ruth Chandler Roosevelt, she brought an elderly white lady to take care of her—Mrs. Ewull, I believe she spelled it.

When her little family had grown to three children, she came with two nannies, Gertrude and Genevieve, both black. The other two children were Elliott Jr. and David Boynton.

FDR was again shocked when Elliott got a divorce and married a movie star in 1944. We heard that at first Elliott had greatly enjoyed the attention that being with a Hollywood star, Faye Emerson, gave him. But then he got a little miffed because she was the center of attention, and he was shunted aside by the crowds.

Around the White House, we all loved Faye Emerson. She never put on airs with the help and was very generous with all of us. We noticed that Faye tried to play down her glamour and be more like Eleanor Roosevelt. We would seldom see her hair out of that little bun she wore on the back of her head.

Elliott and Faye were still together when FDR died, and they went to his funeral. Of all the children, only Elliott and Anna got to the funeral in time.

For a time Elliott and Faye went to live in FDR's hideaway-without-a-telephone, Hilltop Cottage, but the marriage didn't last, and they too got a divorce. Making news, Elliott then was shown dating a nightclub singer, but when he married wife Number 4 in 1951, it was to someone named Minnewa Bell, a California oil heiress.

I don't know anything about that marriage, but it couldn't have been perfect because of what happened next. Elliott went to Phoenix to find a place to live. He married the real estate agent

Patricia Whitehead Peabody, after divorcing Minnewa. That marriage, in 1960, found Elliott again estranged from his own children, but with a whole new brood to raise—his wife's three—and he adopted them. From what I heard, the Roosevelt family wasn't too thrilled when one child changed his name to James Roosevelt III, when he had no blood relationship to "Uncle James." Some of the maids who had served the Roosevelts wondered if this would mean the adopted Roosevelt children would inherit money from Eleanor Roosevelt some day.

The answer came in just a few years when Eleanor died in 1962 and stipulated that only blood relatives would benefit from the family trust fund. Her will gave half the family wealth to the children and half to the grandchildren upon the death of their Roosevelt parent—with the provision that only the "natural" offspring of her children would be beneficiaries.

It was hard to keep up with Elliott's career. When some of us White House regulars met, we would exchange notes on all the Roosevelts, keeping abreast of their adventures. Elliott made more news than anyone. First he was a newspaper man with Hearst. Then he was a radio commentator. Then he was a radio tycoon. Then he worked for Howard Hughes. Then he was in the fertilizer business. Then he was a rancher. Then he went to Miami to manage a convention center.

We thought Elliott's checkered career had finally ended when he landed a job in the career that seemed to come naturally to Roosevelts—politics. Elliott, while married to Patty, was elected mayor of Miami. We speculated that maybe Elliott would use the office as a springboard to land in the U.S. Congress, as two brothers had done. But Elliott seemed destined to do everything to thwart success. First he joined a country club that excluded Jews, and topping that, wife Patty made some remarks considered so "unjudicious" about Jews, that in reaction, the city of Miami swept Elliott out in the next election and installed a Jewish mayor, who won by a landslide. So it was goodbye, Miami.

Then Elliott tried raising horses and operating fruit groves. He seemed to be successful but as usual, it didn't last long. He pulled up stakes and moved to Portugal. Disaster struck and his property was grabbed by the Communists, who took over the government. Elliott fled to England, still not a poor man.

Vows Are Made To Be Broken

The last I heard was that he and Patty were living on an estate that had been owned by British Prime Minister Macmillan. As for Elliott's children with Ruth Chandler Googins, I have heard that all are doing well and that at least two are married.

We noticed that the wives of the Roosevelt sons seemed much more interested in protocol than their husbands. I remember when the President's mother, Sara, died, the White House was almost deserted. Only Gladys Seldon, an extra maid, and I were there, looking after things on the third floor. Suddenly Elliott's wife Ruth arrived at the White House and came up to the third floor, wandering around and looking at the book. She didn't seem particularly sad, but vaguely bored as she rummaged through the books. I said, "Can I help you?"

She said, "Is the Emily Post book here? I can't find it."

I said, "What do you want to know?"

She said, "I want to know whether you put the black crepe band on the sleeve before the funeral or after the funeral."

I said, "The funeral isn't until tomorrow. Are you going out tonight?"

She said, "We're going to a friend's for dinner."

It was as if I had been struck in the chest. It hurt to know that Elliott would be going out to dinner the night before the funeral of the woman who had loved him so and had done so much for him. I'm afraid I sounded a little cold as I said, "Well, put the band on Elliott's sleeve when you go to Hyde Park before the funeral."

They went to the dinner party and made it on time to the funeral at Hyde Park the next day.

The Roosevelt children were certainly not pleased with the treatment they got from their mother at the White House. Eleanor laid down the law. They were to bring their own nurse-maids and not bother her servants to go chasing after spoiled brats, or babysit, or "feed or change."

Of course, now and then some of us would be cajoled into helping by one of the sweet talking daughters-in-law, but they would usually tip us nicely for it.

Other guests seemed to get the best guest rooms, and the children were forever insulted by the rooms that their mother assigned them. John felt slighted to be put on the third floor, which he considered the servants quarters. He was so tall, incidentally, at six-four, that his mother eventually ordered a special bed for him from the Val-Kill furniture factory. Someone pointed out to Eleanor that the Lincoln bed would be the right size for him, but the suggestion fell on deaf ears. Tiny Louis Howe had said that he would like to sleep in the Lincoln bed, so that was the bed that Eleanor ordered carried to his room. It remained his bed all his years at the White House.

Anna Dall wasn't surprised at any room assigned her. She was still talking about the great injustice that had been done her as a blossoming teenager, when she had been yanked out of her lovely bedroom and bath in New York because Louis Howe was moving in. Eleanor had wanted Louis to have the best of everything, and Anna found herself in a tiny, unattractive room.

Eleanor hadn't changed. When too many guests arrived, she ordered her children to go stay in a hotel. And they did.

Eleanor would sometimes fume at the President in the White House and tell him that it was all Sara's fault that FDR Jr. couldn't live within his budget. She had spoiled him. Even though Franklin Jr. was married to Ethel Du Pont, he was still getting an allowance from his father. Of course, he was also still going to law school.

FDR had told Eleanor that no Roosevelt man was going to be supported by a Du Pont. At any rate, the story circulating among the servants was that the First Lady had suggested the President himself pay young Franklin's bills, and then have FDR Jr. pay him back a little at a time out of his allowance. Backstairs, we said that was "real hardship."

Eleanor might have resented her mother-in-law's visits to the White House, but we understood that the matriarch was paying about $100,000 to subsidize her son's lifestyle and his generosity to his children. We used to say Sara had as much right to be at the White House as anyone—she was paying for the privilege.

No wonder the sons needed to be subsidized. Upon graduation from Harvard, young John took a $17 a week job at Filene's department store in Boston. After he came out of the service, he went to work for another department store, this one in Los Angeles. It is a pity that FDR didn't live to see John come into his own and form his own investment company with some partners in the 50s, later becoming a vice president of Bache and Company in New York.

John was the only Roosevelt son who didn't take a crack at politics. Franklin Roosevelt, Jr., the "Sunshine Boy" as his brothers called him, ran and won a seat in Congress first—serving the state of New York—but was considered around Washington to be close to the world's worst as far as attendance goes. At the Truman and Eisenhower White House, we, who honored the Roosevelt memory, wished it was otherwise and that FDR Jr. would add luster to the Roosevelt name. Speaker of the House Sam Rayburn was quoted as being disgusted with FDR Jr. for not paying attention to the job or doing his legislative homework.

Even so, he won a second term. He might have won a third as well, except that he decided to run for governor of New York, like his father had. It was all downhill from then on, as far as Junior's political career was concerned. He lost, and then went on to lose his bid for the attorney generalship of the state.

Had FDR Jr. treated his Congressional career seriously and not racked up one of the poorest attendance records ever, he might still be in Congress today. Also, had President John F. Kennedy not been assassinated, they might have gone into some business together. FDR Jr. spent a great deal of time at the White House and on JFK's sailboat, and they enjoyed each other's company.

The White House was abuzz when FDR actually went to attend the big social wedding of Junior and Ethel Du Pont in 1937. We heard that he had a splendid time mixing and mingling with the 400. We also heard that he and Pierre Du Pont eventually became bitter enemies over New Deal policies that put restrictions on the Du Pont company. That couldn't have helped the marriage, either.

As far as I can remember there was only one other family wedding that FDR attended during those years at the White House. That naturally had to be the highly social wedding of FDR Jr.'s sibling rival Johnny.

It took place exactly one year after Junior's in June 1938 at Nahant, Massachusetts. From what I heard, it too was a wingding, and FDR was in his element, secretly enjoying the fact that he was surrounded by non-New Deal Republicans. Anne came of a rock-ribbed Republican family.

At one of these weddings—I believe it was Ethel's and Junior's—someone made off with a top hat that had the initials "FDR" in it. The embarrassed hosts had the case investigated. They finally traced the hat to someone's house and retrieved the "souvenir."

FDR just roared. It wasn't the hat he wore, but one he didn't want, and he had given it to one of his boys to wear to the wedding. He hadn't expected ever to see it again. The investigators had gone to all that trouble and expense for nothing.

Eleanor and the President were much relieved when John finally, at age twenty-five, made up his mind to marry and settle down. But they weren't happy that he was marrying a Republican. Anne Sturgess Clark was her name. She was the daughter of a wealthy financier of the Boston firm of Scudder, Stevens and Clark.

John was the level-headed one and had dated his girl several years, so we thought it would last forever. It didn't. Even he eventually divorced. It was so sad because he had been the one who had teased his brothers and sister about their crazy mixed-up lives and had bragged that he would never get a divorce.

He not only got a divorce, but he remarried in 1965 to someone named Irene Boyd McAlpin. John's marriage to Anne had been dealt a staggering blow when one of their daughters, Sally, was killed in a fall from her horse while she was just a teenager. Anne was never the same after that, and divorce was inevitable.

The story has a strange twist. When movie star Faye Emerson divorced Elliott, she and Anne went to live together in Spain. Anne still didn't recover, and she seemingly lost her will to live, and died.

The saddest marriage in the Roosevelt family, from what we maids saw, was that of Franklin Jr. and the lovely Ethel du Pont. It started out so beautifully. She was a delicate and delightful creature when she first came to the White House as a bride in 1937. A little haughty, but a joy to watch. We noticed she was drowned out by the rough and ready Roosevelt family at gatherings, but she seemed happy enough. Then her look started to change as she grew lonely. Franklin Jr. was studying law and spending little time with her. She seemed full of anxiety, and she would even ask the maids, "Why can't he be here?"

Even before FDR Jr. went off to war as an ensign on a destroyer, Ethel was developing nervous mannerisms. The worst of these was twisting her hair, and I do believe she actually pulled out bits of hair. She also became careless of her appearance, and even left used personal items about the bedroom instead of disposing of them. And she wouldn't open her mail.

As she went downhill, FDR would look at her in a puzzled way, and behind her back called her "our hothouse flower." Eleanor tried to sit and listen to Ethel's complaints, but she had too much to do and was off and running within a few minutes.

Ethel would wander around the White House and sometimes even come into my sewing room, in search of a sympathetic ear. One of her complaints was Franklin Jr.'s bad temper. She told Lizzie that she didn't know what to do. Once, while Ethel was there, a woman friend was a houseguest at the White House. The woman was very aggressive and kept giving maids messages for FDR Jr., that she was waiting for him in her room. The maids took the messages but never delivered them on the grounds that the guest would have to handle her own communications.

It was interesting that, when Junior and Ethel got their divorce, he didn't marry that aggressive socialite, but Suzanne Perrin. He had two children with each—Christopher du Pont and Franklin Delano with Ethel, and Laura Delano and Nancy with Suzanne—two sons versus two daughters.

With Ethel, Franklin Jr., had lived in high style on Long Island. With Suzanne, he lived on a huge farm of several thousand acres near Poughkeepsie, and raised cattle and sheep.

Farm life didn't work out, and Franklin Jr.'s third wife was Felicia Schiff Sarnoff, who had previously been married to RCA President Robert Sarnoff. Felicia was related to the female publisher Dorothy Schiff, who in the seventies announced that she had been carrying on a flirtation and romance with Felicia's late father-in-law, President Roosevelt, for many years.

Franklin Jr. seemed fabulously in love with Felicia. He married her just two days after he got a Mexican divorce from Suzanne. After a fabulous wedding party, they flew off to spend four fabulous days with Jackie and Aristotle Onassis before sailing off on a private cruise.

Everything was fabulous at first—like a fairy tale. Even so, that marriage also ended in divorce. There were no children.

As I started working on this book, news came that FDR Jr. was trying marriage still another time. This time, perhaps to change his luck, it was an equestrian marriage—he arriving on horseback, his bride arriving in a horse-drawn carriage. And afterwards, they both rode off into the sunset—he in riding garb astride his horse, and his bride Patricia Oakes riding sidesaddle on her horse, wearing her wedding gown and veil.

The year was in its spring and so was his bride, who was twenty-six and never-before married. Franklin Jr. was sixty-two when he married for the fourth time that May of 1977, at his Clove Crook Farm estate, at Poughquag, New York.

Of course, by then I was no longer at the White House.

I was also gone from the White House when I heard the sad news about Ethel du Pont. During Lyndon Johnson's administration, poor Ethel killed herself. She had remarried, but evidently hadn't found peace of mind. Memories of Ethel flooded back to me as I had last seen her, nervously pacing and twisting her hair.

Anna and James

The White House always seethed with one or two behind-the-scenes hostilities or feuds.

And jealousies. On and off Eleanor was jealous of FDR's secretary Missy. But not as jealous as she was of Anna. Anna in turn was jealous of Louis Howe, who made himself so at home at the White House. Servants who went to Hyde Park overheard Eleanor's mother-in-law fan the flames by telling Anna matter-of-factly, "I've always told you your mother cares more for Louis than she does for you."

Anna was bitter that at the White House, Louis got all the good service and Eleanor always made her second to him and his needs. The other children also resented Howe because they were put out of the White House when there was a shortage of room. But Howe never was. And James, as on-and-off unofficial aide to his father, resented the fact that FDR listened to everything Louis said but brushed his son's opinions aside. Sometimes FDR's attendants gave high marks to James for being so loyal to his father in spite of it.

Anna always sided with her father and openly showed her preference for spending time with him rather than even trying to develop a closeness with her mother.

The two eldest offspring, Anna and James, both worked for their father at various times and did so for love, not money, because he refused to put them on the public payroll. But to the end, their first loyalty was to him. The other three, especially Elliott, seemed to lean more toward their mother.

Eleanor was jealous of only one of her children—her daughter Anna, their firstborn. Eleanor didn't care how much attention FDR paid to his sons, but she seemed to take it as a personal affront if he spent too much time talking with Anna. Mrs. Roosevelt didn't even seem to mind so much that Missy spent more time with the President in his relaxed moments than Anna did. It was just Anna that she felt in competition with.

Sometimes, we backstairs felt that there was a little tug of war over FDR between mother and daughter. It began with the President's arrival at the White House, when Anna's marriage was on the rocks. Anna moved in at the same time the President did and acted as hostess for her father at the White House a little more often than her mother liked.

After Anna's divorce, we could see that Eleanor was really pleased when Anna fell in love with the newspaperman John Boettiger and was going to marry him and move out. Eleanor even commented that she had helped the romance along.

Boettiger was covering FDR for the Chicago Tribune, and Anna's closeness to her father helped push them together. Both had to get divorces before they could marry, and Eleanor put up smoke screens so the romance could go on undetected right at the White House. They made a handsome looking couple, Anna and John. She was slim, with honey-blonde hair, and he was tall, dark, handsome, and a little heavy set, somewhat like FDR.

The marriage didn't work. We heard that Anna was too aggressive in trying to advance her husband's career. And John was embarrassed that people were saying he had gotten the job from Hearst as managing editor of a Seattle newspaper, the *Seattle Post-Intelligencer* because of his Roosevelt connection. Anna got into the act herself by being women's page editor.

It may have been too much togetherness from the start. We heard Boettiger say he missed his old days of straight reporting. Now he had a lot more headaches, a lot more responsibility.

Of course FDR was not happy that Boettiger was working for William Randolph Hearst, who was called a "yellow journalist" around the White House, but he swallowed his pride in the interests of his daughter's happiness, financial and otherwise.

From what the helpers reported, he wasn't too surprised though, when Hearst got rid of Boettiger as Hearst soured on FDR. Boettiger and Anna were out.

Anna and James

At first Anna and John were cheerful about it. They would publish their own paper and show the world, especially Hearst. They went to Phoenix and bought a little weekly paper—I believe it was only a shopping guide—and tried to make a go of it as a daily. It was rough going.

Again, Anna was on the doorstep, this time asking for money. We knew that Eleanor and FDR were having many discussions about it—whether to lend or give Anna and her husband money, or whether to let them sink or swim. FDR had once become very upset with Boettiger while he was on the *Seattle Intelligencer* because Boettiger had published attacks on the President and his New Deal policies. Eleanor had tried to be a little more open-minded, saying that just because the *writer* said it didn't mean *Boettiger* meant it. We backstairs figured Eleanor must have said something to her daughter, because eventually Boettiger sent FDR a nice letter, saying how popular the President was in Seattle and how he personally backed him. FDR showed this flattering note around.

One good thing resulted from the marriage, a darling boy named John Jr. We maids fussed over him and couldn't believe that his mother wanted him to be barefoot all the time. I recall one cold day when his father carried little Johnny to the President's Oval office in the West Wing, with his little cold feet hanging over his arm.

I seem to recall that a press conference was in progress in the Oval Office that day, so little barefoot Johnny ended up holding his first press conference and receiving a press pass.

Anna seemed to have a thing against clothing. The maids reported she slept in the nude and hated the constriction of clothes. She also hated the constriction of speech, and she would cuss like a sailor. Since she would later become Missy's successor as the confidante of FDR, sitting in on his happy hour with his cronies, it was just as well that she didn't mind a little salty language or off-color jokes. She could dish it out as well as she could receive it.

As I remember it, Anna kept their news enterprise going while her husband went to serve his country in the European theater during the war. Before he went overseas, he came East for six weeks of officer's training school at Charlottesville, Virginia. Anna came with him. Lizzie McDuffie took leave from the White House to care for little Johnny.

Things didn't go well for Anna and her husband after the war. John Boettiger got more and more depressed as he got more and more in debt. Eventually they divorced, and the ending to the story is that John tried to find happiness in a new marriage but ended up throwing himself out a hotel window in New York.

The tragedy brought Anna and her mother closer together. I heard that Eleanor Roosevelt helped Anna get rid of the debts still hanging over her from the ill-fated marriage.

Anna remarried in 1952 and finally found the peace and security that had so long eluded her. This time she married a doctor, James Halsted, and moved to Berkeley, California, where he was attached to the Veterans Administration Hospital. Later Halsted resigned from government and went into private practice in Hillside, New York.

Anna became more like her mother, concerning herself with charities. After her mother died, Anna became involved in the Eleanor Roosevelt Museum at Hyde Park.

Then came Anna's own decline. She developed throat cancer and was slowly dying. I had kept corresponding with her. Her last letter, dated July 26, 1975, was just a post card. But she was interested as ever in Roosevelt affairs. She wrote that she hoped the plans for an FDR Memorial in Washington, D.C., would be "drastically simplified." She signed it, "Always ever affectionate, Anna R. Halsted," and I shed a few tears because she did not mention her condition. She died in November.

James was the apple of his father's eye, and the son he leaned on most, figuratively and actually. When FDR became President, he wanted James around him. Eleanor, I heard, felt it was unfair to single James out for attention. But James was the steady one, the dependable one, and he was the one who would drop everything to help his father, while the others were off doing their own thing. Backstairs, we wondered if it wasn't this eagerness to please his father and his wife Betsey, while at the same time trying to earn the kind of money Betsey and he were both accustomed to, that resulted in his severe stomach ulcers.

FDR so loved and leaned on James that he wanted him around for fun sometimes, even if his rank did not warrant it. After the 1936 election, when FDR used the excuse of the Pan-American Peace Conference to take an ocean voyage, he insisted James come along as his aide. He even gave him the rank of lieutenant colonel in the Marines to justify his being there. Of course, after the trip, the title melted away.

FDR was always using James for his own purposes. In 1939, FDR wanted to make sure that everything would be to the King's liking during his visit, but he didn't want the American public saying he had spent tax money to send an official to England. Fortunately, he didn't have to. James was then a publicist for Metro-Goldwyn-Mayer, involved in promoting the movie *Wuthering Heights* and had to go to England to publicize its release there. FDR had the American ambassador, Joseph Kennedy, arrange for James to meet King George VI and Queen Elizabeth.

James ended up staying at Windsor Castle, becoming as one of the royal family after prolonged anxiety. Jimmy made his father laugh when he got back, telling how he got hopelessly lost trying to find his way to where the family was gathered. And the first night, he walked miles down corridors searching for his room, afraid to open any door for fear he'd bust in on the King and Queen together in bed.

James had almost as checkered a career as Elliott. First and foremost he was on tap to his father, who never stopped trying to keep him at the White House as his secretary or aide. Before, during, and after the White House, James made a lot of business deals.

Grandmother Sara was willing to send James to law school, but for once he turned her down, saying he would make his own way selling insurance. His father voiced the opinion that James might get so interested in making money that he would give up school. That is exactly what happened.

FDR's eldest son never completed his law degree, but for a time he did make a lot of money in insurance, thanks to the golden name of Roosevelt. We heard discussions around the White House about FDR recommending James to friends of his who needed insurance, but we were sure the President wasn't the kind of man to do anything unethical. FDR might mention his son's business, but he wouldn't twist arms.

James didn't do too well trying to make big money. He saw how much movie producers earned and tried to copy them, but his judgment was poor and his first and only movie, *Pot of Gold*, starring Paulette Goddard, ending up making him richer only in experience.

He accepted a big job with a grain and yeast company only to find, through an investigation by Treasury Secretary Morgenthau whose department chased "revenooers," that there was evidence the grain was being diverted into bootleg liquor.

He saw another chance to get rich quick, but he again stubbed his toe. He went into the jukebox business but not only were there unsubstantiated stories of his involvement with underworld crime lords, but the advent of war cut nonessential production short and closed him out.

When Louis Howe died in April 1936, FDR was lost and insisted that he needed son Jimmy to be his new Louis. We heard rumors around the White House about how adamant Eleanor was against having her son underfoot at the White House, as well as his wife and family. She said it meant a loss of privacy and that it was nepotism, a dirty word to the American public. Other people were crying for jobs. FDR, I heard, told her plaintively, "What good is the presidency if I can't even have my son near me?"

Eleanor gave in, but she told James in no uncertain terms that he was not going to live in her White House, but would have to find a home elsewhere and come to work each day like everyone else. The White House servants shook their heads. Louis Howe could live there, requiring all kinds of care and service. Lorena could live there, Anna could live there and bring her kids with her, but son James couldn't live there.

FDR took it hard, and we felt sorry for him. It was just one more nail shutting the door between FDR and Eleanor, they said.

We wondered how much jealousy of Betsey had to do with it. FDR and Betsey hit it off, and he liked her to serve as his hostess.

Anna and James

He also liked to have cocktails with her before dinner. They laughed and talked together, and James admitted he sometimes felt like a fifth wheel.

At any rate, James did find a home elsewhere, in George-town, and the first thing he did was have a ramp built so that FDR could go and relax with James' family. FDR would have a good time with the little ones, Sara Delano and Kate, when he visited. And we heard from FDR's office that he was fed the foods he loved there, both game and delicious roasts of beef.

Would James have needed an ulcer operation if he hadn't worked for his father at the White House? We used to debate that point backstairs. It was obvious that Louis Howe was a hard act to follow. To be FDR's secretary was to have no life of one's own. Eventually, because of his health, James had to stop working for his father. He went to the hospital and came back to the White House only as a guest. He got rid of the ulcers through an operation. He got rid of Betsey through another kind of opera-tion, a divorce.

As I've said, after the divorce from Betsey, he married the nurse who had taken care of him when he had his operation, Romelle Schneider. She was the only daughter-in-law Eleanor didn't seem to take to. It could have had something to do with all the things Jimmy was doing for Romelle's family. James found himself with added responsibilities, and in the Roosevelt family, children's responsibilities had a way of involving the parents.

At any rate, James did things for Romelle that made the Roosevelt family gasp. He sent her brother to college, gave her sister a job as his secretary, and even brought her widowed mother to live near them.

From what I heard around the White House, the rest of the family couldn't agree on whether Jimmy was a saint or a chump for all the things he did in trying to please his wife. The other sisters-in-law didn't have much in common with her because she was a career girl. They couldn't understand her discontent with her fine home. Jimmy finally acquiesced and moved into a finer one.

The maids around the White House said that Romelle just didn't act like a Roosevelt wife. She didn't even like politics, and from what James said after, politics had been the thing that finally broke them up. She didn't like it when he ran for Governor—a race he lost—and she didn't like it when he ran for U.S. Congress—a race he won and continued to win through five terms. Still the marriage lasted through three children—James Jr., Anthony, and Anna Eleanor.

Once, when one of the maids said that Romelle just didn't belong in the Roosevelt family, another retorted, "What poor girl does?" The consensus was that the Roosevelt boys were handsome and so oozing with charm that they were irresistible. But when they got the girl, they didn't know what to do with her. Only Johnny Roosevelt, when he finally got married, seemed to know how to make his wife feel secure and important to him. I once heard Anna try to explain all the divorces in her family, including her own. She said, "We never learned how to make a mate happy. We only learned how to be individualists."

But to return to Romelle Schneider, the problem seemed to be that she was trying to live up to some image of perfection that she thought was expected of her at the White House. She was very impatient with the maids once because she didn't like the way they were pressing her evening dress for that night's White House dinner. She made them do it over and over, getting more annoyed each time. She finally wore it, but was still dissatisfied.

Even after James and Betsey divorced, FDR would invite Betsey to dinner and have cocktails with her alone.

Betsey bounced back after the divorce and made a second marriage with John Hay "Jock" Whitney. She presided over the Ambassador's residence in London when her husband became U.S. Ambassador to the Court of St. James's.

I wasn't there the night Betsey came back to the White House during the Eisenhower administration. Wilma Holness waited on her and told me afterwards she had looked most impressive and beautiful as an Ambassador's wife. It had been seventeen years since she had last set foot in the White House. She had asked Wilma where I was, sounding as if she wanted to see me. When she heard I wasn't on duty that night, she sent her warmest regards. I was so happy that a divorce from a Roosevelt hadn't

Anna and James

wrecked Betsey's life as it seemed to do to several other castoff wives.

But getting back to Betsey's ex, James, it was politics that brought him his third wife. I was still at the White House. As one of the butlers laughingly commented, when James married Irene Owens, his receptionist, just months after taking office as U.S. Congressman from California in January 1955, "That poor boy seems to have an occupational hazard—when he gets near an occupation, he marries it."

The other occupation he had brushed against was nursing, of course, which had given him Romelle, his second wife.

We watched James' career from afar while we served other presidents, even after we retired from the White House service. I met Irene when James and I appeared together on the Chicago TV talk show "At Random." I had heard that James and Irene had failed to produce a child of their own so I rejoiced for him that he had adopted a little boy, whom he named for his mother's brother Hall, and for his father's family, Delano.

However, as it turned out, the little boy did not benefit from his grandmother's will because he was not a blood Roosevelt.

But this was the least of James' problems with Irene. The worst of his problems hit the newspapers and made headlines around the world.

It happened after James was out of Congress and had moved to Switzerland, where he was vice president of a company. Irene was bitterly unhappy and proved it forcefully. In a rage, she stabbed James with one of his cherished souvenirs, a Marine knife from World War II. Only then it came out that her father had also resorted to violence years before, shooting himself in front of Irene.

James admitted that his wife had accused him of infidelity. Whatever, he managed to escape her and never looked back.

But he did manage to see quite a bit of his son, Hall Delano ("Del"), and again meet an *occupational hazard*. He married Del's teacher, an English girl thirty years his junior, Mary Winskill.

Actually, she was Del's New York teacher. What happened is that James phoned her from Geneva, Switzerland, to come help

Del because Irene was too overwrought to look after the boy following the knife incident. Mary flew to Switzerland, bringing her mother.

They were married in New York in 1969. It was her first marriage and James' fourth. James became a father again at age sixty-three in 1971. The span between this youngest child, Rebecca Mary (called "Becky"), and his oldest child, Sara Delano, was thirty-nine years.

Everything was new and different for James. He sent his wife to the University of California to improve her teaching credentials, and he became a university instructor there, teaching government.

That is the story of James.

I still keep in touch with Anna's daughter, Sistie, who is now Eleanor Seagraves and still lives in the Washington area.

When the Hollywood producer Ed Friendly gave a luncheon for the opening of the TV mini-series based on my first book, Sistie came to represent the Roosevelts. She sat at the head table with me and sounded as public spirited as her grandmother had been.

I miss the old days when I kept track of the Roosevelt family through Anna Halsted, who died in 1975.

That story had a strange twist. Anna's husband, the following year, at age seventy-one married that child we and Anna's mother, Eleanor, had all helped raise in the White House—Diana Hopkins. By then, 1976, Diana was forty-nine.

I remember that Diana came back to visit us at the White House once with one child, when she was Diana Baxter and living in Georgetown. She had gotten a divorce some time before Anna's death from cancer.

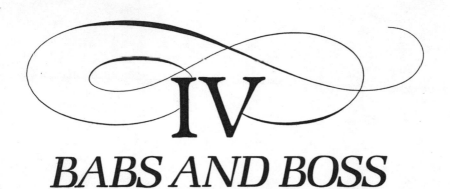

IV
BABS AND BOSS

Babs and Boss

The Roosevelts all had nicknames, like it or not. FDR called Eleanor "Babs." Babs, however, did not believe in nicknames and sternly called the President "Franklin." She was the only one I knew of to do so.

The staffers called him "Boss." The kids called him "Pa." But now and then one or two of them would also call him "Mr. Bean" or refer to him as "the Old Bean," meaning, I surmise, the *head*. I was told that in Britain, calling someone "Old Bean" was a mark of respect when speaking to a familiar.

Various intimates had other names for FDR. Gus Gennerich, his friend and bodyguard, called him "Pal." But he was the only one. In fact, FDR called Gus "Pal," too. It was their own private joke.

Every president is called "The Old Man" by his top aides, but it is surprising how few people not connected with the White House know this. Sometimes the outsider, such as the wife of a houseman, would overhear this name at a gathering and ask, "What old man are you talking about?"

We would answer in a hurry, "Oh, an old man who is getting ready to retire" or "You don't know him, he's a temporary." We had our fun with it.

Sometimes we did the same thing with the First Lady, calling her by the President's nickname for her, "Babs." No outsider in a million years could connect Babs with a woman whose real name was Anna Eleanor Roosevelt. The First Lady told Lizzie the nickname had been given to her by Franklin on their honeymoon, as short for "Baby."

We didn't get the connection, but if she did, it was all right with us. We said it sounded like an abbreviation for *Babies,* and maybe it was because they had a slew of them in a hurry—six children in about ten years, one of whom, the first Franklin D. Jr., died in his first year of a respiratory ailment.

Eleanor's children called her "Mother," and were always more formal with her than with the President. The Secret Service gave Eleanor a less formal name, "Rover," so they could talk about her on telephones and handle her travel plans.

FDR had a still less formal name for his wife when he spoke of her in radio broadcasts, and he knew it went over well with the public—he would say, "My Missus says..."

We had still another name for her, "The Unofficial Vice President." That's what it really amounted to. The word around the White House was that Roosevelt hated to ask his Vice President, tough old "Cactus Jack" Garner, to do anything—so he just asked Eleanor.

After one false start, the metamorphosis into a kind of government official began almost immediately.

I don't know whether it happened just as they arrived at the White House or just before. Apparently, Eleanor wanted desperately to be helpful to her husband—a true working partner—and she asked whether she could work for him, opening his mail.

The story was that FDR gave her the strangest look, probably remembering the last time she had looked at his mail, years before, and had found the love letters from Lucy Mercer, and answered a firm no. Missy, he said, would not like the interference. FDR had come a long way in his emancipation.

After this attempt to be part of the Oval Office, Eleanor quickly emerged as a public figure. In the spring of 1933, the Roosevelt administration had barely begun, and already there was violence brewing in the form of angry World War I veterans.

Eleanor's first important act was a dangerous mission—calming the new Bonus Marchers, who had returned to Washington after Hoover had thrown them out. They were angry.

FDR was too busy to give them his full attention, but he wasn't going to do as the former president had done—order General Douglas MacArthur to get rid of them. FDR had the new Bonus Army greeted with friendliness and proper meals. He ordered that they be housed at Fort Hunt, near Washington.

Still there was danger of their becoming ugly and militant. Eleanor went to visit them, without an army of protection, and with only frail Louis Howe to lean on. She showed a friendly interest in the men, talked with many of them about their individual problems, and persuaded many of them to help themselves and their country by joining the CCC—Civilian Conservation Corps—clearing land and planting trees.

She ended up singing songs with the no longer angry young men. We were proud of her the next day when the bonus marchers were quoted in the papers as saying. "Hoover sent the Army. Roosevelt sent Eleanor."

They could have added, "His unofficial Vice President."

As we saw it, this was the real beginning of Eleanor's acceptance as an important voice of the New Deal.

Howe, we heard from Missy, had told Eleanor that he could make her the first woman president of the United States, after FDR was out of office. Of course, Howe died before FDR's second term so we'll never know if he could have talked her into running or if he could have pulled it off. But I'll bet he could have done both. In his gruff way, he was very persuasive.

The general public, I'm sure, doesn't know how much Eleanor shaped the New Deal and the policies of the nation. And women don't know how much she did for women's lib.

She helped get the first woman into the Cabinet. That was her friend Frances Perkins, who had been labor commissioner in New York State, also at Eleanor's insistence. We heard Eleanor twisted her husband's arm to get him to include Frances in the top echelon of Washington government.

Under Eleanor's nurturing, "Ma" Perkins rose from a social worker to a top position, just as Harry Hopkins had.

Secretary of Labor Ma Perkins turned out to be one of FDR's hardest working and most effective cabinet members. Eleanor and she both had a finger in the Social Security Act, which Perkins helped write.

Just as other presidents sent their vice presidents on fact-finding tours, FDR sent Eleanor. In 1934, his second year in office, he sent her to Puerto Rico to check economic conditions. She came back with a complete report on the desperate poverty of the island under our protection.

The public thought that Eleanor must be thick-skinned to flaunt the bad publicity she received in the anti-Roosevelt newspapers and still do her own thing. We knew differently. She did cringe when, for example, everyone had fun at her expense about her traveling to the far corners of the earth. It didn't stop her, of course, but it did hurt when, for example, there was a story that Admiral Byrd at the South Pole had set an extra place in his icy shelter in case Eleanor showed up.

Even the liberal *New Yorker* ran a cartoon showing Eleanor going down into a coal mine, and the shocked coal miners saying, "Good gosh, here comes Eleanor." That happened before she made her famous "descent into the coal mines," but it didn't stop her. She went anyway to inspect mine conditions.

From what I heard, in real life they wouldn't let her go down into the shaft. Their rule was that no women were allowed. And surely they didn't want trouble with a First Lady getting stuck underground.

Eleanor was soon getting a lot of mail.

Some letters were a little scary and the social office had to decide whether to turn them over to the Secret Service for investigating. One such letter was from a man who had written to bless Eleanor Roosevelt, and in answer, Edith sent some simple note of thanks saying Mrs. Roosevelt appreciated his letter.

In return came a vile letter from the same man saying he withdrew his blessing and was asking God to put a curse upon Eleanor. I asked Edith what the man was so upset about and she said he was furious because Eleanor Roosevelt had not signed the letter and had let someone else answer it.

The funny thing was the man had piously protested that he was definitely not a "crank" but a "servant of God." I believe that "servant of God" did receive a visit from the FBI or Secret Service.

Meanwhile, FDR was having his own mailbag problems.

I had never seen a man so praised and so insulted. So worshipped and so hated. Letters would come to the White House addressed to "Benedict Arnold II" and to "Judas," and we would hear about it. But now and then we also heard that FDR was angry and showed it.

About the most shocking thing he did one day was to present a Nazi Iron Cross to a reporter who had written nasty articles reflecting on FDR's patriotism. Yes, FDR could be nasty, too.

But always very human.

Babs and Boss

People have asked me whether FDR loved the song, "Happy Days Are Here Again." They wonder how it happened to become his theme song. I'm sorry to say the original idea for that song wasn't his. Somewhere, some nameless person deserves a lot of credit for a song that may have had much more to do with FDR's career than all those people who do take the credit.

"Anchors Aweigh" was the song that he liked and that was what the band played when his name was mentioned at the Democratic Convention in Chicago in 1932. But finally Louis Howe, who didn't much care for the song, and had had a bellyful of it at Navy, could stand it no longer. He sent word for the band to play something else, for God's sake, something less heavy.

The band played "Happy Days Are Here Again" because it was the first cheerful song that came to mind. FDR liked it and felt it was lucky. That became his theme song from then on.

FDR was superstitious about all kinds of things. He had his lucky hat for campaigning, for example.

It was certainly unlucky for his opponents for whatever FDR wanted, FDR got—including an unheard of fourth term.

Eleanor didn't feel her clothes were particularly lucky. She was very matter of fact. Actually, she didn't care much what she wore unless others were pushing and cajoling her.

To show how little Eleanor cared about clothes, once the zipper in the back of her dress got stuck and the First Lady said, "Oh, just go ahead and cut it. I simply don't care." Mrs. Roosevelt had no patience when she was in a hurry to get somewhere, and she was in a hurry that day.

I did a lot of sewing that required a few words with Mrs. Roosevelt. I checked with Mabel, her personal maid, and as Eleanor got involved in the war effort, Mabel would often say, "Lillian, Mrs. R. is so busy, I can't approach her. But I'll ask her as soon as she slows down."

Sometimes I had to wait two or three days. No wonder. She was busy with civil defense. She was writing her column, "My Day," which she dictated to Tommy Thompson. She made speeches, sometimes traveling hundreds of miles to make them. She flew around the country seeing her children and grandchildren any-time they called for her—and sometimes just to check up on them.

She juggled a houseload of guests—some official, such as

Churchill—and some personal, such as Joe Lash and Nancy Cook or Marion Dickerman. She answered hundreds of letters a day, wrote notes to her husband for his pillow reading, and kept a correspondence going daily with Lorena Hickok while Hicky was traveling as an investigator for the New Deal.

She was also catching trains or flying off somewhere— sometimes meeting Hicky, more often investigating something for her husband.

The public didn't mind Eleanor knocking herself out to investigate things for the President for free, but they certainly minded when they learned she was making money on her column, "My Day," on articles for *Woman's Home Companion* and other magazines, on books, and on the radio, sponsored by Sweetheart soap.

Columnists attacked her periodically. Editorials were written defending her sometimes but usually blasting her for using the White House for commercial gain.

Eleanor blasted right back, asking whether a woman was supposed to close off using all her talents just because she was now located in the White House.

At the time of the second administration. Eleanor let it slip to one of the staff that she had earned $75,000. This spread like wildfire backstairs, where grown men were earning $2,000 to $3,000 a year and had to pay rent out of that.

The point Eleanor had been trying to make was that her salary was equal to the official salary Congress gave the President. Soon after that, we heard that the Republican members of Congress wanted to investigate her income tax returns and her charitable deductions. I don't know what came of it, but I know she was always writing checks to charities and just plain needy people.

In fact, FDR was known to complain about Eleanor's generosity and said within an attendant's hearing, "It's a good thing Eleanor doesn't own the White House or she'd give that away, too."

Eleanor wrote about almost anything a publisher asked. She ran around the White House, with Tommy Thompson trailing along behind, dictating on any number of subjects.

Babs and Boss

Once she even wrote a children's book, a guide to all the wonders of Washington.

We knew part of the reason Eleanor kept so busy was to avoid thinking of herself as a tragic figure. More than once, in a slightly bitter mood, she commented to women friends within our hearing that she and Missy were both victims of FDR's ego. Or, as she put it, his total absorption in himself and his goals.

It was true that it seemed the whole world centered around him, much more than with other presidents I had known, but we felt somehow it was right and fitting in his case because he had a heavier burden than any of them.

And we were pleased that he rose above the wheelchair and still maintained a great pride in himself—it was part of his charm.

He seemed to do everything with flair and style.

He wore a cape instead of a coat when nobody else did. He used a long cigarette holder and learned to clench it between his teeth at a jaunty angle, or hold it aloft to the delight of the crowds.

And finally, he wore a pince-nez strictly for effect, the only man around with this elegant touch—except his copycat treasury secretary, who mimicked everything but his sense of humor.

It was sad, but seldom did the President and First Lady hit the same mood at the same time. He worked by day, she worked by night.

After a day of leg braces, he wanted to relax.

Eleanor drove FDR wild with her notes and messages and the work pile she left beside his bed. He wanted to think of pleasant things in the evenings—stamps and Missy and Fala and cocktails and good conversations filled with anecdotes and jokes.

She wanted to talk of serious things like the solution to unemployment, housing for the poor, and an idea she is never given credit for—medical help for the poor. I once heard her talking about free health care when she made the impressive point that we are as healthy as the least healthy among us, adding that the rich could and did catch diseases from the poor.

She pointed out that FDR, all his life, had been well-off and well cared for. Yet, he had caught polio and no one knew from whom.

Babs and Boss

Another incompatability between Babs and the Boss was food. One of the butlers used to kid that Eleanor must be extremely interested in sex because she certainly wasn't interested in food. She really didn't care what she ate.

One of the cooks had a theory that Eleanor had defective taste buds because she didn't notice any difference no matter how hard they tried to make something especially good. And so they sometimes just didn't care and quit trying.

The President did care, but he was not in charge. Looking back, it was ridiculous that the First Lady and Henrietta Nesbitt got together and decided what food should be cooked and delivered to the Oval Office in the West Wing at one P.M.

They didn't eat it. Only the President and his luncheon guests ate it—people like poor Missy—and they groaned. Eleanor had her theories of good nutrition. Nesbitt was only concerned with her authority. She wanted iron control. When a cook said, "But Mrs. Nesbitt, the President doesn't like broccoli," she would say, "Well, fix it anyway."

This went on for years, and only the death of FDR's mother brought relief. FDR sent for his mother's cook to come to the White House and cook only for him.

Eleanor was furious. Nesbitt was furious. Backstairs we laughed as this battle raged. Eleanor insisted the cook was killing the President with kindness by smothering everything in a pound of butter. The First Lady prevailed on Dr. McIntire to call in a nutritionist to teach the errant cook how to make things as tasteless as the other cooks did in the name of health.

FDR sent Missy to check up and make sure his own orders were being followed. They weren't.

Once, the President was entertaining some royal guests, and he knew they preferred hot coffee. Missy happened upon the butlers bringing trays of iced tea. She said, "The President ordered hot coffee."

They said, "Mrs. Nesbitt ordered iced tea."

"Didn't she know that he wanted hot coffee?" she persisted.

"Oh yes," they said, "but she said it was better for them."

FDR was much more sensitive to the decor of a room than his wife was. In fact, he always checked over anything important that was ordered for the White House. Once it was new glassware, and FDR's discerning eye immediately spotted an error in the presidential crest etched on the glass. The eagle was facing in the wrong direction.

The President also worked out the arrangement of photos and prints on his study walls. Woe to the person who took them down for cleaning and did not get them up in the right order. He knew immediately. The same went for the little objects he arranged on his desk. Each was an old friend with its own little spot.

FDR was so jovial and jolly that few realized he suffered from allergies. He couldn't stand house dust and had attacks of asthma now and then. Because of this, his bedroom had to be spartan in its decor. Dr. McIntire ordered the rug and the draperies removed. It looked so austere that linen drapery, to which he was not allergic, was installed.

The physician chosen to look after FDR at the White House—Vice Admiral Ross McIntire—was an ear, nose, and throat specialist because FDR was considered to be a healthy man except for his sinus trouble and his allergies.

He was prone to colds. Eleanor was prone to nothing but good health. I only knew her to get sick with a bad cold once—she recovered the next day.

FDR was especially allergic to the lint from cotton and wool. We also had a special problem with his allergy to paint. We had to wait until he was going on a long trip before daring to paint a wall. The odor of newly applied paint drove him up the wall. Now and then the walls of his room would be washed down to get rid of any loose specks

It's too bad Eleanor chose to turn her back on Warm Springs and never accompany him there.

To understand the true FDR, you would have to see him at Warm Springs, Georgia, at the Georgia rehabilitation center, which he founded in 1927 to help those afflicted with polio. What drew him there in the beginning were the natural springs that never dropped below about 80 degrees.

Only among the patients at Warm Springs was FDR himself, not hiding the fact that he was badly crippled, proudly showing how skilled he was at getting along in his wheel chair. Not that he ever gave up hope. Oh no. Once I asked Dr. McIntire if there was a chance the President could regain the use of his limbs. He said, "No, but we must never let him give up hope, so I shall never tell him, Lillian."

We would hear heartrending stories now and then about how FDR imagined new feeling in his toes. Missy always said that if only FDR had spent full time at Warm Springs and waited just another year or so before getting back into politics, she was sure he would have been a walking president. It was one of her sadnesses that he had given up too soon.

Though the sensations in his toes always proved to be imaginary, FDR never tired of urging others at Warm Springs to keep trying and never give up. Several times, with his good humor and optimism, he pulled young patients, and old, out of deep depression. He teased them, prodded them, showed them how he had learned to use his shoulders and arms. But most therapeutic of all, he would take them, singly, for a spin in his hand-controlled Ford and discourse fervently on the beauty of nature, which required *only their eyes* for its enjoyment.

Patients worked long and diligently so that when FDR arrived on his next visit, they could show him some new skill they had mastered. FDR never disappointed them. He made as much fuss as if they had climbed Mt. Everest.

He was always shouting encouragement to patients in the pool and took the scare out of the water experience by giving nicknames to positions that would keep them from drowning— "dead man's float" and "the floating mare."

How much he loved the patients was brought home to us just about every Thanksgiving when FDR left his own family behind and went to Warm Springs to act as a father for all the patients, sitting at the table and carving the holiday turkey.

When people cursed FDR, calling him a "pinko" and "a traitor to his class," I would think of this FDR, the FDR of Warm Springs.

A president in those days received $75,000 salary and an entertainment allowance of $25,000. Pour soul. That didn't begin to keep FDR and his sons going in the fashion they had become accustomed to. FDR would often mention that he just didn't know how he was going to make ends meet.

According to scuttlebutt, Eleanor felt a little downcast that she had to support herself in the White House. In their occasional clashes, she would be heard telling FDR that was the reason she had to take a particular writing or speaking engagement that he was objecting to.

FDR would get terrible letters from the public objecting to the First Lady cashing in on her position in the White House to make money. Some members of the public seemed to feel Eleanor should give her time and efforts free of charge. But FDR and Eleanor both knew that, given both their lifestyles, FDR could not afford Eleanor any other way.

We knew that for years they had agreements of who paid for what—Eleanor using her independent income for her own needs, as well as partially supporting the household in the pre-White House days.

FDR had his personal income, too, and we heard it was about $60,000 a year during the White House years—and this, after taxes, went for entertainment, supporting family and friends in and out of the White House, travel, and whatever else came up.

Now and then it would hurt that in spite of their finances, FDR would not hesitate to spend a small fortune on some collector's item—a rare stamp or manuscript that came on the market.

There was growing competition between the President and First Lady, and each would try to outdo the other in little ways. For example, when the President had some speeches bound in fancy covers and gave them to family members and Missy as gifts, Eleanor waited a suitable length of time and had a series of articles she had written for the *Ladies' Home Journal* bound and presented to the same people.

It was one upmanship! She had earned good money for hers.

No wonder Franklin preferred to eat with Missy.

FDR grew to resent Eleanor's pressure on him. He told Missy and other people around the White House, "She only sees me when she needs me." Eleanor would phone the President to say she needed to talk to him about someone's problem or someone's good idea. The President would suggest they make an appointment for a conference the following morning when he would be rested. Eleanor would say no, it was important, and the person involved would be gone from the White House by then, or she needed to answer a letter immediately.

FDR would sigh and ask what Eleanor suggested. She would suggest they talk about it at dinner, adding that she hated to bother him while he ate, but it seemed to be the only time she could get him to listen.

So FDR would show up for dinner at eight and feign great interest in whatever Eleanor and her group said. Sometimes he really was interested, but as he himself admitted, he had to be an actor to get along. The First Lady would talk rapidly in a voice that grew a little high-pitched as she warmed to the subject.

The President would give her his full attention as she talked, and she seemed quite flattered by it. It was a serious talk between two friends, two business acquaintances. It would be the guests, usually, who would give FDR something to break into laughter about as they related their adventures with hard-headed congressmen, for example.

FDR was always quick to laugh. Backstairs we said that for FDR it wasn't apples, but a laugh a day that kept the doctor away. He needed laughter to survive.

Eleanor could be persistent, to put it mildly, but FDR could be stubborn. The housemen and valets said it was the President's Dutch blood that made him unyielding once he'd made his mind up. They would know by the way he clenched his cigarette holder between his teeth that he had made up his mind and wouldn't budge.

Unfortunately, they didn't teach this to FDR's mate, and Eleanor kept butting her head against his strong will. She would fire memo after memo, hoping to get FDR to change his mind, but that rarely happened.

Sometimes FDR would get so annoyed at his wife's persistence that he would no longer answer the memos. Then Eleanor would take to the telephone and corner him that way. We would be filled in later about the fact that FDR was dodging Eleanor. Sometimes we would know it was going on at that very time.

I recall one time FDR was dodging Eleanor by phone when he had made a decision against interfering in a state case. Eleanor was very agitated about it because it involved a life—even though, as she acknowledged, it was the life of a murderer.

When she could no longer get through to FDR because he was dodging her, Eleanor phoned Harry Hopkins, who was living at the White House, just days before his wedding to Louise Macy, and tried to get him worked up so he would pressure FDR. It didn't work, and the man was put to death. Eleanor grieved, one in spirit with those who were keeping a deathwatch.

The case was that of a black sharecropper who had been sentenced to death for murdering the farm owner. I don't remember his name or the state where it happened, but the family had appealed to Eleanor as he sat in death row, and time was running out.

There was no question of his guilt, but Eleanor wanted his sentence commuted to life. As she told Tommy, "If this were a white man he would have gotten a small sentence or life at most. It's one more case of racial injustice."

Eleanor had done her bit and memoed FDR to contact the governor to suggest giving the man life. FDR had reported to Eleanor that the governor had already been generous in giving several reprieves, and that the man's case lacked merit. FDR said he didn't feel he should push the governor further.

But Eleanor felt *she* could push the President further. She switched to the telephone. Again he told her the governor had the power under the Constitution to do what he thought was right and suggested she lay off the case.

But she wouldn't, and at that point FDR avoided her calls.

That's when she switched her phone calls to Harry Hopkins. Missy was gone. Had she been around, she would have been the one Eleanor turned to, and perhaps there would have been a different ending to the case.

The Mystery of Missy

The woman who sacrificed most for FDR was not Eleanor or Lucy Mercer but Missy LeHand. She gave her love and dedicated her life so completely to Franklin Roosevelt that it broke her health and led to her early death.

Backstairs we said that Missy was the substitute wife, and we honored her for it. I hate to say it, but when Missy gave an order we responded as if it had come from the First Lady. We knew that FDR would always back up Missy.

It was a weird situation. Missy could have gone ahead and made decisions on her own, knowing that FDR would stand behind her, but she was diplomatic enough to give notes to Eleanor asking for her "decision." We really had two mistresses in the White House.

After you accepted the situation, there was no shock in seeing Missy come to FDR's suite at night in her nightgown and robe or sitting on his lap in the Oval study. But she was discreet, and was never still there the next morning when FDR's breakfast tray arrived.

People who were new on the scene and didn't understand the relationship would sometimes be shocked when the family was getting into a car and the President made sure Missy and not Eleanor sat beside him. Of course, he could have sat in the middle with one on each side, but because of his weak legs, he sat just inside the door so he could hold on to the strap.

We loved Missy—all the household help, that is—because she was so much fun and so kind. She only got tough if she thought someone was trying to shortchange or take advantage of the President. She was very protective of him and looked out for his best interest at all times.

The world viewed FDR as a lonely man whose wife was sent

out by him to be his eyes and ears and legs. It was a beautiful picture and no one disputed it. But the truth was far different. Even if Eleanor was home she did not see her husband for stretches at a time, except for a "Good morning" as they passed in the hall.

The way the Roosevelts really communicated was through notes. Eleanor would swing by his bedroom while he was still in the office, and drop off a note for him on his night table. Sometimes it would be very affectionate in tone, beginning, "Dearest Honey," and ending, "With love," or "Much love," but in between it would be just a businesslike message about a letter she had received from someone who needed help, and would he please do thus and so.

Or it might be a compliment to him about a fireside chat he had given. Or about something nice she had heard about FDR during her travels—how much he was loved and how much they respected him in Appalachia.

Eleanor frequently left criticisms by his bedside as well, with her comments on what she disapproved of in his handling of some problem or warning him about certain people.

FDR never bothered with this stuff during his cocktail hour with Missy. According to the valets, he called it, "My homework." But sometime in the night, if he couldn't sleep, or early morning while waiting for his breakfast tray, he would tackle it.

The public would have been surprised to see Babs and Boss in the halls like ships that pass in the night. Surprised to see FDR dictating his answers to his wife to Missy. Or to Grace Tully, who was Missy's assistant.

It was through Missy that FDR waged his war against the food he was served. For all the good it did!

Missy was a tease. She could always find the humor in things. And she made every day exciting for FDR. They always had bets going, and FDR would get up pools and cheat to win, before he was found out and had to pay up.

Once McDuffie, the valet, heard FDR telling how opposed Eleanor was to any form of gambling. FDR said that when they were first married, Eleanor had refused out of principle to play bridge for small stakes at their social parties.

The Mystery of Missy

Eleanor didn't like Warm Springs and didn't go there. Missy was his hostess there. Missy was also FDR's hostess in Hyde Park, especially at the hideaway the President was building—Hilltop Cottage.

Few people knew that Missy actually listed her permanent address for voting as Sara's Hyde Park mansion. And she told Mama and others that she used the White House address for income tax purposes.

Mama used to say that Missy should not work as hard as she did because she had had rheumatic fever as a child. Doctors had told her not to overdo. But she did anyway. She was the President's cheerful shadow.

I recall few times when I saw Missy without a smile on her face. Only when there was trouble did she frown.

I know she had a dream. It was that after the White House, FDR would live in Hilltop Cottage and write books and she would be there to help him. Hilltop Cottage was FDR's answer to Val-Kill. Val-Kill was Eleanor's hideaway where FDR never went unless invited. It was where Eleanor stayed with her friends, a little more than a mile from the big house at Hyde Park, and out of reach of her mother-in-law's watchful eye.

Then FDR built his own hideaway where he could entertain his friends without his mother's supervision. And *Eleanor* never went there except on invitation.

Eleanor, through the years, actually stayed or lived at her cottage for stretches at a time, but FDR stayed at the main house at Hyde Park and only drove to Hilltop Cottage for a few hours now and then with Missy and other friends.

When the King and Queen of England came in 1939, Hilltop was close enough to being finished for the outdoor picnic to be held there, so they would have the cooking facilities inside, and rest rooms, and yet have the picnic effect of eating outdoors.

However, for swimming, FDR still used Eleanor's Val-Kill, several miles away in another part of the Hyde Park estate.

Hilltop Cottage did not even have a phone. And that's the way FDR wanted it.

At the White House, Missy had a suite of rooms on the third floor, where my sewing room was. I would see her darting back and forth, almost dancing sometimes in her vivacity, not waiting for the elevator half the time, but just tripping down the stairs.

Missy's suite was lovely and consisted of a living room, or study, as we called it, a bedroom, and bath. Anything Missy wanted for her quarters she could have. FDR doted on her and liked to see her in fine fashion. But she had so little time that Eleanor, we were shocked to learn, would frequently go shopping for her.

As everyone backstairs agreed, it was a complicated situation.

Missy had her own breakfast in the same style as FDR— served on a tray in bed—in her own bedroom. She read the newspapers and knew what everybody was saying about the Boss and his New Deal programs before she got to the office.

Missy did all the things the average housewife might do— paid the personal bills, wrote FDR's checks, gave Eleanor money. The Roosevelt children were used to going to her. She gave them their weekly allowances growing up, and she was still writing checks for them and their expenses. Even at the White House they came to her with problems, and she served as intermediary.

Eleanor would come to her to solve problems, and to get some additional spending money. Eleanor knew that if Missy asked him, FDR would not object, but if she did, they might get into an argument over how much money the children were spending, or the price she was paying for something.

Backstairs, we knew that one reason Eleanor was so anxious to have her own column and earn her money was that she hated to ask FDR for money. She liked showing him how independent she was, and even before she started earning money, she used her inheritance money to help with household expenses, as well as pay for her own travel and clothes.

Missy was somehow involved with everything FDR did for fun. Eleanor never showed any interest in FDR's stamp collection. Missy was an excited assistant collector, working on his collection with him and reminding him of where he had stashed some missing stamp.

She tore out funny items in the papers that would make him laugh and collected Eleanor cartoons, as well as cartoons about the President.

The Mystery of Missy

Her name was really Margaret, but FDR cared too much about her to settle for a nickname like Maggie. "Missy" seemed just right.

Missy was one of the few people around the White House who could talk about how it used to be when FDR could walk. She had been working for him for some time before the polio attack and had been in the New York office writing to him at Campobello asking for a raise at the very time he went swimming in the cold Canadian waters there and came out feeling strangely tired and weak.

The way we heard the story, the affair between Missy and the Boss had begun soon after the traumatic incident involving Lucy Mercer. For some reason, Eleanor was not so jealous of Missy. Maybe she just gave up. Also, Lucy came from a high social strata, and perhaps this bothered Eleanor. Missy had no pretensions.

Whatever it was, somehow Eleanor made up her mind to accept what she could not change. She simply pretended that Missy was another of her children and included her in all family things. When Missy's niece got married, it was Eleanor who went shopping for the gift Missy would give her.

Just before the election of 1932, Missy's mother died, and it was Eleanor who went with her to Massachusetts to the funeral.

But human nature is human nature, and now and then something showed through. But less at the White House than before.

Eleanor had been a little jealous of Missy back in the days when they had lived in the Governor's Mansion at Albany because even then Missy presided at FDR's all-male gatherings and dinners, which were off limits to Eleanor.

FDR was generous only with those very close to him, such as Missy, whom he would pamper and encourage to buy things at his expense. But he was never overly generous with the household help.

Eleanor was always on the lookout for things to buy for the children of the maids and other staff members—toys or whatever was appropriate for their ages, which she had in a list. She always bought up pocketbooks at Christmas and put a little money in each of them for us maids.

In the summer, Missy would wear shimmering whites that were slim as a stove-pipe and clung to her knees before belling out a bit at her ankles to give more room for movement. Missy was an asset to any group, smiling and tossing her head with its rich, almost taffy-colored hair.

The White House waiters always wore tuxedos and black bow ties to serve at family dinners no matter what the family wore. But at a formal party, the waiters wore tails and white ties, just as the guests did.

The President's valets wore white coats, white shirts, and black bow ties. So did the housemen and busboys. As these white jackets showed signs of wear, they were mended and kept for temporary help who used them during lawn parties at the White House. One of my jobs was finding something wearable for the men coming in for a particular party.

The President would be seen talking and laughing with the guests, as would Eleanor—Missy would be somewhere in the background.

Missy and the President enjoyed a tray of delicacies with their evening cocktails—things that Eleanor had no interest in and considered extravagant—caviar, smoked turkey, smoked clams, and imported cheeses.

Missy would sip her favorite Haig & Haig while FDR mixed his own martini, or sometimes an old-fashioned. When they had guests, FDR would insist on mixing the martinis for everyone, and he would brag that he was the best martini mixer in the East.

There was a mystery about certain flowers that Missy received once a year just before she would go home to Somerville, Massachusetts, for Christmas with her family. They were always white lilacs and smelled heavenly. We never found out if they were from FDR or some old flame.

She would leave them behind and usually Lizzie got to keep them.

One of my first assignments for FDR was to sew extensions on some blankets for his bed. He had a wire contraption across the bottom of the bed to keep the heavy blankets from putting extra weight on his legs. As the President's male attendants explained, this didn't mean he didn't want a nice young warm body next to his, he just didn't want anything heavy pushing on his legs. According to the valets, he led a normal sex life.

The Roosevelt children were not shocked to see Missy in FDR's bedroom at night. They treated her with a warm affection and told their wives (who told us maids) that Missy had always been around FDR in her nightgown, ever since she had come to live with them. They remembered her in the Governor's Mansion—she in her nightgown and the Governor in his pajamas.

They had seen Missy on their father's lap. They had seen her give him a little smooch. FDR and Missy did not flaunt their relationship, but the kids, young as they were, understood that this was just part of their own special family setup and they accepted it.

Lizzie told me about the bedroom arrangement at the Governor's Mansion. FDR had the master bedroom and Missy had the closest nearby bedroom. Eleanor slept away from them in a back bedroom that was smaller than Missy's.

Even then, Eleanor spent her time with her women friends, especially Marion Dickerman, with whom she ran the Todhunter Private School for Girls, and Nancy Cook, who for a time ran the Val-Kill furniture factory, as I've told before.

At the White House, they were still guests now and then, but it was said that Eleanor was not as close to them as she had been in the past.

As for FDR and Missy, the question arises, what did Missy have that Eleanor didn't have? And what did he need? Eleanor was brusque and firm and businesslike. On the other hand, Missy was soft and yielding and always agreed with him, looking at him as if he were the sage of the century—except when she would teasingly bicker with him. The important thing was that for FDR, Missy was, among other things, a playmate who could make him laugh. Eleanor herself admitted that she didn't know how to play or let go enough to be frivolous.

Just as Henrietta Nesbitt was her own worst enemy in the housekeeping department, Eleanor was her own worst enemy in the marriage department.

One of FDR's greatest joys was to get behind the wheel of an automobile so that he could forget his handicap. He was a terrible driver, but Missy didn't mind riding with him in his specially-outfitted Ford, which was completely hand-controlled.

From what I heard, Eleanor refused to ride in it and could not understand the fun they were having.

Eleanor hated water and many times refused to go boating or cruising with her husband. Missy also hated water but went swimming with FDR just to keep him company.

Missy listened. Eleanor talked.

And then, of course, there was that important ingredient of glamour. Missy could be the most glamorous woman in the room with her chandelier earrings swaying and her blue eyes flashing as she talked. FDR was a glutton for glamour and he would watch Missy's performance with obvious delight. He liked the trappings of glamour and Missy made sure to wear high heels that clicked along pleasantly instead of the low heels and sensible oxfords the First Lady wore.

Once the elevator guard at the White House commented, as Missy flipped by, "I'd rather see her walk than anything."

The younger generation does not know that FDR actually had a feud with Joseph Kennedy, the father of President John Kennedy, over something concerning Missy. What happened is that FDR had appointed Kennedy Ambassador to the Court of St. James's but had been concerned about the gossip that Kennedy was romantically involved with movie star Gloria Swanson.

The President called Kennedy in and suggested he terminate his association with the glamorous movie star. Kennedy snapped back—and it quickly made the gossip rounds—"I'll give her up if you give up Missy LeHand."

The story was that FDR had been furious and he bided his time until 1940 when he had a good excuse to fire Kennedy, who had held his London post since 1937. FDR recalled him for making public statements that he did not think the British could defeat Hitler.

And then, with typical FDR humor, Roosevelt took his revenge. When Ambassador Kennedy arrived in Washington, en route to the White House to receive the bad news from the President, FDR purposely didn't send someone of high rank to greet him at the airport and escort him to the Oval Office.

The Mystery of Missy

It would have been the proper thing to do, but FDR had a plan. When the Ambassador stepped off the plane, who was there with a White House limousine to greet him but Missy LeHand. Just Missy and no one but Missy, looking all sweetness and innocence.

As for what attracted Missy to FDR, it was the need to know she was making an important man happy. Seeing FDR laugh was her greatest happiness, she sometimes said. She worked as long as he, simply for the joy of their evenings together and the bits of humor throughout the day.

She really loved him deeply, and he was the only life she knew. She was automatically a part of any family gathering or dinner if FDR attended. When FDR left the table, she left the table. Usually they were the first to go. They had been together since July of 1920, though the affair didn't start immediately.

But it started long before the White House. As a matter of fact, they had shared lazy weekends and vacations aboard a yacht in a group that did not include Eleanor.

Since Eleanor did not want FDR for herself, she had been, in a way, relieved to have Missy around to keep FDR happy while she herself lived her own life, free to come and go as she pleased.

At the White House, she was still free to come and go without explanation. I know that now and then someone would ask FDR where Eleanor was and he would say, "I have no idea," in such a tone that the rest of the sentence could have been, "and I don't much care."

We sometimes thought, backstairs, that Missy was going to try to have a life of her own away from FDR. For a time she dated Earl Miller, who we heard was romantically involved with Eleanor. He had served as Eleanor's bodyguard in the days when FDR was Governor of New York. For a time, Missy also dated the wealthy William Bullitt, whom FDR made the first Ambassador to Russia and later appointed Ambassador to France.

We wondered if FDR engineered these romances just so Missy would see how much better off she was with him. Some speculated that FDR used Missy to get Earl away from his wife, just for his own amusement. It gave us a lot to think about.

Was it FDR's way of getting a subtle revenge for Eleanor's

having broken up his romance with Lucy Mercer years earlier? It certainly added to the mystery of Missy and her importance in the Roosevelt family saga.

When Missy was stricken the first time at the White House, all she could talk about as she lay in her bed was how much she loved FDR and how worried she was that he needed her and she couldn't go to the office to help him.

It happened suddenly in the spring of 1941 that Missy's health broke. I remember it well because I had to find the chef's apron I had made for the office party FDR always hosted with Missy. FDR was proud of that apron and loved to wear it. With it he wore a tall chef's hat from the kitchen.

Actually FDR had not made a single thing his intimate group of top staffers were eating—it had all been prepared at a nearby hotel. FDR didn't even trust the White House kitchens to do a good job on this.

What has never been told, to my knowledge, is what happened that night at the party. Missy suddenly started screaming. She had an intense pain in her head, and later I was told that she had an undiagnosed brain tumor.

It had been FDR's typical annual office party, held for his most intimate staffers such as Steve Early, Hacky (Louise Hackmeister), who handled his personal switchboard, Bill Hassett, the presidential secretary, and Grace Tully, Missy's assistant.

I was told that a piano was rolled in and Marvin MacIntyre, another top aide, played all the old songs FDR loved as the gang serenaded him. When Missy started to scream the party ended. She was helped to bed and sedated.

The next morning, when I arrived at the third floor sewing room, across from Missy's suite, a distraught nurse was outside her door. She said she needed Lizzie.

I asked what was wrong, and she told me what had happened and that Missy was refusing to stay in bed. "She's gotten up and I can't get her back in bed. I need Lizzie to help me."

I told her that Lizzie was not around, and maybe I could help. I went in and said sternly, "Come on, Miss LeHand. Come get into bed."

She meekly climbed in, and I stood by her so she wouldn't get up again. Missy held on to me and lay stroking my arm. In a few minutes the President's doctor, Ross McIntire, arrived with a second doctor and stood watching us from the doorway. "My, she's very affectionate this morning," McIntire said, walking over. He, too, told me what had happened. Then I left to start my own work, across the hall.

That's how it began. With head pains. Dr. McIntire said Missy was exhausted and needed rest.

It was his opinion that she had been working too hard and had been too upset about the war clouds hovering over America. She had been by FDR's side constantly for twenty years.

My mother, Maggie, who had been retired for two years, received a call from Eleanor Roosevelt. "Missy loved you," she said, "would you come back and sit with her at night? She is so lonely."

And so, although Maggie had been gone from the White House since June of 1939, she sat all through the night, every night, listening to Missy's ramblings, her calling for FDR. She couldn't understand that the President was so busy keeping track of Hitler's war in Europe and considering possible U.S. intervention that he couldn't spend much time with her.

I remember Palm Sunday in April of 1941, Mama did not come home at all but stayed at the White House with Missy. Mama came away saying, "It's sad to love a man so much."

Then, as I recall it, came the first stroke. In later years, before her death, she would suffer several other strokes as well, but at the White House Missy was simply agitated and slightly impaired.

Poor Missy could hardly be kept in bed. She was like a war horse and wanted to keep marching. Her speech was slurred, but she kept talking, worrying about the Boss, muttering all night. Three shifts of nurses were brought in to look after her at FDR's personal expense.

It may have been the hopelessness of her love for FDR that helped bring about Missy's stroke—the strain of loving and knowing nothing could come of it. Mama thought so and I agreed. Missy had to know that she could never completely have the love of FDR, and that even the little part she had was shared with Lucy Mercer.

Was Missy LeHand jealous of Lucy Mercer? Maybe she was,

and maybe it helped bring about her breakdown. There was the strain of her job, of course, and there was also the strain of not knowing how secure her future was—whether FDR would always keep her with him.

From her ramblings after the stroke, it was obvious she was not as emotionally secure as she pretended to be.

Meanwhile, Missy's job was taken over by Grace Tully, who did not, however, move into the White House. It was strictly a business relationship.

Missy became unmanageable, and it was agreed that she would be better off away from the White House. She would not hear of it. If she couldn't be near the President, she seemed almost bent on destroying herself. Once she set herself on fire.

Of course, what Missy really wanted was for the President to stay with her all the time. He tried to visit her, but it made him so miserable to find her in that condition that he stayed away. As usual, Eleanor was the saintly person who filled the gap when someone was sick.

One night Missy was smuggled out of the White House to a hospital so that no one would know she was gone. Her illness was kept a secret from the press. Mama said she was sedated so she wouldn't make a fuss about going.

Then, for a while, FDR sent Missy to Warm Springs. He visited her and stayed with her awhile, but from what I heard, it was a fiasco and very sad for both of them.

We heard that Missy was on the phone all the time trying to get through to the President, but he avoided the calls more and more as her pitiful conversations depressed him, and as he became more deeply involved in the world crisis. On Pearl Harbor Day she tried to reach him, but he did not take her calls.

Eventually, Missy returned to the White House to be near FDR and try to work, but she wasn't up to it.

I remember Missy made a big fuss when she returned, saying the blackout curtains I had made for all the windows depressed her. We explained that blackout curtains were the rule for the whole nation, and no light must shine through windows at night that would serve as a beacon to enemy planes.

The Mystery of Missy

Missy was still so upset that Mrs. Nesbitt had someone come in and fit the blackout curtains in Missy's rooms with white liners so that she would not have to look at the dark color.

Missy spent a lot of time in a wheelchair, just like FDR, and we would roll her into the sun porch so she could sit in the sunlight. I was the one who unpacked for Missy when she returned to the White House, and it gave me a start when I discovered a leg brace in her suitcase, just like FDR's. The doctors at Warm Springs had fitted her with a brace to help her walk, but she was too weak and upset to use it.

FDR didn't know what to do with Missy, and finally he sent her home to her own family in Massachusetts to continue recuperating.

Some of our backstairs crowd thought FDR was callous about Missy, but the truth came out after FDR died. His will gave half the income from his estate to Missy. The other half went to Eleanor.

As it turned out, Missy did not survive FDR. She suffered a final stroke and died July 31, 1944, in Boston, never knowing that she could have become rich. Or did she know? The world will never know. It is part of the mystery of Missy.

FDR received the news of Missy's death while he was attending a conference in the Pacific with General MacArthur and Admiral Nimitz on war strategy. Backstairs we were sad that FDR could not even attend Missy's funeral. As usual, it was Eleanor who had to step in and do all the right things.

A standard statement was issued by the White House about how the President had lost a fine secretary: "utterly selfless in her devotion to duty...Hers was a quiet efficiency..."

We could just see the hand of the White House Press Office turning it out.

Eleanor went alone to her funeral.

It was the final irony of Missy's life.

The Lucy Mercer Affair

If I'm going to be frank and honest about what I learned of Eleanor Roosevelt's private life, I must be equally open about what I learned of the President's private life. Some think that there was only one real love in his life, the beautiful Lucy Mercer.

False. I think his love for Missy LeHand was just as great and deep, and just as tragic.

I don't even think his first affair was with Lucy Mercer. The story we heard backstairs was that on his honeymoon, FDR had already been bored with marriage and had strayed—and Eleanor had not been dumb. The way the servants closest to FDR told the story, it had happened in the Alps, or somewhere near the Alps, when they were motoring to St. Moritz.

Eleanor, even then, was not the kind of wife who bowed to her husband's whims, and her husband's whim was to climb a certain mountain. Eleanor refused to go. FDR, being an only child, wasn't used to adjusting to anyone else's whims and desires either—especially a female of his own age. He insisted on climbing the mountain.

A woman named Kitty, whom they'd met at the hotel, offered to go in Eleanor's place, soothing Eleanor's apprehensions by saying that her husband was going to meet them somewhere along the climb. Eleanor received her first lesson in jealousy when she waited all day for their return, only to have them show up minus Kitty's husband.

Backstairs it was said Eleanor never really trusted FDR after that, and that her own attitude might have pushed young Franklin into the arms of other women. It was easy for him, because he was so debonair, handsome, and rich. Even in his wheelchair, he was the handsomest man I had ever seen in the White House. He exuded charm to the very end. The maids agreed that his sons, although handsome, couldn't hold a candle to him. However, FDR Jr. did look the most like him and did have the most charm of the younger Roosevelts.

The Lucy Mercer affair was the first serious liaison that the handsome FDR involved himself in. At the time, he was well on his way in his own career and had come to Washington to be assistant secretary of the Navy, during the Wilson Administration, under Secretary Josephus Daniels.

After FDR got into the White House, he brought in Jonathan Daniels, the son of his old boss, to work for him as press secretary. FDR was very loyal to friends who had helped him along the way. Maybe one reason FDR was so close to the Danielses was that they both knew all about his affair with Lucy.

So, of course, did McDuffie, FDR's valet, and Lizzie, McDuffie's wife, and Maggie, my mother, and others close to the Roosevelt family. There was a theory backstairs that one reason Eleanor Roosevelt decided to have only black servants was that she thought they would be less likely to spread tales of what they heard and less likely to understand it.

If so, she was right on the first point but certainly wrong on the latter. We understood, all right, but we only talked among ourselves. The help would often have a private chuckle about what we had heard, and how obvious it was that those speaking must have thought what they were saying went over our heads.

Only the brightest survived at the White House. We had schoolteachers working as maids, for example. We learned to act dumb as part of the job!

The people who really aren't too bright are those who refuse to believe that a man is a *man* first and a president, second. I am thinking of all the people who say it was impossible that Franklin Roosevelt could have had an affair with Lucy Mercer. As one woman put it, "Oh, he might have kissed her or written her a mash note, but that doesn't mean they were having a real affair."

I smiled and said nothing. But I wanted to ask if it would mean anything to her to know that FDR and Lucy actually stayed in a tourist cabin together one night. That entry from a tourist cabin at Virginia Beach showed them registered as husband and wife, and Eleanor, so the story went backstairs, had a copy of it.

Also, FDR took Lucy along on two cruises. Eleanor knew about one of them at least—and this was before she discovered the love letters from Lucy. What happened in 1917 was that FDR got up a party of friends to go with him on a naval yacht cruise, and he included Lucy Mercer.

Eleanor got suspicious and came racing after them in another boat, though she hated sailing. The way the story goes, the rest of the cruise was prim and proper and dull—and everyone was slightly embarrassed. But FDR was secretly seething at having his wife check up on him. He retaliated by having Lucy assigned to his office as a female yeoman volunteer. Then he took her out on another naval cruise, one to which Eleanor wasn't invited, and which she didn't find out about until much later.

Then Eleanor did something that was out of character for her and infuriated her husband. She had quietly pulled strings to get Lucy discharged from the Navy on orders from the Secretary of the Navy, Josephus Daniels, himself. The excuse was that Lucy's father had died. It made no sense, but FDR decided not to fight it. Eleanor was suspicious and he knew it.

I don't know how Alice Roosevelt Longworth found out about Lucy and FDR, but considering that she had one of the best social spy systems in Washington, it isn't surprising. And perhaps it is not surprising that Sweet Alice took the opportunity to drive another wedge between Eleanor and Franklin either. She invited Lucy and Franklin to dinner, without telling Eleanor, of course, And, of course, Eleanor eventually heard about it.

Years later, Alice would brag about her role in helping Franklin see Lucy Mercer, and was quoted as saying, "Franklin deserved a little fun. He was married to Eleanor, wasn't he?" Even while encouraging the romance between the assistant secretary of the Navy and the lovely Lucy, Alice had teased Eleanor, hinting she might have trouble holding on to her handsome husband.

So it was clear Eleanor already knew something was going on, or had gone on, and may have been looking for evidence when FDR came down with pneumonia in September 1918.

You could hardly fault her for feeling a little jealous of Lucy. Lucy was bright, beautiful, and footloose in her early twenties. Eleanor was thirty-four and saddled with five kids, including a yearling. And she had never been footloose or beautiful.

At any rate, she looked through FDR's personal papers while he was sick and found the love letters from Lucy. The excuse given in write-ups about the finding was that it was strictly accidental.

The story is that Lucy Mercer, being Catholic, was horrified at the thought of divorce and promised Eleanor that she would never see Franklin alone again. And, so the story goes, Eleanor gallantly offered Franklin a divorce.

First of all, let me point out that Lucy's mother had been divorced when she married Lucy's father. So that takes care of that. She was also separated from Lucy's father, but that's another story. And secondly, Eleanor's offer of a divorce can also be challenged. Another version of the story—and the one that seems more logical to me—is that Eleanor simply talked about how the scandal of an affair becoming public would ruin the lives of their sons. For the moment, that was enough to stop FDR and Lucy in their tracks.

Then, bringing in the big guns, Eleanor told FDR's mother, Sara, what was going on, knowing Sara would know how to handle her son and could threaten to cut the purse strings. FDR loved his luxurious way of life too much to endanger that. Years later, Louis Howe, who was sick in bed in the White House, would reminisce about FDR's wild youth and wondered what would have happened if the affair had continued. As Louis told it, FDR sought his opinion on what to do.

Howe had known FDR for years and had guided his political career. FDR hadn't always listened to him, such as when he ran for New York senator in 1914 against Howe's advice. But he listened to Howe this time, and what Howe warned him was that any scandal now would wash out any chance of a political career, including the dream they shared of FDR's following in the footsteps of Teddy Roosevelt to become assistant secretary of the Navy, governor of New York, vice president, and then president. Howe warned him that he was on the bottom rung of the ladder as assistant secretary but he was about to blow up the ladder he was standing on.

So, it seemed that FDR sadly gave up Lucy. In fact he didn't *really* give her up.

I have never told this before, but I knew that Lucy came to the White House to see the President. Her name then was

Rutherfurd, but I didn't know her full name. I remember one day a valet said to some of us, "Oh my, I have just delivered a lovely lady to the President's room." Later I was told her name was Lucy. Eleanor was not at the White House that day. In about an hour, the President called for the valet, who slipped her out the back door to a waiting limousine.

I was told that Lucy wore the most feminine of clothes and smelled of heavenly expensive perfumes. Once she wore a black ribbon around her throat that was very dramatic and sort of sexy. Cesar said the President told her the ribbon reminded him of the ones she had always worn in the past, and she had said that she had hoped he would remember. At that point Cesar had backed out of the room.

From what I heard from the men who took care of FDR, he and Lucy never stopped seeing each other. He saw her every chance he could, even though she eventually married a wealthy, but elderly, North Carolina socialite, Winthrop Rutherfurd, in 1920. He would dream up excuses for trips that Eleanor wouldn't be interested in so that he could meet Lucy on neutral ground, such as at the home of a friend.

One of those friends was Bernard Baruch, who lent his estate in South Carolina for the rendezvous. Eleanor thought Baruch was her friend, and he was in a way. But most of the Roosevelt friends were lined up on one side or the other. They were loyal either to FDR or to Eleanor. And they protected one from the other.

Eleanor, in her glory at the inaugural in March 1933, would have had a fit had she known that the President-elect had sent for Lucy and placed a limousine at her disposal so she could share his moment of glory, even though she couldn't come to the White House for the reception after the inauguration on Capitol Hill.

And after Lucy's husband died, just a year before FDR himself died, FDR was as romantic about Lucy as ever, still arranging meetings.

There was a cartoon in the newspaper with a caption saying "Hoover was dead from the waist up and Roosevelt was dead from the waist down." McDuffie said, "I'll be damned if he is!" and walked away.

A man has no secrets from his valet. The valets knew there

was nothing incomplete about FDR's love life. Only his legs were paralyzed. The polio had not impaired the trunk of his body. We servants understood that when he arrived at the White House, and for several of his terms, FDR was in excellent health. As they put it, he never slowed down to the bitter end.

The way we understood it, backstairs at the White House, Eleanor hadn't been exactly happy, but was relieved to have an excuse not to share FDR's bed anymore, after learning the truth about Lucy, because she didn't want more children, and the whole thing was a chore to her. To her, sex had been a wifely duty only, as she once told Anna, her daughter.

So, with the excuse of Lucy, Eleanor turned her marriage into a platonic relationship. But even so, now and then, there would be little flashes of jealousy between the women around FDR. It was the old story of the dog and the bone—she didn't want it, but she didn't want anyone else to have it.

And in his way, FDR tried to be discreet, even though he wasn't going to give up the joys of manhood completely, or stop seeing Lucy.

The story backstairs was that if Lucy Mercer had been as rich as Eleanor, FDR quite possibly would have asked Eleanor for a divorce, married Lucy, and let politics go hang. FDR definitely needed his wife's money and his mother's bounty to live in the style he enjoyed. He could have gotten along on his mother's wealth, but when Eleanor turned his mother against him, and Sara insisted he give up Lucy, he turned chicken.

Poor Lucy was rich in refinement and beauty, but the family had lost its money. She even had to help support her mother. FDR had not been raised to rough it.

So Eleanor won. But during the time Lucy thought she'd never see FDR again, she at least saved her pride in one matter, as we heard it. Lucy had been a volunteer with Eleanor in the social Navy League's "wool Saturdays." They made warm things for sailors. Eleanor tried to pay Lucy for the help she had given and sent her a check.

Lucy was not to be bought off and returned the check. Eleanor mailed it again, received it in the mail again, and gave up. Washington was a small society and some of Lucy's friends knew what had happened and were on her side. Some insiders were on Eleanor's side, but not all.

The Lucy Mercer Affair

The fact that Lucy Mercer's love affair with FDR before and during the White House years didn't get around was a tribute to the loyalty of the White House employees. So many people knew and saw them together, the black household staff included.

But the white staff knew and kept the secrets as well. Grace Tully, FDR's private secretary after Missy, knew. Bill Hassett, who had various titles in working for FDR, such as correspondence secretary and press aide, knew everything, and even went with Roosevelt when he visited Lucy at her estate, called Tranquility Farms. Jonathan Daniels, who also held various positions both in and out of the White House and was for a time FDR's press secretary, knew all about it. And of course, Ross McIntire, his personal physician, knew, as well as his heart specialist, Commander Howard Bruenn, who was with him that fateful day in Warm Springs, as was Bill Hassett.

But while he lived, none of them, not a soul, told it to the press. As I said, in those days we kept our secrets well.

Years later, on her eightieth birthday, Grace Tully broke her silence about Lucy admitting that sometimes she personally had slipped Lucy through her office to visit the President. And she added that she was aware that Lucy would have lunch at the White House.

Aunt Polly also entered the conspiracy of covering for Lucy Mercer when Eleanor was safely away from the White House on one of her trips. She would come with Lucy if it was more than a sneak visit with Lucy being slipped in and out by the valet, for an hour or two. At the dinner table, if Lucy stayed on there, Daisy and Polly would be there too, and sometimes so was Anna Roosevelt.

But as far as I know, from what the valets and others said, Aunt Polly and Daisy didn't go to Bernie Baruch's Hobcaw estate in South Carolina. They didn't have to. The estate was thousands of acres large and gave FDR all the privacy he could want.

The way it worked, Lucy could slip away to Hobcaw because she and her family vacationed near there in Aiken, North Carolina. FDR needed no excuse but his friendship with Baruch and his need for a rest.

Once, when we knew FDR was with Baruch, Dr. McIntire had cooperated by spreading the word that the President was having sinus trouble and that he had told him to go south. Later, the word among the most trusted servants backstairs was that the President had seen his lovely lady Lucy not once, but many times, and that somehow he had managed to have Eleanor come down for a short visit without the women meeting each other. I seem to recall that the First Lady didn't go there alone, but took several traveling companions with her.

But the most surprising thing of all is that FDR managed to visit Lucy right in her own home without the world knowing. The way that was done, according to what FDR's trusted attendants told me, is that the press pool that traveled with FDR would be told that a wartime blackout was being imposed on the President's movements. In other words, they wouldn't be able to write anything about where he was going.

FDR had gone to Tranquility Farms, the Rutherfurd estate at Allamuchy, New York, not too far from Hyde Park. His train stopped, and he was simply taken off the train and disappeared for a few hours.

I heard that he had even said once or twice that he was meeting an old friend whose husband was ill, and once, that he was meeting an old friend whose husband had died.

And when Lucy came to Washington, even when Eleanor was at the White House, the word was that FDR's chauffeur simply drove him out into the country where Lucy was waiting, and they would drive around a while.

There was no way to avoid the conclusion that FDR still cared deeply about Lucy.

It was interesting that FDR seemed destined to love Catholic women. Missy was Catholic. Lucy Mercer Rutherfurd was Catholic. The girl he first loved, and whom his mother stopped him from marrying, had been Catholic. An attendant once heard FDR comment that he had found the most warmhearted women to be either Jewish or Catholic.

Lizzie—who went to Hyde Park—knew that FDR had once almost married a Catholic girl, or at least had entertained serious thoughts. His mother had had a fit about it and had made him promise not to marry the girl on religious principles. The girl had been a very fine person with impeccable credentials, for anyone but his mother. Frances Dana's ancestors included Richard Dana, the author of *Two Years Before the Mast,* and the famous poet, Henry Wadsworth Longfellow.

We wondered if FDR had been so angry at his mother when Frances Dana finally married someone else, that he became biased toward Catholic women from then on—Lucy Mercer, Missy LeHand, and even Grace Tully, who was his trusted secretary after Missy, though not a romantic interest.

There was one thing FDR demanded in all his females—he liked them tall. Eleanor was very tall, in fact, only son John towered above her at six-foot-four. Lucy Mercer was five-foot-nine. Missy LeHand was only an inch shorter. All were slim and had an aristocratic bearing. "The Boss likes proud women," the valets said.

He also liked blue eyes. Eleanor had blue eyes. Lucy had blue eyes. Missy had huge blue eyes that could look flirtatious or haughty, as her mood changed.

And they all had healthy looking brownish hair, with just a glint of red in it. Missy's hair was the lightest, sort of strawberry blond.

You would have to be blind to be around FDR at the White House and not know that he liked women. A few he truly loved—Lucy and Missy, and in his own way, undoubtedly, Eleanor—but he also liked to make a play for almost every pretty woman. Or pretty girl. One of the butlers told how FDR had actually put his hand under a pretty guest's dress as they sat side by side at the table. FDR was an expert at fondling knees under the tablecloth, but this, we agreed, was the boldest yet.

The butlers laughed and said the Boss was probably the only man who dared pat royalty on the bottom. He kiddingly patted the derriere of Queen Elizabeth. He played kneesies with princesses under the table, especially Princess Martha of Norway.

We concluded that he was infatuated with the royal princess, who, with her small children, was sitting out the war in Washington. She was married, of course. But then, so was he. Her husband came and went during the war years, but she stayed on in Washington without him.

Eleanor seemed to be more disturbed by FDR's flirtations with royal figures than with pretty secretaries or American society matrons. Backstairs we tried to figure that out. We decided that Eleanor hated phoniness and was annoyed that FDR was so impressed with royalty. She herself treated them as if they were the people next door.

Martha was the most obvious in vying for the attention of the President, even at the dinner table right in front of Eleanor. The butlers reported her putting on a little girl act, even though she was the mother of young children. FDR seemed to eat it up. Eleanor would be tight-lipped when she turned her conversation to someone else, pretending she didn't hear. FDR even proved how he felt about Martha by giving himself a nickname that she could call him—no one called him any nickname but "Boss."

He told Martha to call him "the Godfather," and she did, usually changing it to "Godfather, dear," or "Dear godfather." The help could tell that this made Eleanor slightly sick to her stomach, and she quit inviting Martha to things. At the White House, the help wasn't too surprised to see the ardor with which the President kissed Princess Martha at every opportunity, including when he said goodnight to her.

Servants would hear Eleanor use the name "Martha" to mean any woman who made a fuss over her husband—referring to the female as "just another Martha."

At first Eleanor made Martha very welcome at the White House, but eventually, she saw her as a competitor and got jealous. Thereafter, Princess Martha would come quietly into the White House to visit the President when Eleanor was away. We knew that the President had helped her find a house outside of Washington in nearby Maryland and slipped out to see her now and then.

Even so, we were a little shocked when FDR took Princess Martha to Hyde Park some time after his mother's death and had her installed as a house guest for a while. He even took her house hunting in the Hyde Park area, to see if he could find her an estate near him.

The White House servants returned saying, "It looks like the Boss has found a new Missy."

The strange thing was that after Missy died, all the family pitied FDR the rest of his life for being a lonely man. Maybe he was. As we saw it, he was doing the best he could to be even more convivial and happy-sounding than ever. His flirtatiousness increased. It seemed he was trying to convince himself that he had stepped up a notch in life and now was in love with a princess.

That's how it seemed to us as we watched the life stories unfold in the private family quarters.

We would know when Princess Martha had appeared to visit the President at the White House. Eleanor would be safely out of town, and we would fervently hope the First Lady wouldn't make any surprise returns. But it was bound to happen and it did, once. In this case once was enough.

What happened was that Martha had appeared in Eleanor's absence and had been installed in one of the guest rooms. In the middle of the night, Eleanor returned and went to the room where she had left one of her own favorite guests, Joe Lash, a young liberal who was executive secretary of the American Youth Congress, and one of her protégés. Eleanor and Joe were great friends and would talk far into the night. So she went over to his door, gave a quick rap, and walked in. Had she checked the Usher's Office, she would have known Joe had been moved. What she found inside was a startled naked man. It was Princess Martha's bodyguard.

Eleanor was furious. This time she didn't wait to write FDR a note about it. She told him in person, the next day. And she warned the staff that *her* guests were never to be moved from their rooms again without contacting her—no matter where in the world her travels had taken her.

Princess Martha never became queen. She died in 1954, when she was fifty-three years old. Her husband, Prince Olaf, mounted the Norwegian throne in 1957 and ruled alone.

Eleanor and Hicky

I really think FDR and Eleanor both wanted the world to know the truth about their relationship with each other and with Missy and Lorena Hickok. I think, that having read of the tangled lives of historical characters, they wanted history to understand them.

If FDR didn't want the world to know about Missy, he would have changed his will after she died. He had plenty of time to do so. The will treated Missy and Eleanor alike, and that was the way he must have wanted history to record it.

If Eleanor hadn't wanted her relationship with Lorena Hickok revealed, she would have insisted Lorena destroy her letters. It sounded to me, from hearing Lorena talk—and other White House maids agreed—as if Lorena adored Eleanor to such an extent that she would do anything Eleanor requested. The fact that Lorena stipulated that her letters not be opened until ten years after her death shows that she very well knew how revealing the letters were, but wanted to set the record straight.

And what this all says to me is that Eleanor and the President wanted to leave the message that they were not just sad and estranged from each other—though they were that—but that they also had found fulfilling relationships elsewhere. The message from each could be summed up in just three words: "Don't pity me."

As I write this book, there is speculation about whether or not Eleanor Roosevelt had a lesbian relationship with Lorena Hickok. If she did—and I am no eyewitness to such a relation-ship—it wouldn't be the first time such a thing happened at the White House.

As a matter of fact, I happened to be just outside the door on one such occasion. I will not tell names, but one particular

Roosevelt in-law—no longer in the family—and a female office employee were caught together in bed. The maid hadn't barged in. The in-law had rung for service, asking for something, and it was being delivered. When the maid opened the door, they jumped apart in bed, and then one leaped out of bed and dashed into the adjoining sitting room, stark naked. The one who remained in bed didn't seem too upset. I guess she knew that we maids would keep our mouths shut, and she was right.

One woman who didn't worry about keeping her mouth shut lived in the White House in a different Roosevelt era—Teddy's daughter. Alice Longworth always said exactly what she thought, and she didn't care who heard. She frequently talked about women's sexual adventures, even commenting on women having poodles as sex partners. She said that nothing shocked her, and that when she was living at the White House as a president's daughter, "lesbianism and homosexuality were very popular." She commented that some woman had fallen in love with her, but didn't go into detail on how the thing turned out.

Had she or hadn't she? Probably not, because she said her own immediate family would have been horrified. Backstairs, however, we wouldn't have been amazed at anything Alice claimed to have done.

Now to tackle the relationships of Eleanor and those dear to her heart. It is painful for me to write of this because I don't like to disturb the dreams of many people. But I do owe a debt to history, and I was a part of history for many years—before and after Eleanor was in the White House. And I must remind people that Eleanor Roosevelt was a woman *first* and a First Lady *second*.

I also think she knew that someday all things would be made public. She once said in my hearing, "History has few secrets." Even her own sons are now helping history fill in some of those secrets.

I am amused when I hear people say that the kisses exchanged between Lorena Hickok and Eleanor Roosevelt, and discussed in letters finally published in a book by Doris Faber, *The Life of Lorena Hickok—E.R.'s Friend*, have no meaning, that Eleanor kissed everyone.

Not true. In fact, that's ridiculous. It reflects the desire of such people to hide their heads in the sand like ostriches. Eleanor wrote Lorena soon after she had moved into the White House, "I can't kiss you so I kiss your picture goodnight and good morning! Don't laugh! This is the first day I've had no letter and I miss it sadly but it is good discipline..."

And Lorena wrote to Eleanor in a letter a little later, "Most clearly I remember your eyes, with a kind of teasing smile in them, and the feeling of that soft spot just northeast of the corner of your mouth against my lips. I wonder what we'll do when we meet—what we'll say..."

I'm glad these letters finally came out and became part of the public domain, housed at the Franklin D. Roosevelt Library in Hyde Park, New York, where any interested person may study them. And let me tell you why I'm glad. It's simply that now we don't have to feel so sorry for Eleanor, the picture of the lonely long-suffering wife, whose husband, the President, dies in the arms of another woman.

Eleanor had her own life, and she lived it fully. The servants who kept up with these things decided Babs and the Boss had a sort of agreement that they would not interfere in each other's romances. Still, now and then, there was jealousy on both sides.

But returning to the innocent public and what it knew and didn't know, it didn't know that Hicky was with Eleanor on election night. It didn't know Hicky was with Eleanor at the Mayflower Hotel in Washington on Inaugural Eve.

As I have said, I never saw Eleanor and Lorena Hickok in a compromising situation. That is, I never saw them in bed together. But I was at the White House on many occasions when Hicky, as we all called her behind her back, slept in the First Lady's bedroom suite, on the daybed in her sitting room. Supposedly, the reason was that there were so many guests, Eleanor had to reshuffle the sleeping arrangements.

Where Hick usually slept was in the tiny sitting room behind the larger room where Louis Howe stayed. Hicky lived, in fact, in the northwest corner of the house, across the west hall from Eleanor's suite, which was in the southwest corner. Eleanor ran back and forth frequently. Lorena's job was to stay out of sight, according to the backstairs crowd who knew these things.

FDR wasn't to know she was there. It was our job to help her stay hidden, because Hick wasn't just a guest now and then, but she came and stayed for months and months.

When the Roosevelts first arrived in 1933, there was a short honeymoon stage around the White House when Hick was an open guest, welcomed by the President, joining the family for dinner. But eventually, so the sub rosa story went, he got the drift and feared the situation could give the White House a bad reputation.

The President was heard raising his voice to Eleanor, telling her, "I want that woman kept out of this house." *That woman* meant too much to Eleanor, and instead of keeping her out of the house, she simply kept her out of FDR's sight. Now and then Eleanor, with the help of people like Louis Howe and Harry Hopkins, would arrange for a job to get Hicky out of the White House, preferably a traveling job.

The perfect job of this sort was arranged by Harry Hopkins, who got Hicky a job investigating how relief was administered nationwide under the FERA, the Federal Emergency Relief Administration. This kept her out of the White House for long stretches of time, but she sent plaintive letters to Eleanor about how she missed her, as well as plaintive reports on the suffering of the hungry, and often cold, masses.

Since her reports went to Harry Hopkins, with a copy to Eleanor Roosevelt, the President would be told some of the most touching items. We, the household family, would be told how lucky we were to have such good jobs, with good meals furnished by the White House. One report told of a family who took turns wearing the only warm clothing they had. Another told of little children working in beet fields to earn pennies to help support their families. Lorena would come back and tell us many things.

Eleanor Roosevelt would meet her now and then away from the White House, and they would travel together. Once, for example, they met and sought anonymity in San Francisco, having dinner together in a hotel room and traveling around in the area in Hick's car.

Eleanor and Hicky

We were amused that Lorena Hickok named her automobile after one of the maids at the White House—Bluette, who was, as I've said, very protective of Hicky, and who, incidentially, helped keep her hidden.

We were also amused at the jealousies aroused by the friendship of Lorena and Eleanor. There was, as I have said, FDR's jealousy of Lorena. Then there was Lorena's jealousy of the time and attention Eleanor Roosevelt gave other friends, such as the "little dancer" as we called her around the White House, Mayris "Tiny" Chaney. We considered Mayris to be a protégé of Eleanor's, and they, too, had done some traveling together. She wanted to be a famous dancer. She, also, came to the White House as a guest and stayed for fairly long visits.

Mayris was so cute and funny that she became a favorite of some of the Roosevelt daughters-in-law, as well. She even made hats for some of them. The daughters-in-law didn't want to hurt her feelings and later would give most of them to the White House maids.

Once, when Tiny was in Washington with her dancing partner, the First Lady had the team entertain at a White House function. As I recall, it was mostly to give Tiny more exposure and to showcase her talents. Guests who saw her dance didn't realize how well she knew the White House. She stayed in whatever room was empty. If there was an overflow, a niche was made for her somewhere.

A second attempt of Eleanor's to help Mayris' career didn't fare so well, and in fact, got Congress up in arms. Eleanor was a hot shot volunteer in Civil Defense, after Pearl Harbor, and she used her position to appoint Mayris Director of Physical Fitness at a salary considered quite handsome at the time, $4,600. Federal employees were happy to be getting $2,600 to $3,000 in those Depression days. In comparison, the President's personal secretary, Missy LeHand, was getting only a little over $3,000 and the highest her salary rose before her stroke forced her into retirement, before Pearl Harbor, was $5,000. Congress had a field day tossing snide and licentious barbs at Eleanor and her "fan dancer," as they insisted on labelling Tiny. One Congressman suggested Eleanor try to get Sally Rand.

Congress made sure that Eleanor wouldn't have her dancer, voting to ban the use of Office of Civilian Defense tax money for teaching dancing as an aid to physical fitness.

We, at the White House, were not surprised when Eleanor resigned her position as a volunteer assistant director at the Office of Civilian Defense. In her place stepped her husband's friend and press aide, Jonathan Daniels, but he could only stand the turmoil and pressure within that organization for a few months before resigning.

We maids at the White House felt sorry for Mayris' troubles because we liked her. She was always a lot of fun to have around the White House, and we never knew what to expect next. Once she did a daring thing. She went out of the White House wearing slacks, something frowned upon in those days. When she returned, the ushers didn't want to let her into the front door. There was nothing they could do with a friend of the First Lady, but their disapproval was obvious.

Mayris Chaney also visited with Eleanor in Eleanor's hideaway apartment in Greenwich Village. The way we heard it at the White House, Eleanor Roosevelt had enlisted Tommy Thompson to get an apartment so Eleanor's mother-in-law and husband couldn't be in her hair or keep tabs on her.

FDR and Eleanor had a lovely big home on East 65th Street, a graystone, but Eleanor hated it and spent as little time there as possible, just as she spent as little time as possible at the Hyde Park estate.

Tommy knew every secret and was, in fact, part of Eleanor's hidden life, helping her maintain her privacy. Tommy needed privacy for her own life, as well. She had been married, but had gotten a divorce in the late thirties. Her name had been Scheider. I don't believe I ever saw her husband around the White House.

Or at her apartment in the Dorchester.

The way I got the story, Tommy Thompson had first introduced Eleanor Roosevelt to Lorena Hickok, sometime in 1928. Eventually the three spent a lot of time together, and together they celebrated Tommy's birthday just before Eleanor moved to the White House—taking Tommy along, of course, as her secretary. After Tommy's divorce, she started going with a Treasury Department official, Henry Osthagen, who then became a part of Eleanor's magic circle that included Hicky and Mayris Chaney and Earl Miller, whom Eleanor had met when he was assigned to guard her in the days when Franklin Roosevelt was governor of New York.

Eleanor and Tommy actually shared two homes, the Village apartment and the Val-Kill cottage, so near and yet so emotionally far from her big house at Hyde Park. Maids who went to Hyde Park to take care of Val-Kill got used to the fact that Tommy Thompson used the downstairs as her apartment, while Eleanor Roosevelt used the upstairs. Each entertained her own friend. Or friends.

Since Tommy had the downstairs living room, cocktails would be served down in her quarters before dinner, although Eleanor didn't drink. What she did do, by all accounts, was knit, and the needles clicked along with the conversation. Or Eleanor might read poetry aloud to the group as they sipped. Eleanor was interested in poetry, and she often carried bits of verse with her.

That is another way in which she and the President weren't compatible. He liked humorous verse, but couldn't appreciate a beautiful line the way she could. He also wasn't as concerned with religion as Eleanor was, who kept little prayers on her dresser and in her purse.

Eleanor and Hicky sometimes stayed together at Val-Kill, too.

The public didn't know that Eleanor and Hicky were already inseparable when Eleanor moved into the White House. They had spent the day before the Inauguration together. They spent Inauguration Day together.

The public didn't know that it was Lorena Hickok who went with Eleanor Roosevelt to see the White House just before the start of the Roosevelt Administration. But she didn't come in. She waited at the iron gate in front—the Northwest Entrance on Pennsylvania Avenue—for Eleanor to come out. This wasn't too significant, except that Eleanor had refused to have the White House car pick her up to bring her to the White House—probably to protect her privacy. We watched Eleanor from afar, not realizing that the incoming First Lady was going to fire all the white help and make it an all-black staff.

It was somehow sad to see how eagerly Hicky tried to do

things that would endear her to Eleanor. Although she was rather heavy set, she tried to learn to ride a horse. That phase didn't last long.

But Hick and Eleanor did walk around Washington, sometimes driving to places where they could have more privacy, such as at a certain cemetery in Rock Creek Park where they would sit and gaze at a statue entitled "Grief." Eleanor hated to use White House limousines because she didn't want people spying on her.

She refused Secret Service protection. She didn't just turn it down gently, but roughly informed the Secret Service to stay out of the way. They tried to get the President to put his foot down, but he said it was hopeless and just to let Eleanor have her head. Backstairs we laughed when we heard people say how noble it was of the First Lady not to permit the Secret Service to waste the taxpayers' money in protecting her. Our theory was simpler. Eleanor didn't want the Secret Service keeping tabs on her and Lorena Hickok when they were going around together—which was pretty steady in those early White House years.

One letter that has survived through the years was written by Eleanor to Hick, and it says, "I wish I could lie down with you tonight and take you in my arms." It certainly would have been possible for the wish to come true—not that night, but on many other occasions—because they did often sleep in Eleanor's suite, Hickok being assigned the couch in Eleanor's sitting room.

But the word was that Eleanor didn't like only Lorena. There were other women with whom she was said to have a romantic alliance, before, during, and after Lorena.

And in this same period of time, there were several men with whom Eleanor was intimate, or so the servants believed. Earl Miller seemed to be the most important of them, just as Lorena Hickok was said to be the most important of the women. The servants didn't condemn Eleanor. They said she might as well try to get some happiness as best she could, because she certainly wasn't getting it with FDR.

FDR certainly had his own romantic involvements. And the servants didn't blame him either. They said that was life, even in the White House.

One young man made himself very much at home in the White House. Eleanor was seen kissing him goodnight and wandering with him in and around the White House like young lovers.

Backstairs some said this was why Eleanor wasn't so upset about knowing Missy LeHand was in the President's bedroom—Eleanor was in the young man's room, visiting with *him.*

Servants occasionally did see that FDR would try to embrace Eleanor, but she would recoil and back away.

The alienation wasn't all one sided. Eleanor held Franklin at arm's length, and as their children have recorded, refused to share his bedroom.

FDR also got on his high horse. One time, for example, he was in his Oval study on the second floor near his bedroom, having cocktails with Missy.

Suddenly Eleanor popped in, something she rarely did, and asked if she might join him and bring in a few of her lady friends. The Boss gave her a loud and clear, "No, you may not." And after she had nervously hurried off, FDR exploded with, "I can't stand those she-males."

In the thirties and forties, and probably even today, children didn't discuss the love lives of their mothers. Especially if they are at all offbeat. I was interested in what Elliott Roosevelt had to say in his book, *An Untold Story: The Roosevelts of Hyde Park,* concerning Eleanor's female friends.

Elliott wrote, "... I suspected that some of the women, all dead now, who flattered my unwitting mother with their attentions were active lesbians."

Through the years we saw quite a few females who seemed to be unusually attached to Eleanor. We always wondered what the various relationships were—we assumed that Hicky was not the first woman in Eleanor's life.

Backstairs the word was that Eleanor's interest in Hickok left her no time for other friends. At any rate, sometime during the second term, Eleanor ended her business relationship with Nancy Cook and Marion Dickerman. To get full possession of Val-Kill, she traded her share of the Todhunter school. They were welcome at the White House and at Val-Kill, but the three were no longer inseparable. Now and then I did a little sewing for Nancy, but none that I recall for Marion.

There was no way one could get away from saying Lorena

Babs and Boss

Hickok looked mannish. We heard it constantly around the White House. And it was true. She had a masculine stride, and she dressed in a masculine style. Lizzie once said, "Put a seam down the middle of her skirt, and I swear, old Hicky will be wearing a man's suit." She wasn't a bad looking woman and had she kept her weight down and tried to act and look feminine, she could have been most attractive.

No ruffles and lace for her: she wore masculine looking suits, flat shoes, and dark cotton stockings. We fretted and muttered that she looked out of place in the White House, but if it didn't bother Eleanor, what could we do? Nothing.

Well, maybe something. At least one maid tried. It happened the time Hicky bought a white linen skirt as her bow to the summer season. But in Washington, summer season ended abruptly with Labor Day. To be caught wearing white after Labor Day was considered very bad taste.

But Hicky didn't know or didn't care about seasons. She would lay out her outfit for the next day and a White House maid, usually Margaret, would press it for her. And one day, after Labor Day, she laid out the white skirt. Margaret pressed it hoping she would change her mind, hinting that she might want to change to something else. The subtle hint fell on deaf ears. Margaret was too polite to tell Hicky right out what was socially correct. But the next day, Margaret thought she may have made headway when Hicky asked, "How is the weather?"

Margaret said, "Very chilly and damp."

A little later Margaret came to me almost in tears. "Don't you know, Hick went out the front door of the *White House* with that skirt on." She was so upset that at first I thought Hicky was going out the House with a *sheet* on.

We really cared about the impression everyone connected with the White House made on the public. And it wasn't just the maids. It was also the ushers and doormen who cared.

My mother, Maggie, used to take care of Lorena Hickok until Mama retired, so she knew how much Lorena and the First Lady meant to each other, and how affectionate they were. After Mama retired, the job of looking after Hicky fell to other maids.

Eleanor and Hicky

Eleanor did not seem to mind that Hicky wore things that were considered very unstylish. She saw only the beauty within Hicky. Eventually Eleanor saw that Hicky didn't seem to have stylish clothes, and she started giving her things right out of her own closet.

Hicky hated to buy things for herself, but she was wonderfully generous, buying little presents for Eleanor and even for us. For example, someone told her it was Mama's birthday, and Hicky told Eleanor's personal maid, Mabel Haley, "Buy something nice for Maggie and wrap it for me." Mabel bought a beautiful slip, and Hicky added a nice note of thanks for all Mama had done for her.

We knew, backstairs, that Eleanor was spending a good deal of money dressing Lorena in clothes as good as her own, and often better. Eleanor, many times, bought very fine materials—sometimes handwoven—and had them made into the man-tailored suits that Hicky always wore. Hicky hardly dared admire something Eleanor was wearing for fear that Eleanor would have it altered for her. I know. Hicky proudly told where her clothes came from, and several times I was the one to let out seams and shorten something of the First Lady's for Hick.

One of Hicky's favorite evening gowns was a black velvet, unadorned, floor-length dress that Eleanor had worn. It would be steamed in her bathroom after each use.

Once Hicky laughed and said it was a good thing she and Eleanor weren't built the other way around, because I would have a jolly hard time making her clothes fit the First Lady. I would have to do drastic things like add ruffles to the bottom in a different color.

Some of us maids wondered if Eleanor was so generous with Hicky to make up for all the things she couldn't invite her special friend to, for fear of the President's ire. For example, she was never invited to State dinners. The only formal White House party she was invited to annually was the First Lady's party for the ladies of the press, even though she was no longer one of them.

In the early days at the White House, Hicky would join Eleanor at breakfast. Hick always had her coffee in a special, huge, blue and white mug that Eleanor had given her. It was a joke between them that this was a proper cup for a reporter. Later, when Hick was staying out of sight because of FDR, Bluette would bring the special mug full of coffee to her bedroom.

I think one thing that shows how Eleanor felt about Hicky is that she bought her a car—the one they named Bluette, after the White House maid. Hicky was truly thrilled at this show of generosity, according to Mama and others in whom she confided. Mama said it was a miracle they both survived riding in the car because neither was a good driver. Lorena learned to drive in Bluette. When they went on trips together, they would take turns driving.

Hickok, as long as she stayed in the little sitting room that was her domain, was safe from detection. Even if there was a guest in the big room, the Lincoln room, the door would be locked between them. I'm sure some guests would have been surprised to know that Lorena and the First Lady were visiting together on the other side of the door.

It was only in the early days of her White House stay that Lorena would slip across the West Hall to visit Eleanor in her room. Afterwards, it was Eleanor who came to visit her.

But both Eleanor and Lorena slept in single beds. The President's bed was only a little larger than a single. It was a semihospital-style bed, specially made for him at Val-Kill furniture factory.

Eleanor's sitting room was decorated with framed photos and snapshots of family groups and groups of friends. In one group shot was Lorena Hickok. But the President never came to Eleanor's sitting room so there was no danger of his finding the picture there.

At first, of course, it wasn't that way. Before he realized that Lorena was taking up residence at the White House, FDR would exchange a friendly greeting with her, and now and again talk with her at family group dinners and even at cocktails. But as his animosity increased, maids conspired to make sure Hicky didn't leave her room when FDR was around. She was careful to stay out of the President's path. She would leave the White House after early breakfast with Eleanor, and slip into her room before the President got back from his office in the West Wing, in the evening.

Eleanor and Hicky

Eleanor sometimes wore a sapphire ring. Hicky told me and Bluette and other maids that she had given it as a birthday gift to the First Lady. I had wondered about that ring because Eleanor didn't like jewelry and rarely decorated herself with anything sparkly, except for the diamond studded watch her husband had given her, and this sapphire ring. I was interested to learn more about the ring in Doris Faber's book about Eleanor's relationship with Hicky, *The Life of Lorena Hickok, E.R.'s Friend.*

Faber's research confirms that Lorena did give the ring to Eleanor and indicates that Lorena didn't pay for the ring but had received it years before from an opera singer. But what surprised me a bit was reading in one of Eleanor's letters to Hicky how much that ring meant to Eleanor, who had diamonds and pearls galore if she chose to wear them.

Eleanor's letter, to Lorena on her fortieth birthday, March 7, 1933, addresses Hicky as "Hick darling," and promises that on another birthday they will be together, adding, "Oh! I want to put my arms around you, I ache to hold you close."

Then Eleanor gets to the ring: "Your ring is a great comfort. I look at it and think she does love me or I wouldn't be wearing it!"

It was ironic, looking back, to compare two gifts Eleanor received about the time she came to the White House. It helps explain why Eleanor would cling to another woman for emotional satisfaction.

That March 1933 marked Eleanor's first birthday at the White House as well as the Inauguration.

FDR had taken pen in hand and written Eleanor a "Dear Babs" letter, using a humorous approach to tell her that he couldn't think of a thing to give her for her birthday—laxative pills, etchings, whiskey or beer—and so was enclosing a check for $200. Lorena Hickok had simply given her a ring from her very own finger—something Eleanor could keep and cherish.

As I look back, I feel sorry for Lorena Hickok, who traded a great career as a newspaperwoman for a half-hidden life in the shadow of Eleanor Roosevelt. She had been the top female reporter for the Associated Press, even covering political campaigns we were told, before tossing it away to be closer to Eleanor.

Actually, she lost her usefulness to the wire service when she switched her allegiance from the public to Eleanor, rather than sticking to her stories as a tough and unbiased newspaperwoman should have. So her choice had been either to move away from covering politics, or to quit her job and move closer to Eleanor. She chose the latter.

We, backstairs, knew that Lorena was secretly helping Eleanor with her writing. She never got the credit she deserved for helping make Eleanor's column, *My Day,* as successful as it was, or for her help in Eleanor's article writing. Nor did she get the writing reward she had been waiting for. We knew that she fully expected to be permitted to write Eleanor's life story. It would have given her a handsome income. As it was, Eleanor wrote her own. Of course, eventually Eleanor became a fairly polished writer, but we at the White House sewing room wondered how much credit Hicky deserved for having made a writer of the First Lady.

I had thought that after FDR died, she and Hickok would live together full time. Hicky had always said that someday she, Hicky, would live and write at Val-Kill. And Eleanor would be there whenever FDR didn't need her and would write.

But it didn't happen. After FDR died, Eleanor lived exactly the same kind of life as at the White House—dedicating herself to public life, such as the United Nations, and never settling down with any one person.

For years, Hicky lived all alone in a house in Mastic, Long Island, still at Eleanor's beck and call—but Eleanor seldom called. Then, in 1955, when Hicky's eyesight started failing due to sugar diabetes and her finances were equally shaky, Eleanor invited her, at last, to make Val-Kill her home. It lasted only a year.

The story that friends told, who saw them at Val-Kill together, was that Eleanor had grown more conservative and didn't like seeing Hicky slopping around in masculine pants and old sweater. And it didn't seem right for Hicky to be addressing the former first lady as "Darling," in a very proprietary way, no matter who was there. Eleanor had Hicky moved to a little log cabin nearby that was part of a motel. And finally, in 1958, she was moved to a rented room in Hyde Park, where she lived out the rest of her life.

Eleanor and Hicky

To the end of Eleanor's life, Hicky waited in the wings. When Eleanor lay in the hospital dying, she wrote a note to Hicky saying that she would phone her soon. It didn't happen.

And when Eleanor died in 1962, Hicky was too weak and distraught to attend her funeral. Instead, in the dark of night, she was driven to Hyde Park so that she could lay a wreath on the tombstone, unseen and unsung.

Eleanor's will left Hicky $1,000.

Hicky survived Eleanor by six years and died of sugar diabetes.

Eleanor's Day

Eleanor's day was not FDR's day.

We maids could not believe our eyes as we came to the conclusion that Eleanor and the President were like ships that passed in the night—exchanging signals but seldom stopping to visit. Each led a completely separate life.

As the backstairs people saw it, Eleanor had not been physically awakened until quite late in life, and then only outside of marriage. Had she felt a real sexual attraction toward her husband, she would have forgiven him, as so many other wives do, after finding love letters from another woman. Had she wanted her husband, she would have been more aggressive.

In our opinion, Eleanor liked certain women as well as certain men. The men seemed to be considerably younger than she. Important among them was Earl Miller. It was amusing to the household staff that Eleanor did not want Secret Service body-guards at the White House, but that is exactly what Earl Miller had been for her in New York, and she had loved it.

One day the joke around the White House was that Eleanor had made a funny, telling Tommy to notify Earl that if he wanted to "protect" her, he could come to Val-Kill that weekend.

Maggie and I had seen a lot of first families, but this was something unique. Two independent worlds within the White House. Their schedules for the day reflected this.

Take the morning hours. First Eleanor. She might go horse-back riding at five A.M. The latest she'd stay in bed would be seven-thirty. Often she was gone from the White House by eight. If Lorena was there, they would have breakfast together in the West Hall sitting room. Sometimes another guest would join them—Nancy Cook or Marion Dickerman. And occasionally

Eleanor ate breakfast alone at the table which would be set up whenever a meal was served there.

Sometimes we saw famous people at Eleanor's breakfast table. Once it was one of the richest women in the world—Doris Duke— who was a guest at the White House. Eleanor got out of bed early to take a trip with her to Arthurdale, Eleanor's experiment in low cost housing.

After breakfast, Eleanor had three quick conferences. The first to see her was Henrietta Nesbitt, who came with her black book of menus for the day. The First Lady and she huddled over it and Eleanor gave any orders relating to arriving guests or something the President wanted.

The First Lady did not kiss Henrietta, but she did kiss her next two visitors. At first we thought it strange, but then, it wasn't *our* business. She kissed her social secretary, Mrs. Helm, and her private secretary, Tommy Thompson.

Eleanor kissed few people, seldom even her children, where we could see. She hardly kissed anybody. She rarely even kissed her husband, as the White House help well knew. And son James, in his book, *My Parents: A Differing View,* comments, "Mother was formal, perhaps prudish. She was not given to open displays of affection…"

What James says is certainly true. Eleanor was not a demonstrative person.

Tommy brought the mail, and Helm brought the invitations that had arrived, as well as the plans for the next formal party. Eleanor worked at her desk in the sitting room next to her little bedroom.

As long as the First Lady was at her sitting-room desk, Tommy would come back and forth from their cubbyhole of an office behind the elevator on the second floor, across the West Hall sitting room to Eleanor's suite. Many times Tommy and she would stand in the West Hall, each with a stack of papers, talking loudly at each other.

Eleanor had one bad ear. You had to shout if she had the wrong side aimed toward you.

As for FDR, he would seldom see with whom Eleanor had breakfast because he was still asleep in his bedroom. He would wake up at eight or eight-thirty, and only rarely did his valet have to awaken him when he came into the bedroom at 8:30 with the newspapers.

Incidentally, Eleanor hated to have servants awaken her and so she had a little alarm clock that she set herself.

FDR's valet, who was McDuffie when Roosevelt first came to the White House, phoned for the President's breakfast. It would be brought on a tray at nine. Then Mac would help FDR out of bed and into the bathroom to help him shave and bathe.

Usually, while FDR was still eating, he had his first callers—his doctor, Ross McIntire, his press secretary, Jonathan Daniels or Steve Early, and Marvin McIntyre, his appointments secretary. The others stayed awhile, but the doctor would just pause long enough to ask how the President was feeling that morning.

FDR hated the sight of a doctor's little black bag, so McIntire didn't carry one. If FDR needed his blood pressure or legs checked, he stopped at the doctor's office on his way to the Oval Office.

One of the things the President enjoyed most each morning was making his own coffee—even grinding his own coffee beans. It was his little coffee ritual, as he and Fala enjoyed breakfast in bed.

The President was in no hurry to get to the office and he would finally get there at ten-thirty or eleven.

As I've said, around the White House some called Mrs. Roosevelt the "unofficial vice-president," because she took an interest in every phase of government and tried to help run it. Some said this was good. Some said this was bad.

It may have been good for the country, but it was certainly bad for the marriage. FDR got very tired of the memoranda she fired off to him and left in his room as a kind of pillow talk. It was not the kind of pillow talk a warmblooded man needed in the night.

But rather than upset Eleanor and the balance they had established in their marriage, he grinned and bore it, answering almost everything. His male aides called it his price of freedom. Eleanor would not bother him if he just kept her happy with answers to her questions and gave her plenty of assignments.

Babs and Boss

Or, as the servants closest to him said, "He treats her just like any president treats his vice president." And as FDR changed vice presidents—from John Nance Garner, to Henry Wallace, to Harry Truman, the servants said, "It doesn't matter anyway—Eleanor is still vice president."

In the mornings, after she was sure the President had gone, she ran into his room and picked up any messages he had left for her. Most of the time if he had an answer of any length, he would take Eleanor's note to the office with him and dictate his answer.

All through the day, he didn't come back to the Mansion, but stayed in his office in the West Wing. At about one P.M. lunch would be rolled over to the Oval Office in a specially built hot and cold steam table. It would be filled with whatever Eleanor and Henrietta had decreed he must eat.

Missy always shared his usually dismal meal, and sometimes they inflicted it on a few guests as well.

Meanwhile, Eleanor was eating at the Mansion—again in the West Hall. She didn't have to watch her diet because she didn't enjoy food that much and never overate. Her figure was really excellent. I knew because I sewed for her.

Eleanor was more concerned that her luncheon guests enjoy their food. She almost never ate alone—neither did FDR. It's just that they seldom ate together. The exceptions were when the far-flung family visited or when there were special guests of importance to both of them.

Then, of course, they ate in a dining room—either the family dining room or the state dining room.

The family dining-room table was most comfortable with sixteen persons or less, but it could accommodate twenty-two. Eleanor was so hyperactive that she usually drank Sanka coffee while guests had the real stuff.

Not often, but just now and then, Mrs. Roosevelt would be in the shopping mood, and she would dash out one block from the White House and go shopping at Garfinckel's, the most expensive department store in Washington.

It had elegant clothes. But we would comment that it was a good thing it wasn't the cheapest store in town that was located one block away, or surely, with her lack of concern about clothes, she would be shopping there—"at a fire sale."

Eleanor's Day

The First Lady's clothes were very conservative. When she shopped in New York, which wasn't often, it was usually at Arnold Constable's. She once bragged about how she had done her whole season's shopping in two hours. Frankly, I thought her clothes looked it. She simply didn't know how to pick flattering styles.

It was my job to make Eleanor's blouses. I did it in my own time, staying late at the White House and being paid out of Eleanor's private funds. She was meticulous about paying her bills, insisting I make out a bill for what she owed.

I would have preferred she just give me what she wanted.

The worst thing that Eleanor did was wear hairnets. It drove us frantic. We wanted to tell her to let her lovely hair fall free but she insisted on this kind of neatness even when going out in the evening in long gowns. The hairnet would fall down over her forehead.

I remember once when the First Lady went to England to visit the royal family. We cringed as we saw a newspaper photograph that showed the detested hairnet halfway down her forehead.

I think it was Hicky who finally prevailed on the First Lady to quit wearing a hairnet. Relief all the way around!

A time we all groaned was when the British King and Queen visited Hyde Park and had that infamous hot dog picnic. But that isn't what we groaned about. We groaned because the First Lady chose to wear a gingham dress—something that signified *housedress*—while the Queen dressed regally.

Eleanor did not use cosmetics, and many of us would comment on how nice it would be if she just put on a little "warpaint" to emphasize her good points. Her lovely blue eyes, for example. But she liked no artifice. Not even nail polish, though her hands were beautiful.

The only thing she did do was wear the faintest bit of perfume. You had to be very close to notice it.

There were many friendly arguments backstairs about whether the First Lady could be called pretty. Some said she could be. Some pointed out her lovely skin, especially on her shoulders when she exposed them in her evening gowns.

We agreed that it was a shame that her grandmother, who took care of her after her mother died, hadn't bothered to have her teeth straightened or have reconstruction done on her chin. A plastic surgeon could have made her beautiful, some said. I had to agree.

Eleanor did not wear much jewelry, except for her husband's wedding present, which she wore even when it didn't look particularly good with the outfit. I noticed she always wore this little decorative watch with diamonds forming her initials.

And she wore the ring Hicky had given her.

She had another wedding present that she didn't wear. That was her mother-in-law's present of a pearl necklace of five strands. Typically Eleanor, she had given a strand each to her children or their wives, until she ran out of strands.

Incidentally, one of the daughters-in-law did return the pearls after her divorce, but I don't know who fell heir to them.

The one time Eleanor pulled out all stops and wore jewelry worthy of the name was when Queen Elizabeth came on her famous visit with King George. Then, as if to compete with the queen's tiara, Eleanor wore a family diamond necklace, set against her gown of ecru lace.

Eleanor did not indulge in small talk. Even while entertaining, the First Lady was busy making converts to a cause, usually by talking about conditions she found around the country. Once, after a trip, she was talking about the need for housing and expanded jobs for the depressed mining area of West Virginia to a group of guests that included William Bullitt, whom her husband made an ambassador.

Eleanor told about visiting tar paper homes in which there was little to eat and little joy. In one shack, a little boy clutched his sole treasure, a white rabbit. His older sister whispered loudly to the lady visitor, whose identity as first lady was unknown to her, "Ha, ha. He thinks we ain't gonna eat his rabbit but we is!"

The little brother heard every word, as he was probably meant to hear, and rushed crying out of the house with his rabbit.

Eleanor told the story to show the frightful condition of poverty. But to Bill Bullitt, there was another message from that poor little child. Quickly he wrote out a check, begging Eleanor to send it to that family immediately to save the life of the little boy's rabbit.

The general public didn't know that Eleanor had a gun. She didn't want it. The Secret Service had insisted on giving it to her when she refused to let them protect her. She took lessons on how to use it and was supposed to keep it with her at all times.

I know she kept it in her dresser drawer and I never knew her to take it along with her. It was just as well. The President roared with laughter as he told friends what J. Edgar Hoover had told him in a tongue-in-cheek note after Eleanor had practiced shooting targets at the FBI Firing Range. "If there is one person in the United States who should not carry a gun, it is Eleanor. She cannot hit the broad side of a barn..."

She might not be able to hit the broad side of a barn but there was one skill she did learn to relish.

Eleanor learned to knit—not well, but profusely. She knitted day and night. In airplanes, cars, during parties, during conversations with friends. She even knitted as she listened to speeches as a member of the audience in a public place. She even knitted in a congressional hearing room. And from the speaker's platform before she rose to say a few words.

The White House staff was a little distressed by the places Eleanor suddenly started knitting—almost ostentatiously. Being chosen to receive one of her vests or sweaters was a mixed blessing. No two were alike, considering the dropped stitches. I was one who helped pretty them up for gift-giving.

When she was at the White House and not traveling, Eleanor received people at tea time. She grew up with this tradition because she had gone to school in England.

Usually tea would be served in the Red Room on the first floor, one flight below the family quarters. She poured the tea herself. There would be little platters of cakes and cookies.

If there was a huge gathering at tea time, they would be served in the State Dining Room. Mrs. Helm sat at one end of the long table and she at the other. There were never any wines or hard liquors served around Eleanor. She was a complete teetotaler and heartily disapproved of the President's drinking. If he ordered drinks served, she didn't complain, but she didn't like it.

At Eleanor's teas, three beverages were served: coffee, tea and cocoa. Once a diplomat with a thick accent was given cocoa by mistake and asked if this tea was grown in the U.S.

Before tea, Eleanor sometimes scheduled official conferences, and these she also conducted on the public first floor, and not in the family quarters where her study and office were.

Now back again to the President's Oval Office. Leaving work at six P.M., FDR frequently took a dip in the White House pool before coming to the Mansion. The pool had been funded by public donation in an outpouring of love toward the man who had overcome polio to become the thirty-second president of the United States.

Missy jumped into the pool too, as would Fala. Then Missy rushed to her room to change for the happy hour while FDR enjoyed another luxury—a long rubdown. It was administered by George Fox, who came from the physician's office and was the pharmacist.

FDR and Missy frequently ate dinner alone late in the evening.

Dinner at eight was the rule for Eleanor. She ate with her many guests in the first floor small private dining room located next to the State Dining Room. When there was a formal or state dinner, this room was used as a serving room by the butlers.

Missy and FDR and his cronies might still be in their cocktail hour upstairs in the President's study. If there was a guest he particularly wanted to chat with, FDR would make an effort to get to the table downstairs at eight or a little after—and the diners would wait for him and Missy to arrive.

If his sons and daughters-in-law were there, he would definitely make the effort. One favorite of his—as long as she lasted in her marriage to son James—was Betsey Cushing, who was a lot like Missy in being an expert in light-hearted banter.

Betsey would be the first to arrive at FDR's study for cocktails and was always welcome.

If Eleanor's table was full of her female friends, FDR and Missy had dinner in his upstairs sitting room. often asking someone like Harry Hopkins—Harry the Hop—to stay and eat with them.

Eleanor was the night owl. She often stayed up until two, talking seriously with guests, such as Joseph Lash, who was very important in the antiwar youth movement.

Her energy wore everyone out. The secretaries left so tired at the end of the day that they almost shuffled along, but Eleanor was only nicely started. She spent half the night enjoying friends, catching up on reading, writing letters, making phone calls, planning benefits to help needy musicians, or youth groups who wanted to keep America out of the war, or black organizations wanting better jobs and equal pay for Negroes.

Suddenly she might jump up and race down the stairs to see how things were in the new servant's dining room.

Looking back, I could almost say that Eleanor did not have a real life. She was hardly a mother because she let the servants and nursemaids raise her children. As a result, her children turned to their grandmother, Sara Delano Roosevelt, into their surrogate mother.

She didn't have a real husband. She turned her back on a normal married life and insisted it be only a friendship and a business partnership. Into that role stepped Missy LeHand, who became the surrogate wife.

So all Eleanor had was her public life and her private affairs.

Most of the time she kept so busy that it seemed to be a very happy life. But now and then, when she slowed down, we could tell she was a little wistful or sad, and even a little bitter.

On many occasions, we who watched first families come and go, felt sorry for her. But there was nothing we could do. She had chosen her own path. It was her destiny.

DEATH HANGS OVER THE WHITE HOUSE

Death Hangs Over the White House

I remember someone once commented that the Roosevelts seemed to be a charmed family. People dropped like flies around them, but *they* remained strong. I remember it was twisted into a warning to some visitor, "Don't let your life get too entangled with the Roosevelts. It might end tragically."

This was during the third term, and a list of names was ticked off of aides and intimates who had had nervous breakdowns or strokes, had committed suicide, or died mysteriously.

It seemed to me that we had more than our share of shocks during the Roosevelt administration—surely more than I had seen connected with any other presidential family.

It started even before the Roosevelts moved into the White House with the assassination of one of FDR's political enemies, Anton Cermak. How strange that Roosevelt's administration started with one death and ended with another—his own.

Mayor Anton Cermak of Chicago was one of those delegates who was against Roosevelt's nomination in 1932 and had booed him. In fact, Cermak and his followers joined Al Smith's supporters to boo Roosevelt just as the California delegates put him over the top and he won the nomination. The bitterness continued to the point where Al Smith refused to let the nomination be unanimous by releasing his delegates.

FDR, I heard, was still licking his wounds over that insult when he moved into the White House. He remembered the fact that his nomination had not been unanimous.

But getting back to that tragedy that spared the charmed FDR. It happened in February, just a month before the Inaugural then held in March. There was a big American Legion convention in Miami, and all kinds of Democratic leaders were to escort the President-elect's motorcade to the park where he would speak.

White House aides explained later that Cermak rushed to Miami to try to get FDR to promise help for his cold and starving Chicago poor, who were foraging through the city tearing up city property for firewood.

FDR had given his speech and was in his open car when Cermak approached him and was gunned down by a mysterious figure named Zangara, who seemed to have no reason except that he hated all presidents, as he later said.

Four people were slightly injured, but Cermak was the only one to die of his wounds. FDR was untouched. Though he protested he had been after the President, there was talk around the White House that Zangara had been used by Chicago mobsters to bump off the mayor. FDR himself was quoted as saying he didn't believe Zangara had been after him but had been aiming at Cermak from the beginning.

Zangara did not survive to write his memoirs. He was convicted and executed within the month.

A second tragedy hung over the White House as the Roosevelts moved in. That was the strange death of the man slated to be FDR's Attorney-General, Senator Thomas J. Walsh of Montana.

Walsh had just gotten married and was on his way to Washington by train after a honeymoon in Miami when he dropped dead.

All of this gruesome news was enough to give the White House staff a bit of a chill.

Then there was the personal tragedy hanging over FDR's head. Few people knew, as he entered the White House, about the suicide of his sailing buddy. It affected Missy almost as much as it did FDR.

In fact, Missy, who was known for sunshine and laughter, cried about it, remembering how close they had once been with Livingston Davis, whom they called "Livy," and who had been FDR's favorite pal since they had gone to Harvard together.

I was told Eleanor did not approve of Livy and called him "strange" and "different." And he certainly was. One day he took off his pants for no apparent reason when both Missy and another woman were on board. Another time he took off all his clothes—to exercise, he claimed. The others claimed that was just Livy. And with Livy, it was anything for a laugh.

Missy said FDR refused to get rid of a good friend just because he had "a little peculiarity." FDR had so many good laughs with Livy, whose humor consisted of more than just throwing off his clothes, that he lost no opportunity to spend time with his moneyed friend from Pride's Crossing, Massachusetts, and always made sure to have him around. When FDR became assistant secretary of the Navy in 1913, he lost no opportunity to combine official duties with a visit to Livy.

For example, when Assistant Secretary Roosevelt attended the launching of a new battleship, the USS *Nevada,* at Quincy, Massachusetts, he combined it with a game of golf with Livy at a country club.

FDR eventually made Livy "special assistant to the assistant secretary" in 1916 so that he could have him around full time at the Navy.

The way Missy told it, starting in the 1920s she would go out on cruises with FDR and Livy and others of that yachting circle and be "one of the boys," making it a rule to show no sign of shock no matter what the irrepressible Livy did next.

Missy talked a lot about Livy when she first came to the White House because she was still upset by what had happened. The very month Franklin Roosevelt announced that he was going to run for president, Livy put a gun to his head and committed suicide.

There was no connection, of course, but FDR and Missy were both terribly upset. FDR was touched that Livy left him a token gift in his will and included with it a statement that it was in memory of their happy times.

Then, before the Roosevelts had enjoyed their first Christmas in the White House, Mary Foster, Eleanor Roosevelt's personal maid, died. She had been her friend as well as her maid, and Eleanor took it very hard. She had gone for an operation and never came back.

Then Ike Hoover went home one night and didn't come back. The chief usher died in the night. Now it was FDR who took it hard. Ike had been the most famous man in the White House besides himself. Ike had travelled with President Wilson to the famous peace conference. FDR consulted him on matters of protocol, and the President enjoyed learning how things were done correctly, according to precedence.

Ike, I remember, knew how to walk backwards in the presence of royalty, something his successors were not able to master.

Now it was Raymond Muir's turn to be elevated from usher to chief usher. He was a lovely person, a lawyer, who had been in World War I and come back with a French wife. In time Muir realized that chief usher was a dead-end job, and transferred to the State Department where he could advance.

I remember he came back to the White House in 1939 on an official assignment—to check out the White House before the visit of the King and Queen of England and see what was needed from a diplomatic viewpoint.

Howell Crim was the next up to bat. Several days before Ike Hoover died, Ike told him that some day he was going to write his memoir, and he wanted Crim's help. Crim's sentiments on memoirs made him famous around the White House. He said, "I don't kiss and tell."

Ike Hoover's widow did gather up his notes and give them to a magazine, but there were no revelations of the real secrets he knew.

With the appointment of Crim, the office of the usher underwent a great change. Up to that point, an Army officer had always been detailed to the White House to handle the White House budget. He and the housekeeper handed out the money.

The Roosevelts decided they did not want an outsider doling out the money allotted by Congress, and Crim fell heir to the title of "Money Man." I got along fine with Crim, but he was a little stuffy.

We felt very sorry for him when he too started to wither at the White House. We said the White House was a killing job for all but the strongest. He developed some kind of blood ailment, and we thought he was using a sun lamp to keep from having a pallor. However, Crim remained at the White House until the

Death Hangs Over the White House

Eisenhower administration. We all went to Crim's funeral—white and black White House staff alike—and mourned the little man who didn't kiss and tell.

It wasn't just the household help who collapsed under the strain of working for the Roosevelts. Marvin McIntyre, one of FDR's most important aides at the Oval Office and the confidant whom he named appointments secretary, collapsed at the White House in the late thirties and had to take more than a year off before he could continue.

Not only had doctors ordered him to rest but to get out of Washington for a complete change of atmosphere and to stay out of reach of the tumultuous Roosevelt White House. The White House used up people like soap!

There was hardly a time during the twelve years Roosevelt lived in the White House when the family was not in turmoil or experiencing some kind of misery or sadness.

Four times there were bodies lying in state in the East Room, and the fourth was FDR himself. Before him, there had been Eleanor's brother, Hall, Louis Howe, who had been the best friend a president ever had, and Gus Gennerich, who was only a bodyguard and a subject of some mystery.

And there had been the strange and touching case of the secretary FDR had nicknamed Rabbit. Her name was really Margaret Durand, but FDR and Louis Howe had decided her fly-away hair gave her a look of having sprouted rabbit ears, and she was always scurrying off in a hurry. FDR was very fond of her.

Rabbit had been devoted to Louis all through his illness at the White House. She had even helped Mama and other maids make his bed when they got him up for short intervals during the last months. Then after Louis Howe died in 1936, Rabbit's health started to fail.

Backstairs we feared Rabbit had caught something from Louis. For a time she worked as secretary to James Roosevelt when he helped his father, but eventually she was unable to go on. Her lungs were affected and she was taken to a hospital.

There was not a dry eye in the White House when, in July of 1938, we heard that she had gotten married in an oxygen tent. A little later she died. But she kept her spirit to the very end. She kidded with her bridegroom about her unique bridal veil—an oxygen tent.

Tragedy, tragedy. We seemed to be surrounded by it. Carole Lombard visited the White House just before she went on a publicity jaunt that resulted in her death.

Amelia Earhart was an overnight guest before her strange disappearance in 1937. I still have a souvenir of her visit.

Two persons who married Roosevelt children eventually committed suicide.

There were so many deaths. It seemed FDR lost every person he leaned on and cared most deeply about—Missy LeHand, Louis Howe, Harry Hopkins, his mother. Death came in clusters.

Sometimes it wasn't death that took his favorite people away. His valet McDuffie suffered a nervous breakdown. FDR also had grown very fond of some of his daughters-in-law—especially Betsey Cushing—and had lost their company through his sons' many divorces. Once FDR told a valet, "I'm accused of not having a heart, but I'm afraid of caring too deeply. You see how they all go."

He sounded very sad and lonely as he said it, sitting in his wheelchair, getting ready for bed. I don't think he ever stopped missing Betsey—especially at cocktail hour. In the old days, she would be the first in his study for cocktails, and the laughter would ring out. She helped him through the dark days after Missy took sick and had to leave the White House.

Louis Howe was a mess, but FDR loved him because Howe made FDR the center of his whole life. Long before FDR was even a twinkle in the Democratic donkey's eye, Louis was telling him he would someday be president.

This was back in the teens of the century, when FDR was assistant secretary of the Navy. Eleanor accepted him, drew him to her bosom. She wouldn't have had she known that Howe, who was her husband's assistant in his Navy office, encouraged the handsome FDR in his dalliance with Lucy Mercer and helped cover for him.

Maybe one reason Eleanor embraced and felt sorry for Louis was that her mother-in-law, Sara, hated him so and never tired of complaining of how messy and ugly he was.

Death Hangs Over the White House

Messy or not, ugly or not, Louis had the key to FDR and was determined to groom him for the presidency. There had been two Adams as presidents, and Louis was sure there would be two Roosevelts. In fact, Louis and Franklin talked endlessly over drinks, plotting how FDR would follow exactly in the footsteps of his fifth cousin and Eleanor's uncle, Teddy Roosevelt, the famed rough rider.

According to their blueprint, FDR would follow the progression of assistant secretary of the Navy, governor of New York, vice president, and then president.

It didn't quite turn out that way, and things looked dark when FDR jumped the gun and tried for vice president before running for governor. And it had all looked dark when FDR contracted polio in 1921 and seemed relegated to the sidelines.

Two people wouldn't let FDR vegetate—Louis Howe and Missy LeHand, who worked for FDR in his law office. Both badgered Franklin to get up and fight his way back into the mainstream of politics.

The way we heard it at the White House, Eleanor was a regular brick about helping FDR learn to walk again and she and Howe took turns rubbing his legs. But Eleanor merely maintained an open mind about whether he returned to politics, saying whatever he wanted to do was all right with her. She hadn't pushed.

It was Louis and Missy, working in shifts and together, who prodded, insulted, and pushed FDR until he got mad enough to start fighting.

When Louis got sick and could no longer even make it from his bedroom to FDR's sitting room for happy hour, FDR ordered Rabbit to work right in Howe's bedroom and he himself pretended he was still taking orders from Howe.

Louis' telephone bills were atrocious as from his bed he called anywhere in the country at will to check on how FDR stood with the voters of that state and discussed issues FDR would face.

Actually, Louis started going downhill early in 1935, and he needed an oxygen tent in his room part of the time. Even so, he huffed and puffed on the telephone—demanding to be put through to FDR at three o'clock in the morning.

It was Eleanor, ironically, who bore the brunt of his demands, seeing him every day, giving him words to live for, and keeping track of the doctor's orders. Finally, he was too sick even for the White House, and he was moved to Bethesda Naval Hospital. He refused to go by ambulance, and Eleanor saved his pride by taking him there herself, in style, in the back seat of a White House limousine.

Again, his White House secretary Rabbit was close behind and now spent her time handling phones for him and taking dictation from his bedside.

It was only April, and everyone pretended Louis was saving his strength for the Democratic Convention in Philadelphia. The way we understood it in the servants' quarters, FDR could not stand the pain of seeing people close to him slipping away and hid from them, letting Eleanor handle whatever needed handling. But it didn't mean he cared less. He cared too much.

FDR did not beat a path to Louis' hospital bedside as Eleanor did, but just let his cheery voice do what it could. Nor did Louis Howe make it to the convention. The evening of April 18, 1936, while FDR was joking and laughing at the Gridiron dinner, someone came and whispered to him that Howe was dead.

Immediately FDR ordered the White House flag to fly at half-mast, and Louis Howe was brought back to the White House to lie in state in the East Room. It was unorthodox, but it was the least FDR could do for the man who "made" him President.

After the election that year, FDR suffered his next great loss. This time it was his favorite bodyguard Gus Gennerich, who had protected him as governor of New York. Gus had been a well-publicized New York cop who was known for his valor, having engaged in several gun battles with criminals.

FDR arranged for him to be transferred to Secret Service when he came to the White House. Gus was more of a friend to FDR than outsiders supposed, and he was often found arguing politics with the Boss.

It wasn't that Gus didn't respect and agree with FDR on most points, but as he explained to us, "Somebody's got to tell the Boss what the civilians are thinking and he doesn't always want to get it from Eleanor." Sometimes he would even slip some amusing character he had met at a bar into the President's office to brighten up his day.

Death Hangs Over the White House

Whenever FDR traveled abroad, he took Gus and could count on him to jolly up the long travel hours with some of the droll stories of his adventures. Gus was a bachelor, and FDR enjoyed learning, through him, how bachelors operated.

Another thing they had in common was that Gus was buying a farm for his retirement home. He kidded the Boss that he was learning how to be a gentleman farmer from him—that one day they would be exchanging some of that Henry Wallace seed corn. Wallace, whom FDR made secretary of agriculture, was famous for his experiments to improve the corn crop yield.

At any rate, December of 1936 found FDR safely reelected to a second term and on a work-and-play goodwill trip to South America. There was fishing with his son James, who went along as his official aide, partying, and even an official address that FDR gave the peace conference at Buenos Aires. Backstairs, we heard some of what was going on, and it wasn't so pleasant. At the conference, FDR's speech had been disrupted by a pre-hippie-type kid yelling, "Down with imperialism," and heading for the American president. Argentine guards dragged the boy out, and FDR safely finished his speech. (We heard two years later that the boy had been killed in an airplane crash.)

Something else that happened in Argentina was much harder on the President—the mysterious death of Gus in a night club. Gus had gone to a nightclub and met some girl with whom he danced for several hours. He seemed to be having a wonderful time. Then, as he sat at his table, he suddenly fell over dead.

There was talk that perhaps he had been poisoned by a jealous boyfriend dropping something in his drink. FDR was awakened and told the terrible news. A shipboard conference was held, and FDR and his advisers considered the possibility of this becoming an international incident.

They decided it would be best to bypass an autopsy and get the body out of there. The officials did not want to release the body, but FDR's doctor, Ross McIntire, through some hocus-pocus had the body delivered first to a funeral parlor and then to the American Embassy, and from there back to Washington, where Gus lay in state in the East Room.

FDR was very upset to lose Gus, and so were his friends backstairs. It is a case still discussed by White House old-timers, who still meet in retirement. Did Gus suffer some terrible concussion when he fell during a rough and tumble initiation as the ship crossed the equator? Is that what affected him later?

Or was poor Gus the victim of something more sinister?

The official word was that Gus had suffered a cerebral hemorrhage. Who will ever know the truth? No autopsy was ever performed.

The year 1941 brought the largest cluster of tragedies—Pearl Harbor and World War II, Missy's stroke, the death of the President's mother in September, and the First Lady's brother in December.

Sara Delano Roosevelt died of a blood clot in her lung in the month of her eighty-seventh birthday. This was a terrible blow to the President, and we would see him sadly touching his armband. It went on and on for months. The President still seemed deeply grieved, and servants around the President said the poor man had nobody to bolster his ego now that Missy and his mother both were struck down.

Missy was still alive, of course, but at this time the situation was reversed, and she needed bolstering from him instead.

I said to George Fields one day, "When is the Boss going to take that armband off?"

He said, "I think he's prepared to wear it for a long time."

I said, "Well, you tell him even widows in mourning for their husbands only take to the veil for a year."

He corrected me and said, "The Boss says when his father died, old Sara wore a black widow's veil clear to the ground for years."

"Well, he's not a widow or even a widower," I retorted, "So tell him enough is enough."

Fields laughed and said, "I'll be sure to give him your message." I'm sure it was no thanks to me, but the armband did come off at the end of one year. FDR's sad look did not. He got choked up every time he told how he had been opening some of his mother's prized possessions and had felt as if he were hit with a sledgehammer as he realized he was looking at all his own little baby clothes.

We felt really sorry for the President for the manner in which his mother died. He hadn't been able to have a last word with her and tell her of his love. She hadn't even known that he was there. She had been failing and was brought from Campobello, her summer home, because of her weakened condition. The story around the White House was that she probably knew she would never return there and made a dramatic exit, refusing to be carried to her limousine, but proudly hobbling to it on the arm of her butler.

She went to Hyde Park, but she didn't get better. FDR went to see her at the start of September and spent one night with her. He came back to the White House saying his mother had a cold. A few days later there was an emergency call for the President to hurry to Hyde Park. Eleanor went with him, and both were at her bedside when she seemed to pass away in her sleep, not knowing they had arrived.

"Isn't that tragic?" we asked each other. "He's never there in a crisis and the one time he *is* where it's happening, it's of no use."

I remember that Eleanor was dry-eyed over her mother-in-law's death in the autumn of 1941. That's the way I saw it, and that's the way the other maids saw it. It also circulated around the White House that Eleanor was most annoyed with Franklin.

Instead of telling his wife directly, FDR had informed Eleanor through his daughter Anna, that he wanted nothing moved in his mother's house. He wanted nothing changed.

Not only did this show how estranged they were, but it showed us again how FDR hated confrontations. Eleanor had said that she would like to change Hyde Park some day to make it "liveable." Now she had gotten the message that it was not to be.

Eleanor told someone within our hearing, "In other words Hyde Park is now to be a shrine and it will still not be home to me. I would have to make changes to feel at home but my hands are tied."

Even as Sara Delano Roosevelt lay dying, another tragedy was brewing. And this was the one that would shake Eleanor to her foundation. Her closest friend, and some said, the person she loved most in the whole world, her brother Hall Roosevelt, was being taken to a hospital in Poughkeepsie.

On the very day Sara was laid to rest beside the President's father in the churchyard of St. James at Hyde Park, the First Lady had her brother moved to Washington to be near her—at the

Army's Walter Reed Hospital, on 16th Street, several miles from the White House.

We sent changes of clothing to the First Lady at the hospital because she stayed there night and day until he died. As Eleanor put it, "He was like a child to me. It was like losing my child."

Eleanor had Hall's casket brought to the White House, where it lay in state in the East Room, as Gus' had. In fact, Eleanor commented that Hall deserved at least as much honor as Gus. A funeral service was held there, and then Eleanor accompanied her brother's body to Tivoli, where a place had been provided for it in the Hall family vault.

Now it was a White House with Eleanor and FDR each silently nursing a personal grief. As best we could we comforted each of them, but we were only servants.

At the time of Hall's funeral, FDR and Eleanor were seen embracing, and it was remarked on by the household help as a novelty. But as is true of all novelties, it did not last. How we wished that Eleanor could continue to cling to FDR as she did for that brief moment.

It almost seemed that every time FDR took a trip, someone in his party died or he received news of someone's death. News of Missy LeHand's death had been handed him in Honolulu. "Pa" Watson, the personal aide he counted on for relaxation and humor, died when they were returning to the U. S. from the Yalta Conference.

It was the final shock for FDR before his own death only two months later.

The Yalta Conference, named for the spot where it had taken place—Yalta in the Crimea—concluded February 11, with FDR and Churchill getting Josef Stalin's commitment that Russia would enter the war against Japan. And now they were steaming back happily aboard the U.S.S. *Quincy,* the President and his friend Pa Watson.

As FDR talked about it later, it hadn't been a happy-happy trio of world leaders, meeting to thresh things out and come to an agreement of great importance to the world. Instead of cooperating, Churchill and Stalin had squabbled and thrust verbal barbs at each other, and FDR had played peacemaker. It had been hard on Watson as well—anything that affected FDR, affected him.

Death Hangs Over the White House

FDR said he had thought of Missy and how much her Catholicism meant to her when Pa Watson, as he lay dying on shipboard, asked to become a Catholic. Fortunately, there was a Catholic ship's chaplain along, and he performed the conversion, as FDR sat sadly by.

A valet heard FDR say, "If only Missy could have been there." Now he faced his sorrows alone.

"I Hate War..."

At the White House we used to imitate FDR among ourselves, saying to a fellow maid or houseman, "Ah hate wa-ah." The other would reply, "Ah hate wa-ah, *everyone* hates wa-ah. Have you got anything else to hate?"

Three times that I can remember Franklin Roosevelt assured the world he hated war and there must have been many more times. But it all ended with our getting into the war.

I remember that Christmas of 1936, five years before he declared war with the "day that shall live in infamy" speech, FDR was so delighted with his "I hate war, I have seen war" speech, delivered that summer at Chatauqua, New York, that he gave it as his Christmas present. Expensively bound, of course.

In 1939, as England faced the raging tiger Hitler, who gobbled up one European nation after another, FDR said, "This nation will remain a neutral nation... I hate war! I say that again and again... As long as it remains within my power to prevent, there will be no blackout of peace in the United States."

But we knew, backstairs, that we were sliding into a war, especially as he started to say thing like, "The hand that holds the dagger has stuck it into the back of its neighbor."

It was a strange time at the White House with Eleanor fighting the notion of preparedness and FDR preparing to go to war if necessary and in spite of a balky Congress that hated to spend the money for munitions to fight other countries' battles.

FDR kept his own counsel. He listened to Eleanor and her young friends talk against preparedness, and he didn't argue. He just kept doing what he had to do, feeling the weight of history on his shoulders.

It was interesting to see how Eleanor's attitudes were influenced by youth groups and then how she slowly came around to FDR's view.

As head of the Youth Congress, Joe Lash had many occasions to come to Washington, and he was always free to stay at the White House. Even if Eleanor was not there, he was free to come. Sometimes his fiancée, Trude, and he would both be there in separate rooms.

Sometimes Joe Lash and Eleanor would have dinner in the private dining room while the President and Missy had dinner in the Oval study.

When Joe was called to testify before a congressional committee, Eleanor was in the audience, listening and taking notes. When the Youth Congress was marching on Washington to protest any American involvement in Europe's war, in February of 1940, Eleanor invited the whole 4,000 marchers to come to the White House lawn and prevailed on FDR to come out and speak to them and explain his position.

Afterwards, Lash and a group of his colleagues went into the White House to eat and have further conversations with Eleanor. FDR made himself scarce. He was furious. This time they had gone too far. He had not been pleased, he told intimates, to look out on the lawn and see such signs as, "WE REFUSE TO FIGHT," "KEEP AMERICA OUT OF WAR," and "THE YANKS ARE *NOT* COMING."

Also, the youngsters booed him as he had tried to talk to them of patriotism and youth's responsibility toward their country. Adding to the insult, his wife, Eleanor, had worked around the clock getting people and organizations to let the youngsters come and sleep overnight. FDR told his intimates how he felt over cocktails, but to Eleanor he tried to keep a civil tongue and treat it with slight humor. It was reported backstairs that he had said to her, "Our young folks certainly are unpredictable these days, aren't they?"

Eleanor, we learned, scolded Lash and his friends for having booed their President, saying it had been disrespectful and a mark of bad manners. They did apologize to her.

Lash rated so highly with Eleanor that she gave him almost anything she gave her children—and sometimes more. As I recall,

"I Hate War..."

I was told that she had let Joe and his fiancée use her beloved cottage Val-Kill, something that she rarely let her own sons do.

At first FDR was very fond of Lash, too, and considered him a bright young man, but the word around the White House was that the fondness wore thin when FDR suspected that the youth group he was associated with was infiltrated by young communists, or at least communist sympathizers.

It developed into some rather bitter arguments between Eleanor and the President, with Eleanor defending the youth movement and Lash as simply idealistic, if perhaps a bit overzealous.

Eventually, she herself got a little disillusioned about Lash's group, but never about him. A maid once heard her defending Lash by saying she was sure he was a "good and loyal American."

What eventually turned Eleanor against the youth group was their attitude in the matter of Russia and Finland. When Russia attacked Finland in 1940, they weren't too concerned about Finland's suffering and didn't want the United States to get involved. But when Germany attacked Russia in June of 1941, they changed their tune and wanted help for Russia. Eleanor, we were relieved to see, withdrew her support of the youth group.

War talk or no war talk, preparedness or no preparedness, politics still kept rolling along on schedule—"like a road show," we said backstairs.

In 1940 the White House was in an uproar because Jim Farley passed the word around that he wanted to be President—that FDR had had the White House long enough.

Even his wife defected for a while.

When Eleanor expressed herself vigorously to FDR against an unprecedented third term, the President asked whom she would like to see as the next president. It was noted and passed around backstairs that her answer had been, "Cordell Hull." He was then secretary of state. She also commented that James Farley certainly deserved consideration after all that he had done to make FDR president in the first place.

As the conversation was reported to me, FDR said Louis Howe had the greater credit, and Eleanor had retorted that it might be so but Louis Howe was dead.

Eleanor had been on Cordell Hull's side since 1924. That was when he was chairman of the Democratic National Committee, and he had made her famous by appointing her chairman of a ladies' subcommittee to make suggestions for political planks of interest to women.

Eleanor had gathered her liberal Democratic friends around her, including Elinor Morgenthau, wife of the man FDR would later make treasury secretary, and had come up with some zingers. They demanded a plank supporting the League of Nations. And a plank strengthening the Prohibition enforcement laws. And wildest of all, a plank demanding equal pay for women!

They didn't get far with the 1924 Convention Resolutions Committee, but Cordell Hull had made a powerful friend. He ended up nine years later in 1933, with the top cabinet job under Roosevelt—secretary of state.

FDR was forever being hurt by his sons' defections in politics. Elliott especially disappointed him. Back in the early days of the administration, when he had gone out West, Elliott got himself a job as aviation editor of the Hearst newspaper in Los Angeles. FDR, we heard, was appalled that Elliott was working for Hearst.

He was even more appalled when Elliott switched to the job of commentator on radio and was tossing barbs at FDR's New Deal on Mutual Network. His White House attendants knew that FDR was hurt to the quick.

Now in 1940, Elliott was again the thorn in FDR's side. He was touting Cactus Jack Garner for President.

At this point, we heard that FDR had decided Garner was the enemy, and he was not going to have him as a vice presidential candidate again, even if he did decide to try for a third term.

Old Cactus Jack had proven to be a millstone around his neck and had not supported his New Deal. The Texan was just too conservative for FDR, but just right for Elliott's acquired Texas taste.

By now FDR was used to Elliott's defections.

What hurt FDR most was that his own wife, Eleanor, started needling him to stay out of the 1940 race and to stop people who were already talking him up as a third term candidate—people like Harry Hopkins.

"I Hate War..."

Word was that he felt more estranged from Eleanor than ever, and she was not welcome at his political strategy pow-wows.

As the time for the Democratic Convention in Chicago approached, we were amused that the President claimed he didn't care who the Democratic Convention selected. For some strange reason, Harry Hopkins set up a Roosevelt third term headquarters in Chicago, anyway.

Eleanor gathered some of her close friends around her at Val-Kill to sit out the convention. Her secret source of information at the convention was Lorena Hickok, who few realized was sitting in for her.

So the convention in Chicago began.

By now, Eleanor had made her peace with the President and was in favor of a third term if that was what he wanted.

FDR was sure Farley couldn't make it because he was a Catholic, and the country wasn't ready for a Catholic president. But FDR watched from afar as Carter Glass, the senator from Virginia, nominated Farley. Of course, FDR was through with Farley and changed postmaster generals in mid stream, selecting Frank Walker.

Cactus Jack Garner was also nominated.

Then Senator Lister Hill of Alabama nominated Franklin Delano Roosevelt, and the hall went wild. Harry Hopkins had done a good job.

But now again came trouble. And again it was from the bosom of his own family.

We heard that Elliott Roosevelt infuriated his father by announcing that he was going to second the nomination of Texan Jesse Jones for vice-president. FDR hated Jesse Jones at this point and wanted only Henry Wallace because he was a liberal. He told Eleanor over the phone that he would turn down the nomination if Wallace was not the selection, and he backed it up by telling her he already had his refusal written out, ready to go.

Farley was the snake in the grass who was going to nominate Jesse Jones for the second place and Farley, still acting the friend, was the one who met Eleanor at the Chicago Airport when she finally arrived to try to help her husband.

From what we heard back at the White House, it was a tense

situation. The First Lady arrived at the convention hall, located her son, Franklin Jr., and sent him to find Elliott. Few even knew Eleanor was there, at this point. Elliott was her favorite, but she read him the riot act about muddying the water and daring to back a man his father didn't want as potential president.

If he supported Jones, and Jones got the vice presidential nomination, his father was going to turn down the nomination, she warned him. Elliott, shocked at this news, tried to assure his mother that nothing would stop "Pa," but said he was committed.

The convention hall had been booing the name of Henry Wallace every time they heard it, but when Eleanor took the floor to speak on behalf of her husband, she gradually made them see that a President giving his life blood to help his nation had the right to ask to work with a man whom he felt he could trust and who he felt was qualified for the gravest responsibility—in other words, had the makings of a competent president.

Although Eleanor never mentioned Wallace by name, the delegates all knew whom she meant, and when the voting started, they gave their leader the man *he* wanted.

Needless to say, Jesse Jones never forgave FDR, and he also hated Henry Wallace, making FDR feel very uncomfortable to have the two men together—his Vice President and his secretary of commerce.

It was ironic that just before he died, FDR finally got rid of Jesse Jones from his cabinet post, the only man FDR ever fired, we were told. And with typical FDR whimsy, he gave his job to his worst enemy—Henry Wallace, who in 1945 was no longer Vice President.

There is one missing link to the story, and that is why Elliott backed Jesse Jones. The backstairs speculation was that it concerned a financial mess involving Elliott. Jesse Jones had bailed him out, somehow arranging a loan, though not an RFC loan—if anyone of the Roosevelt family had gotten a government loan, it would have hit every headline.

The amount of the loan which I heard bandied about was two million dollars, and the story was that some fast-talking Texans had pulled Elliott into a radio deal and had left him floundering in debt.

"I Hate War..."

Poor FDR groaned and said he wished his sons would just take normal jobs and wistfully wondered aloud, "Why do they try to be millionaires?"

There was rejoicing in the family, and even among the servants, when Elliott came to his senses and supported his father's third-term bid in 1940.

But the most interesting postscript concerns Harold Ickes, FDR's crusty secretary of the interior.

Ickes had one desire and he never attained it. That was to be vice president. We wondered how much Eleanor had to do with the fact that he never got a chance. She would have memoed FDR to death to prevent it, we said.

But Ickes remained faithful to FDR, and FDR, in spite of what Eleanor might have felt, remained faithful to Ickes. Ickes remained secretary of interior throughout the whole Roosevelt administration.

Before the first year of his third term was over, FDR, who still hated war, was at war. And so was the nation.

As a footnote to history, it was Grace Tully, Missy's successor as top secretary, to whom FDR dictated the fateful 500-word message to Congress which resulted in the declaration of war.

Grace was home that Sunday morning—December 7, 1941— and wasn't too excited when she got a phone call from FDR's trusted switchboard operator, Hacky. Her complacency quickly faded as Hacky spewed out her message. "Grace, thank God you're there. Get on your high horse. The Japanese have just bombed Pearl Harbor and a car is on its way to pick you up."

The hours flew by, and a nightmare day at the White House turned into a nightmare night. Eventually, what emerged was a speech that would take its place in history books along with Lincoln's *Gettysburg Address* and George Washington's *Farewell Address*.

The following day, December 8, FDR stood before a joint session of Congress and intoned the words that are known to every schoolchild: "Yesterday, December 7, 1941—a date which will live in infamy..."

From then on, Grace would always be close to the President at times of crisis—November 1942, waiting to hear that the invasion of North Africa had begun; June 1944, waiting to hear that the D-Day landings had started on the beaches of Normandy.

It was not until the next administration that we heard strange whisperings that perhaps FDR and Churchill had received advance warning of the "sneak attack" and had let it happen to prod the U.S. into war. We dismissed such things as rumors.

Wartime, at the White House, meant Winston Churchill. He was always underfoot.

People remember Churchill for his rolling phrases, his magnificent voice. I remember him too for his cussing. You could hear him far and wide.

Churchill didn't mind who could hear him but *he* didn't like any noise when he was ready to sleep. He used to use ear plugs while he slept. He was trying to blot out, or at least muffle, the noise of the men working on the underground bomb shelter, night and day. It was, naturally, a very secret project. I didn't personally see it, but I knew it had offices for aides, as well as FDR, and above each desk was a Pullman bed that folded into the wall.

Churchill had a little wartime security problem of his own—the cigars he was never without. We heard that little samples of the cigars were injected into mice. If the mouse did not drop dead, the new box of cigars was safe to smoke.

We used to say, "All Churchill needs is a teddy bear." He would curl up with his hot water bottle even in the summer. Nobody could understand it. We dismissed it as "the British way."

We heard how exhausted FDR was, trying to keep up with Churchill, both in staying awake and drinking. FDR was always relieved when Churchill left and he could stop bending his elbow so often.

But at least FDR was left with a few good chuckles. Sir Winston did not go in for crazy nicknames for the people around him, but he had other ways of cutting people down. To indicate how haughty he thought Sir Stafford Cripps was—the man whom he made ambassador to Russia in 1940 and envoy to India in 1942—Churchill commented, "There, but for the grace of God, goes God!"

During the war, Eleanor used every opportunity to inspect the conditions under which her sons were serving their country.

She flew to San Diego to the Second Marine Raider Battalion and met and talked with son James' commander, learning from him how open-minded her son had grown.

Eleanor came back to the White House proud that James insisted on treating blacks and whites alike, much to the irritation of some of the white Marines under him. "He's getting a reputation," she said, laughing, "my kind of reputation."

She went to England to report to FDR on how the war was going there in October of 1942 and got to see Elliott.

Eleanor took a gift with her for Winston Churchill from FDR. It was a package of two things he really missed from America—a jar of honey and a well-cured ham.

In England, Eleanor was taken to see how women were trained to survive when their houses were blitzed and burned— making tiny stoves out of any brick or tin they could scrounge, and cooking outdoors in rain or shine, using whatever rations the government could spare.

She came back full of civil defense ideas for Americans.

During the war, all kinds of extra precautions were taken to protect FDR. I don't know if his special train is still in existence today, but it was a beauty given to him by the Association of American Railroads for patriotic reasons. I believe before FDR could accept it, the government had to present the company with a check for $1.00.

Anyway, the President could escape wartime attack on it or ride it to a safer place. It was made of bombproof metal even on the underside. The designers had thought of everything, even an escape hatch on the roof, like a submarine has, in case the train was attacked on a bridge and dropped into the water.

Yet the President could look as if he were taking his ease behind his desk. Crowds could look in and see him, not knowing they were looking through bulletproof glass.

Louise Hackmeister used to set up a switchboard in her own bedroom whenever FDR went to Warm Springs. She didn't like it but she did it anyway. And wherever she was, she was on twenty-four hour call. It was a hard life. Of all the help, FDR trusted her most to sound convincing when she said she didn't know what was going on. And sure enough, while FDR lay dying at Warm

Springs, the faithful maestro of the switchboard was still telling reporters she didn't know what was going on.

All during the war years, the nation never knew when FDR was at Warm Springs or elsewhere away from the White House. For security reasons, Hackmeister always made it sound as if FDR was at the White House, with business as usual. Only a small pool of three reporters were allowed to go along to Warm Springs, but there was a rule that they were not to reveal where they were, and stories they got from the President were to be datelined "WASHINGTON, D.C."

Hackmeister, a tall and tough gal, was a master at convincing people that the President was in his Oval Office, no matter where he was, even when he was discussing invasion plans on the high seas or in far-off lands, meeting Chiang Kai-shek at Cairo, or Stalin and Churchill at Casablanca or Teheran. Nobody knew where the President was until he *wasn't* there anymore, and was safely home.

Mike Reilly travelled with FDR on his wartime conferences. When they got back from one trip—I believe, Yalta—a little rumor went around that the Russian NKVD had attempted to tap the palace where FDR was staying and had planted listening devices. Reilly and his men combed the place and found all the bugs—they hoped.

There was great excitement backstairs at the White House in 1943, when word trickled down that FDR had gone to his Casablanca conference on an airplane. Only later did we hear it, and we were shocked.

"How could you let him do that?" I protested to Dr. McIntire, FDR's personal physician, whom I considered a good friend. "He could have been killed."

"True." said McIntire. "He could have gone down in the ocean. But there was less danger of that than there was from U-boats. Nobody expected a president to be flying."

"Did the Boss like flying?" I asked.

"No indeed," said the doctor. "He hated it."

FDR had flown in a Boeing 314 for his meeting with Churchill and De Gaulle in January 1943. And in spite of his not liking planes, we later heard that Roosevelt was having a special plane built for presidential use at Douglas Aircraft in California—a C-54.

All the Roosevelt sons served their country with distinction but received only brickbats from the enemies of their father.

During the whole war, the bad publicity did not abate no matter how devoted and patriotic the boys were. Elliott especially came under fire when his dog Blaze was shipped home on a military plane, and an enlisted man was supposedly "bumped" at his command, to make room for the dog.

Though Elliott had done a lot of wild things, he would not have dared to bump a soldier on his way home. We at the White House were sure that Elliott was telling the truth and really did not know that someone serving under him had given his dog priority over a man.

While it flamed, FDR cringed at the bad publicity and the maliciousness of the press, which insisted Elliott was just a spoiled brat. Even members of Congress took pot shots at the Roosevelt sons' war records, hinting that they were playing it safe in protected posts.

About that time Elliott sent a bitter letter to his father saying he sometimes found himself hoping "one of us gets killed" so the papers would stop accusing the rest of the brothers of goldbricking. I heard that FDR almost cried when he received that letter.

Elliott may have been the wild one of the family, but when World War II started, he insisted on getting into the fighting as an Army reconnaissance pilot, going behind enemy lines to take photographs in unarmed planes.

Both Elliott and James could have kept out of the service. Elliott, we knew, had disabilities that included bad eyesight, but he insisted on signing waivers so he could get into the zone of action.

James had a bad case of ulcers, and a section of his stomach had been removed. He, too, insisted on action and action he got, as part of the famous Carlson's Raiders of the Marines.

In that capacity, in 1942 he was sent by Admiral Nimitz on a sneak submarine attack of Makin Island, which was in the hands of the Japanese. Later, FDR bragged around the White House that Jimmy had had a walkie-talkie shot out of his hands by the enemy as he stood on the beach command post directing the firing of shells from the submarines.

According to his proud father, he had not panicked but had grabbed another walkie-talkie and kept the firing at the enemy gunboats going.

One sniper's bullet did seem to have James' name on it. He was standing with another officer, and he took a step. The other man stepped where he had been and was shot through the head. When we eventually heard of this backstairs, we marvelled again at this family with charmed lives.

Also, before the night was over, James rescued three men from drowning. President Roosevelt was mighty proud when he awarded the Navy Cross for heroism to his son, and Jimmy ended up with a promotion to colonel in the Marines.

Elliott did still better on the matter of promotions, rising to the rank of brigadier general and commanding a wing of 250 planes. He won the Distinguished Flying Cross.

The White House swelled with pride, right along with FDR, when news came that we finally had a *general* in the family. It turned out to be FDR's final triumph, and afterward some of us shed a few tears as we heard that one of the President's last letters had been a "Dear Bunny" letter of congratulations.

John and FDR Jr. were both Navy men.

Johnny was very unhappy when he seemed to be stuck on dry land in naval supply. We heard that he was harassing his father to get him assigned to a ship. Any ship. Any ocean.

We heard that FDR had gotten yet another complaining letter from Johnny asking why he couldn't do something. FDR told Prettyman, "Is this the way to run a war? I'm concentrating on the fleet and I have to stop and think of one sailor bitching at me who happens to be my son."

However, that son did get his way and found himself in the Pacific, aboard the aircraft carrier *Hornet*.

Johnny did not disappoint his father. He received a Bronze Star for bravery under fire, as well as promotion to lieutenant colonel. But unfortunately FDR did not live to see it. Johnny was still Lt. John Roosevelt when word reached him aboard the *Hornet*, cruising near Okinawa, that his father was dead.

By strange coincidence, FDR Jr.'s ship, the U.S.S. *Ulvert M. Moore* was cruising so close to the *Hornet* at the time of Roosevelt's death, that John and FDR Jr. were able to communicate by loudspeaker and find out from each other that neither was leaving his post to go home for the funeral.

Each had decided on his own that their father would have wanted him to stay in the war zone and get the job done. The battle of Okinawa was beginning.

FDR Jr. was a lieutenant commander when his father died. He had been in the Sicilian invasion. In fact, his ship, the destroyer, *Mayrant,* was bombed from under him and five of his men were killed. Others were badly wounded, and FDR Jr., not caring about his own life, carried a wounded man to safety under heavy fire. He received the Silver Star for his bravery, which his father had lived to see.

The fourth election was a wartime one—November, 1944. FDR still hated war, and the theme this time was "get the job done."

FDR fought the wars and Eleanor fought the inauguration crowds that surged through the White House. She had become quite adept at handling inauguration mobs. By the third inauguration, which took place January 20, 1941, she was able to serve over a thousand guests in the space of one hour. Of course, the guests ate standing up and she moved them along at a rapid clip, but they did manage to have a complete meal of soup, roast beef, sliced ham and tongue, tossed salad, plain cake or cake à la mode, and coffee.

That was only the half of it. The other half was a stand-up tea for 4,000 guests. Some gobbled so much food that we assumed it was going to last them for supper. There were sandwiches by the thousands, mountains of little cakes, and hundreds of gallons of tea and coffee.

The final inauguration was a miserable one—January 20, 1944. The joy was gone. We could see and were told by the valets and housemen that the President did not have the energy to take the grand parade route up Pennsylvania Avenue.

The reason given for the decision to hold the inauguration right at the White House was that it was wartime and not a time for frills and pomp. But we knew the truth.

Death Hangs Over the White House

All of us backstairs were distressed that the President refused to wear a coat for his swearing-in ceremony on the South Portico of the White House. It was very cold and bitter, but FDR wanted to look healthy.

He waved off the coat and stood outside without it.

The gardeners, to protect the grounds and perhaps keep people's feet from growing numb with cold, had placed canvas on the ground below the President. The small crowd stood looking up. There was not much room for VIPs to stand near him.

There was one person FDR particularly wanted at his fourth inauguration—his son James. James was stationed in the Philippines, and when FDR sent word that he wanted him, James replied that the only way he could come was if the Commander in Chief so ordered.

The Commander in Chief ordered Marine Colonel James Roosevelt to active duty in Washington. We knew that FDR was delighted that James, on whose arm he had leaned through three inaugural ceremonies, would be there for him to lean on again.

Another special request the President had made—and one that cost him considerable money for plane and train tickets—was to have all his grandchildren attend so that they could tell their children someday about having seen the historical fourth-term inauguration.

There were thirteen grandchildren—an unlucky number for sure, as it turned out, with his death following so soon after.

Eleanor did not hide her displeasure when, following the swearing-in ceremony, she had to stand all alone at the inaugural reception in the White House, greeting all his political friends and advisors, while FDR enjoyed himself in the Green Room.

The only persons admitted to the Green Room were a few trusted friends—among them, the face Eleanor was least happy to see, Princess Martha of Norway.

Last Days of a Giant

In the last days the whole household worried about the President. Daughter–confidante Anna, trying to be like Missy, ran around spreading cheer, smiling and laughing as if he couldn't be better. But we knew differently. We saw the President's shaking hands and we shook our heads behind his back.

We knew FDR was getting a lot more medical care, but we didn't hear any scare words like cancer. Only things like "strain" and "too great a burden for one man."

In December of 1943, FDR came down with the flu and couldn't throw it off. At that point, the rumor from Dr. McIntire's office was that he needed help in caring for the President. He arranged for a complete physical by a heart specialist, a Dr. Howard Bruenn, who was then with Bethesda Naval Hospital.

I remember Dr. McIntire was reported as being happy that the President was in pretty good shape, considering that he had to sit in a wheelchair all day. But the President was supposed to stay out of the swimming pool and give up cigarettes.

The valets and others close to the President knew that the doctors hadn't found anything radically wrong, just hypertension and a slightly enlarged heart.

FDR moaned and groaned that he was now on a low-salt diet. He added salt whenever he could. He didn't obey the smoking ban very well either. I don't believe there was ever a day in his life at the White House when he didn't smoke.

The most important thing was that the President was ordered to get plenty of rest. Rest and politics and running for a fourth term didn't go together. Nor did rest and running a hotel for world leaders and royalty, as well as trying to keep a romance running at the same time: Lucy Mercer Rutherfurd.

Now, instead of eating his meals with Missy, he was eating them with Anna. Eleanor hardly got to see him. Sometimes, when she would be asked something by a member of the family or staff, she would say angrily, "You will have to ask Anna. I am not kept informed."

Eleanor wasn't pleased when her husband insisted that Anna be his most intimate and trusted aide after Missy died. Anna sat in on all his man-talk stag parties and tried to be one of the boys, as Missy had been.

The difference was that Anna was even tougher than Missy. Missy mostly kept quiet and listened, except when prodded by FDR to speak up. Anna needed no urging, but spoke her mind freely and often. Her laughter would ring out. She told a story as good as any man, the valets said.

Missy was a little different. She would pretend she didn't hear off-color stories, and she would be there mostly as a backup to FDR, when he was entertaining. She let him shine. Anna seemed to like impressing her father with how tough she was. A valet said he wished he had a dime for every time Anna said "damn." But that wasn't all she said by a long shot.

Missy was wonderfully witty, but FDR had to push her to repeat stories to his friends. And a lot of his humor involved teasing Missy to get her dander up. In front of friends, she always called FDR "Boss," and only when they were alone, except for valets, would she call him endearing names.

But getting back to Anna and her father, she also became a buffer between him and her mother, trying to do all the things for Eleanor that Missy used to do. The word was that Eleanor was trying to reestablish her supremacy in this triumvirate, and would come bustling into FDR's study with a stack of papers and letters that she wanted to talk to FDR about. FDR understood this power play and he wasn't going to let Eleanor cut Anna out. Anna was taking Missy's place, and that was the way he wanted it.

One day Eleanor pulled this emergency conference bit when his nerves were raw from other problems. According to the valet, he took the stack of papers and gave Eleanor a dirty look. He turned to Anna, who was fixing cocktails for FDR and a few buddies who would be arriving soon. "Here," he said, "you take care of this, Sis." He practically threw the papers to his daughter.

Eleanor, hurt and angry, stalked out.

The valet noticed that Eleanor temporarily cut down on her paper work assignments for her husband.

There came the day that we felt particularly sorry for Eleanor. She suffered a great put-down after the 1945 Inauguration. Eleanor had humbled herself to ask Franklin whether she could go with him on the trip which later became known as the Yalta Conference. The rumor buzzed through the White House that she would finally be going with the President on something important, and some of us speculated that with the sea air and the romance of the high seas, maybe they would finally share the same bed.

But then came the devastating backstairs news that FDR didn't want his wife to go because she would cramp his style and disapprove of his drinking and heavy smoking. But he was going to take daughter Anna along, because she would be "one of the boys" and wouldn't try to dictate to him.

To show the way things were between Anna and her mother, I recall that once the butlers were horrified because as Eleanor was questioning FDR about some decision, Anna burst out at her mother, telling her, in effect, to get off FDR's back and quit pressuring him at the dinner table. She had snapped, "Don't you know you're giving Father indigestion?"

The Yalta Conference had been in February. They came back from Yalta—Fala, Franklin, and Anna—raring to go on a holiday. FDR had promised that they would take off for Warm Springs as soon as possible and have a party.

It was quite an entourage that finally took off March 29th: Lizzie McDuffie, his favorite maid; Arthur Prettyman, his valet; Mike Reilly, his trusted Secret Serviceman; Dr. Bruenn, because it wasn't an important enough trip to warrant Dr. McIntire leaving the White House, and besides, everyone said FDR looked in the pink again; FDR's quaint little relatives, Aunt Polly and Daisy Suckley; and Fala, of course.

As I was told later, Anna had made all the arrangements for

Lucy to meet FDR at Warm Springs. She was going to go herself, but her son Johnny was in the hospital with a gland infection of some sort. So Anna didn't go.

FDR was full of anticipation. When he got to Warm Springs, he drove his own specially-built car to the Little White House. He was delighted at all the spring foliage, and he said he was going to enjoy himself in spite of having to polish his speech. It was to be delivered on the birthday of Thomas Jefferson, godfather of the Democratic party. All across the country, there would be Jefferson Day banquets timed so that they would be able to hear FDR give his speech on radio simultaneously.

Lizzie heard FDR call Anna, and let her know explicitly, without saying so, that the arrangements she had made for Lucy to join him at Warm Springs had worked out. "I have an old friend visiting," he told her joyfully, also mentioning the plans for the barbeque party on the twelfth. Later I heard that FDR had made no attempt to hide Lucy's presence from the local people or the hospital. Lucy's name was on a guest list of those who would attend the festivities. Secret Service would naturally check out everyone, but they could have done so on verbal instructions.

They knew her, anyway. They had been along on FDR's visits at Baruch's estate and on the back roads with them. They didn't have to check up on her anymore.

As a matter of fact, the President had gone in his own car to pick up Lucy at a crossroads on April 9th. Before that, he had kept busy with the stacks of work that came to him daily from the White House, dictating to his trusted secretary, Grace Tully, once Missy's assistant.

Lucy Rutherfurd arrived in a big convertible, bringing two people—the famous artist Madame Shoumatoff and a photographer named Nick Robbins. He was going to take color shots that would help the artist work on her painting later. She was going to rough in a figure and finish the painting later in her studio. Lucy got in the President's car, and the photographer drove her Caddy.

Lucy and the President were like happy kids enjoying golden days—as if there would be no end to them. Even as Madame Shoumatoff sketched and studied FDR, Lucy and he held hands.

Most people don't realize the significance of the painting. It wasn't a portrait slated for the White House. It was a portrait

Eleanor knew nothing about. In fact, the painting was being made for Lucy Mercer's daughter Barbara, born in 1922. Barbara was the only child the elderly Winthrop Rutherfurd had sired with his young wife. Lucy had chosen the artist, who was famous among the social set.

Time flew, and suddenly it was the morning of the party, April 12th.

FDR had planned a happy day for everyone. He had arranged a barbeque and minstrel show for all the patients at his Warm Springs Foundation who were in good enough shape to make it. Among this crowd, FDR's handicaps were so slight they made him seem to be a tower of strength. The host was to be the mayor of Warm Springs, Frank Allcorn.

That morning Secret Service had already checked under every leaf and bush of the picnic area, and a special chair sat ready for the President to sit in while enjoying the minstrel show. The entertainers were all local talent—patients—except for accordionist Graham Jackson, who was coming from the naval base.

My good friend Monty Snyder, who was the President's chauffeur, had already made a dry run of the route he would take, including where he would arrive and where he would park the car. Years after this day, he would take his own life. But this day was just a normal day, and Monty merely exchanged a few words with the Secret Service, who were setting up a shortwave station in a nearby barn, making sure everything was in readiness for the party.

The party was in readiness but the guest of honor never came.

FDR had felt a little twinge of a headache that morning, while posing. Everyone made a little fuss over him, and Lucy Mercer rubbed his head until he said he felt better. The pain was attributed to muscle soreness. He looked at a little mail and was ready to pose a bit more before lunch, which was almost ready.

Bill Hassett interrupted for awhile, bringing in many things that needed the President's signature. One was a bill from Congress, and another was a diplomatic letter.

The President had shown off a bit for the "girls," bragging that he was now going to demonstrate some American history—how you pass a bill. They giggled as he signed with a flourish.

Then he made a joke about the letter put together by the State Department that required his signature. It was, he said, a perfect letter, because it was absolutely meaningless and revealed nothing.

Hassett, too, came in for a little ribbing. As FDR signed each document, including various appointments to government jobs, Hassett spread the sheets out on every chair in the room for the ink to dry. "Well, Bishop," FDR had teased, "are you through with your laundry yet? Is it all dry?"

FDR also worked a while on his speech, especially on the punch line, a last line to leave them thinking. Finally he was satisfied: "The only limit to our realization of tomorrow is our doubts of today."

It had been a pleasant picture, almost a scene out of *Little Women*. FDR, surrounded by the women he loved and trusted— Aunt Polly, dear Daisy Suckley, who had given him Fala and was even now fussing over the spoiled darling of the President; Lizzie; and of course, the passion of his fading years, Lucy.

I was told that Polly was reading something aloud. Lucy was holding his hand. Then it happened. A searing pain in his head— the President just had time to tell them and as he was lifting his hand to his head, he slumped over. Shoumatoff screamed. Lucy screamed and cradled the President's head. It was 1:15 P.M.

The last words the President had said, as he looked into Lucy's eyes were "I've got a terrible headache." Days later at the White House, Lizzie told me between sobs, "At least his last look was into the eyes of a beautiful woman." She said it several times and seemed to derive some comfort from the fact that he had "died happy."

But he didn't die immediately. In fact, it was viewed as only a fainting spell, at first. Prettyman and Dr. Bruenn, who had been summoned, carried him to his bed and worked over him. Somebody realized it might be awkward if Lucy and the artist were found in the house, so they hustled out and drove away.

Lizzie said poor Lucy hardly knew what she was doing and had to be torn away from the place. She wanted to stay and take care of her darling. Would they let her know how he was? Would they call her? Would they tell her when to return?

"Yes, yes, yes. Just hurry. You must go now. We'll call."

"Oh my God. This is terrible," said Lucy, crying. "I don't know what to do."

"Everything will be all right. Just hurry now."

And as Lucy was being shoved out the door, Polly was calling the White House. Everyone warned her not to alarm the First Lady. Polly told Eleanor the President had fainted, but he was being taken care of in the other room.

"Oh dear," said Eleanor, wondering what to do. Should she come right away?

No, it didn't seem too serious.

Eleanor continued her schedule, including going to the Sulgrave Club to a tea.

Meanwhile Dr. McIntire at the White House was having a telephone discussion with Dr. Bruenn. Anna got the word from McIntire that the President seemed to be responding, so she didn't worry.

But suddenly at 3:31 Georgia time (4:31 Washington time) Franklin Delano stopped breathing and no resuscitation could revive him. Adrenalin injected directly into his heart had no effect. That was it.

Now I guess I can tell what was never told before, besides the fact that Lucy was hysterical and was rushed out of the cottage and driven away so that no one would report to the world that she had been there. It concerns Lizzie.

Lizzie was covering up Lucy's tracks when she discovered that Lucy had left behind some articles of clothing in a drawer. Lizzie grabbed them and stuffed them in her own bag. When she got back to the White House, Lizzie showed them to me and pondered what to do with them.

She could simply destroy the evidence. That was one solution. But if she did that, Lucy might not find out and be even more worried about whether her possessions had fallen into Eleanor's hands.

Instead, Lizzie wrapped up the garments and mailed them to Lucy with Lizzie's own return address on the package.

Cerebral hemorrhage was the diagnosis. And twenty-five years later, the doctor who had been with him that day, Howard G. Bruenn, wrote an article saying that had there been the drugs for hypertension then that we have now, and had the President quit smoking and quit exhausting himself, the story might have had a different ending. He might have lived a long, happy life.

The phone call reached Eleanor at the Sulgrave Club tea.

When Eleanor flew to Warm Springs, there was no evidence of Lucy or a painting anywhere. But somewhere along the line, Polly slipped and mentioned Lucy and the truth was out. Eleanor was coldly furious. Later at the White House, she cornered Anna and demanded to know if Lucy had also been at the White House. Anna admitted she had. Now Eleanor knew that even her daughter had been in on the conspiracy.

With head high, she continued saying all the right things about how the country had sustained a great loss, that she wished the new president, Harry Truman, well. I knew the truth from Lizzie. I longed to comfort Eleanor and tell her that I admired her gallantry and her bravery, but I couldn't. She was the general and I was just her soldier, so I simply said how sorry I was and helped her with the packing. She didn't cry.

She got out of the White House as fast as she could, taking only Tommy Thompson with her, and I was told that as she rode away, she kept her gaze grimly ahead and never looked back.

I didn't blame her. He hadn't played the game. He had flaunted his affairs among his friends. Had they been laughing behind her back?

One of the maids overheard her say to Tommy, "They worship him and they don't even know him. I only thought I knew him."

There is a sad note to Lucy Mercer's story. After the President's death, she became more dependent on her sister, Violetta, one of the few persons who really knew her and with whom she could let her hair down. In 1947, Violetta came to live with Lucy at the huge Rutherfurd estate at Aiken. But there was small comfort for Lucy. Violetta became despondent and committed suicide by shooting herself in the head.

Lucy, who had become a recluse, didn't live much longer. She developed leukemia and died almost alone in a New York hospital in July of 1948. She was only in her mid-fifties.

Last Days of a Giant

Fala handled the tragedy as best he could, but he never had the same spirit again. First he went to live with Aunt Polly, the cousin of Daisy Suckley, who had given him to FDR. But that didn't quite suit. Eleanor came to claim him and that made him feel a lot better. They had a fairly good life at the end—not a riotous life anymore, not big conversations and shouting and chasing toys to bring back to his beloved master in bed—but quieter games like pouncing on her knitting. Fala was ready to go when he died five years after his master, secure in the knowledge that he would be buried near him at Hyde Park.

How did Fala know? Because FDR had promised him, and FDR never broke promises to his best friends. And twelve years later, Eleanor came to join them and the circle was complete.

In 1970 the still vigorous artist Elizabeth Shoumatoff was invited to return to Warm Springs to speak on the twenty-fifth anniversary of FDR's death. I didn't hear her speech, but I doubt that it included a discussion of Lucy Mercer.

I enjoyed reading about the artist's sneak visit to the Little White House a few years before that. Shoumatoff told a reporter that she had put on dark glasses and walked in, as if she were an ordinary tourist. She had gone to the place where the unfinished portrait still hangs—thanks to her—and had inquired about it.

Madame Shoumatoff said the guard had given a good description of the painter's technique and had said, "Of course, Mrs. Shoumatoff is a very old lady now—but she still paints."

"Good for her!" said the artist and hurried out, feeling very ancient.

Epilogue

The President did not lie in state in the Rotunda of the Capitol as presidents like Lincoln had in the past and John Fitzgerald Kennedy would in the future. It was thought that he didn't want that, and his supposed wishes were respected.

He did lie in state, in a closed casket, in the East Room of the White House. We servants were not permitted to attend the service. It was too crowded. Instead, at 4:30, we were permitted to file quickly past his casket for our own private moment of goodbye. We were told to walk fast.

It was painful to move along, to hurry, to have just seconds, but I'm sure the outpouring of love from us must have filled the room to bursting.

Some of us knew that the barrier between FDR and Eleanor continued even in death. Eleanor had found a letter addressed to son James with the words, "Funeral instructions," and had not wanted to open it because it was not addressed to her. The Lucy incident had cured her of opening mail. So Eleanor had "winged it," doing only the things she thought FDR would want, such as skipping the honors from Congress, which he felt hated him.

Eleanor also chose to keep the casket closed.

On that point, we knew that only Eleanor had a view of her husband in the casket. Everyone had been ordered out of the East Room and the casket had been opened only for her. She had stayed alone in the room with her husband at last—something she hadn't done for years. We wondered what she said to that sleeping figure, but we hoped it was that she had forgiven him and wanted him to forgive her, too.

She finally permitted herself one tender touch and placed a rose within the casket. Then the casket was closed, forever, and

Death Hangs Over the White House

Eleanor walked out of the room, her face a mask. I did not see her shed a tear.

When I heard of all the instructions that hadn't been followed, I was sorry Eleanor hadn't opened the envelope that so clearly indicated the President's funeral instructions.

He *had* wanted the household people to attend the service in the East Room and had so instructed. And strangely enough, he *had* wanted to be taken to the Rotunda of the Capitol, as Lincoln and others had been. But not for a long lying in state. He wanted to be taken there at twelve noon, the hour when Congress convenes each day, and to remain there only long enough for a twenty-minute service, by his old headmaster at Groton, Dr. Endicott Peabody. He wanted only a short prayer by the headmaster and the singing of two hymns, but no speeches or tributes to him by the Congress.

And then, he didn't want to be surrounded by Capitol Hill characters at the gravesite in Hyde Park either, but only by the Speaker of the House and a delegation of two Senators and two Representatives. Other than these, he wanted only his closest family and associates.

So many things were not done right. FDR hadn't wanted to be embalmed, and he hadn't wanted to be preserved in cement. He wanted only a simple wooden casket, loosely closed. He wanted to return to the earth—as it says in the Bible, dust unto dust. But Eleanor didn't know, so he was embalmed and his heavy metal casket was placed in cement to preserve his body.

And there was one other thing that upset the FDR servants and aides who learned about these things. FDR had wanted to be carried to his grave by the men of the Hyde Park area. Instead, military men carried his casket.

At least the family, knowing how he felt, have not authorized statues to commemorate FDR. There was one placed in Montevideo, Uruguay—but it is gone now—destroyed by terrorists in 1979; one in London; and one in Oslo; but none in the U.S. that I know of. Only a simple commemorative stone for him in front of the United States Archives. I was there at its unveiling.

That day we all spoke of how tired FDR had become of seeing himself in the newspapers in photograph and cartoon. And I remember at the White House, how I would hear that FDR had groaned because still another painting of him had come in as a gift. "I'm tired of the sight of me," he once said.

He had been particularly disgusted when a float had been constructed in New York for a parade. It consisted of a tremendous head of FDR sliding along the street like a decapitated giant's head. It was too much.

One thing Eleanor had used her own judgment about was in not letting any of the grandchildren enter the East Room or view the casket. She had seen too much death as a child to inflict the experience on another child now.

This we knew. But what we learned later, and what Eleanor would have known had she opened the letter concerning FDR's wishes, was that he wanted certain enemies kept out of the room. I never did find out who was on the enemies list. It could have been a lengthy list, for the President, I heard, had many bitter feelings in his last days about people who hadn't been loyal.

Years later in 1980, on her eightieth birthday, Grace Tully reminisced about the Boss and shared a humorous note he had sent her from Cairo during the Teheran conference in November of 1943, which couched his own bitterness about Congress in wit. After assuring Tully that the conference was going well, he said, "My role is that of peacemaker. I've seen the Pyramids and made close friends with the Sphinx. Congress should know her."

Something that touched my heart was hearing about Graham Jackson, the chief petty officer who took care of FDR when he was in Warm Springs, and how he had given FDR a proper sendoff, when his body was leaving Warm Springs. Graham had come at FDR's bidding to play his accordion for the barbeque party the President was attending that day. Instead he stayed to play for the funeral train.

As the train pulled away from the Warm Springs station, there stood Graham, face wet with tears, sending the mournful strains of "Going Home" after it.

Had FDR died before his time? We thought he did. He was only sixty-three.

I thought at the time, and have no reason to change my mind, that had Roosevelt been permitted to rest more in office, or had he given up the presidency altogether and not run for the fourth term, he would have lived many more years.

He pushed himself a lot the last few years. He had been lonely without the old crowd—Missy, Howe, Gus, Livy—and had spent longer hours at his desk, instead of relaxing. Also, he felt the burden of the war and a desperation to get the job done—as if his long hours could do it.

He should have rested, but he went on several far-flung journeys to consult with Allied leaders, and there was no Missy to stop him—or make sure someone was fussing over him.

He did have one person fussing over him, a few trusted persons knew, but he didn't have her by his side often. That was Lucy Mercer, who was back in his life more solidly than ever in those last months. But even maneuvering to see her may have added to his exhaustion.

Where was anyone who could help when the President had slumped in his chair at 1:15 P.M. at Warm Springs? Where was the doctor? Where was his therapist? Where was Secret Serviceman Mike Reilly? Where was Grace Tully? Where was Louise Hackmeister, who could find anyone by phone at a moment's notice? Where was Bill Hassett, his "laundryman"?

Dr. Bruenn had examined FDR that morning and found him in good shape. Doc felt he, himself, could take a swim before lunch with some of the gang. With him were Mike Reilly, Grace Tully, Grace's assistant Dorothy Brady, and Hacky.

Hassett had taken his "laundry" of presidential documents and put them away. He was having lunch at a dining room on the hospital grounds. The swimmers were about to join him.

Hacky had stopped at her cottage to check the switchboard being handled by the Warm Springs Foundation switchboard girls in her absence.

At that moment, Daisy Suckley had called the switchboard from the Little White House saying she needed the doctor. Hacky had gotten the message from the switchboard girls, and in a grim comedy of errors, called the wrong Daisy—Daisy Bonner, the cook—asking if the President wanted Dr. Bruenn to come to lunch at the Little White House.

Daisy Bonner excitedly told Hackmeister to send the doctor

Epilogue

quick because the President had "taken ill." Quickly Hackey called Bruenn at the swimming pool phone.

So sure had he been that the President was all right that he didn't have his black bag with him. He instructed Hacky to locate George Fox, the pharmacist–therapist who was acting as Bruenn's assistant, helping administer the President's relaxing rubdowns even on this vacation. "Tell him I'm heading for the Little White House and to bring my bag," Bruenn said.

By the hand of God, Fox was in view of her window and Hacky didn't even have to use the telephone to deliver the message. Meanwhile, a Secret Serviceman outside the Little White House had jumped into his car and retrieved the President's chief agent, Reilly, who was still at the pool.

Reilly called Tully.

People were converging on the cottage from all directions, as Lucy Mercer and Madame Shoumatoff were exploding out of it. Dr. Bruenn was quickly cutting off the President's clothing as he lay on the bed, to better monitor his heart, and he and Prettyman slipped his legs into a pair of pajamas.

In about an hour—a few minutes after two—Bruenn had a quick consultation by phone with Dr. McIntire at the White House, and the two men kept in close touch. Bruenn told him the evidence of a cerebral hemorrhage was all there—FDR's blood pressure, which had been 180 over 110 to 120 that morning was now over 300 and could not be measured any more on the instrument. The pulse was 104, and one eye was dilating to an extreme extent. He described the loud, laborious breathing.

He said he had injected the President with medications to bring the blood pressure down, and the President was still unconscious.

McIntire said he would locate Dr. James Paullin in Atlanta, and that Mike Reilly could find him on the highway and clear a path. Again, something failed. Reilly couldn't find him, and the famous internist showed up on his own at three twenty-five and rushed right into the bedroom, speaking to no one.

By then Bruenn had started artificial respiration. Dr. Paullin was quickly examining FDR, and within minutes was preparing to inject Adrenalin directly into FDR's heart, which had suddenly stopped. The Adrenalin started it again for only a few moments. Then there was no more of the dreadful breathing, no more snorting gasps.

Grace Tully came in silently, kissed the President on the forehead, and walked out.

The telephone line was still open to the White House. The time was three thirty-five.

How had Eleanor reacted to the message that her husband was dead? In the days that followed, we reviewed it again and again. She had almost not reacted.

A strange calm came over Eleanor, and later she didn't even remember that her first words had been something like, "I am sorrier for the nation than I am for myself."

The phone call she received at the Sulgrave Club had been from Steve Early, the Press Secretary, asking her in a tense voice to please return to the White House, but not telling her why. Later, Eleanor said she knew instinctively that something terrible had happened at Warm Springs.

Instead of rushing out to her waiting car, she returned to the club's tea, held for the benefit of the thrift shop, and even sat down to wait until the pianist had finished her number. It was hard for us to understand.

Eleanor then rose and announced that she was sorry, but she couldn't stay for the rest of the lovely concert because she had received a call and was needed back at the White House. All the ladies applauded her.

She arrived at the White House, went to her sitting room, and summoned Steve Early. He arrived in a minute with Dr. McIntire. Their words, that the President was gone—had "slipped away"—triggered her strange response.

Steve Early recorded the comment that she was sorrier for the nation than for herself. Then quietly, without a tear, she proceeded to do two other things before summoning Harry Truman to the White House to tell him he was president.

Matter of factly, she rang for her personal maid, Mabel, and told her to put a few things in a bag because she was going to Warm Springs. "The President is *sick*," she said. Evidently she didn't want any of the household to know the truth yet.

Calmly, she wrote out a message to each son in the service.

Epilogue

Even without knowing the full story, she wrote a gentle message that would cause them the least pain. I saved a copy of it: DARLINGS: FATHER SLEPT AWAY THIS AFTERNOON. HE DID HIS JOB TO THE END AS HE WOULD WANT YOU TO DO. BLESS YOU. ALL OUR LOVE. MOTHER.

The bitterness would come later.

Anna was at the White House and did not fly to Warm Springs with her mother. She stayed at the White House and made funeral arrangements while Eleanor was on her way to get FDR's body.

I sometimes wondered if Anna did not go with her mother on that sad mission because she was suffering with the knowledge of who had been with FDR at the end, and the fact that she had been the one to arrange it. Maybe she was afraid of what Eleanor would find at Warm Springs. Maybe she was afraid of what she herself might blurt out on the trip.

As for the treachery of Anna in the matter of Lucy, Eleanor did eventually forgive her.

Eleanor always turned the other cheek. After the shock of FDR's death, she reconciled herself to her daughter's human weakness and helped Anna with her debts. Mother and daughter finally achieved a closeness they had not had before when they competed for FDR's attention.

When Eleanor's health broke down in her last years, it was Anna she leaned on, just as FDR had leaned on Anna. It was Anna who took care of her in the dark days when she didn't want people to see how bad she looked. It was Anna who tried to cheer her and make bright conversation.

The sign that she had finally completely forgiven Anna was that she left all her money in a trust for Anna, for use during her daughter's lifetime. Anna, I knew, was also proud to have much of her mother's handmade Val-Kill furniture to put in her own home. She enjoyed that furniture just thirteen years before her own death at the age of sixty-nine.

And what of Eleanor's own bright career, the final stardom as chairwoman of the Commission on Human Rights and delegate to the United Nations? Harry Truman, her husband's successor, had appointed her, calling her, "the First Lady of the World."

Backstairs at the White House we applauded.

Years later, we found it amusing, considering Eleanor's teetotaling ways at the White House, to hear that in a reverse twist, liquor had been at the root of Eleanor's forced resignation from the U.N.

Eisenhower had done it. He had come into office and quietly retired her. We were told that Ike was furious when he heard that Eleanor had engaged in a conversation at a party about his wife, Mamie's, possible drinking problem.

Although we found it amusing that she who didn't drink was *done in* by drink, we still were very sorry that our new boss' sensitivity meant that the world was denied the fine talents of a great lady.

Eleanor still rushed around, appearing suddenly here, there, and everywhere. I was astonished one Sunday to see her arriving at my church, St. Luke's Episcopal, on 15th Street, N.W. We greeted each other warmly and had a wonderful visit.

Eleanor was seventy-eight when she died of a rare disease— bone marrow tuberculosis—in November of 1962.

I attended the memorial services for her at the Washington Cathedral, and sadly greeted some of the members of the family who attended—especially son, James, whom, of all the Roosevelt children, we maids had loved most and felt closest to. He was our pet.

Sometime later, Mabel Webster, who had been Eleanor's personal maid, and I received a personal invitation from Ambassador Adlai Stevenson of the United Nations, to attend a tribute to Mrs. Roosevelt at Lincoln Center, New York. Mabel and I went and were part of an audience of 2,600, which included representatives from sixty nations as well as half of Hollywood.

How Eleanor would have enjoyed it! Mabel and I looked around and wished we could bring our beloved Eleanor back for just an hour to hear what this star-studded gang said about her— people out of her fabled past like Marian Anderson, Leonard Bernstein, Mme. Vihayna Pandit, Helen Gahagan Douglas, Fredric March, Sidney Poitier.

Out in the corridor I was grabbed by Fanny Hurst, one of Eleanor's favorite and frequent White House guests. She held my hand and looked very sad and much older as she said, "Oh, I think so often of the White House days. How far away they seem."

The saddest trip I took was to the dedication ceremony of the Eleanor Roosevelt Wing of the presidential library at Hyde Park on May 3, 1972. I did not want to face it alone, so I took Loretta Deans, a White House cook in the Roosevelt days.

The invitation from the trustees of the Eleanor Roosevelt Memorial Foundation had been addressed to me, but I thought it fitting to take Loretta because she had made many trips to Hyde Park in the old days with the Roosevelt family. In fact, she may well have been the only White House servant to receive a gift of money from FDR's perfectionist mother, Sara Delano.

The senior Mrs. Roosevelt had developed a fondness for the way Loretta Deans made applesauce and would always call for the side dash with "the special touch." I have tasted that applesauce, and it is indeed unique, but Loretta would never tell what the secret ingredient was.

Old Sara had given her a generous tip for making the special side dish. I asked Loretta if Sara had tried to get the recipe, and Loretta had said, "Are you crazy? She wouldn't know what to do with a recipe or recognize a cooking tip if it bit her. She has a kitchen full of cooks and skullery maids and butlers to do the serving."

Now Loretta was thrilled to be returning to Hyde Park as a guest and not to make applesauce. When we approached Hyde Park it was raining and dismal and suddenly, as we arrived, the rain stopped and the sun came out radiantly. It was almost like an omen.

Photographers were taking pictures of the Roosevelt children and when Anna saw me, she stopped everything and gave me a hug, while still holding the trowel with which she was helping to lay the cornerstone.

"I was so afraid you wouldn't get here," she said.

A tent had been erected, and as soon as we entered the tent for the ceremonies, the rain again came down in sheets. And again it seemed a message that only for Eleanor had the heavens held back their tears.

And it still rained as we boarded special buses to take us back to New York and LaGuardia Airport. We spent some time in the FDR presidential library, and it was almost as if Eleanor were still among us. We were a very quiet group as we rode, our minds preoccupied with the Roosevelts and death.

I was told that toward the end of her life, Eleanor's hands shook a great deal, and she was a changed woman. But when I last saw her, it was a private visit, and she was in fine form, bustling around her 74th Street, East, apartment in New York City. The date was February 27, 1961, and I had gone to give her the first copy off the presses of the book she had urged my mother, Maggie Rogers, to write for history's sake, after Mama retired as head maid of the White House.

She was so happy that I had finished the job and finally produced the manuscript Maggie had not lived to write.

We talked of all the drastic changes Maggie and I had seen during our work years, and Eleanor said she could hardly wait to get started reading the book, *My Thirty Years Backstairs at the White House.*

Neither of us could have dreamed that eighteen years later, Hollywood producer Ed Friendly would make a nine-hour mini-series of the book which would receive eleven Emmy Award nominations.

How I long to tell her how we felt about her at the White House and how we echoed her sufferings in our own hearts. I hope, wherever she is, she again understands that I am now finishing the job—again for history's sake.

That I'm finally telling the rest of the story.

Books of Special Interest on the Roosevelts

Some of these books contain only a few interesting comments about the Roosevelts, among a wide array of subjects, and some deal exclusively with the Roosevelts. A few of these books I wrote myself, in collaboration with my coauthor. I list them all now for people who enjoy reading anything they can get their hands on about this fabulous family.

The Roosevelt Album—Letters, Speeches, Documents: The Highlights of His Life and Work. A.J. Ezickson. New York: Knickerbocker Publishing Company, 1945.

The Captains and the Kings: Intimate Glimpses of White House Life by the Social Secretary under the Wilsons, the Roosevelts and the Trumans. Edith Benham Helm. New York: G.P. Putnam's Sons, 1954.

Eleanor and Franklin: The Story of Their Relationship, Based on Eleanor Roosevelt's Private Papers. Joseph P. Lash. New York: W. W. Norton & Company, 1971.

The Life of Lorena Hickok, E.R.'s Friend. Doris Faber. New York: William Morrow & Company, 1980.

In and Out of the White House...from Washington to the Eisenhowers. Ona Griffin Jeffries. New York: Wilfred Funk, Inc., 1960.

They Lived in the White House. Frances Cavanah. Philadelphia: Macrae Smith Company, 1959.

My Thirty Years Backstairs at the White House. Lillian Rogers Parks, with Frances Spatz Leighton. New York: Fleet Publishing Corporation, 1961. This book was turned into a nine-hour TV mini-series by producer Ed Friendly in 1979 that received eleven Emmy nominations. The book was published in paperback by Avon in 1961.

Backstairs at the White House: The Story of Two Generations of White House Servants Who Shared the Lives of Eight Presidents. Gwen Bagni and Paul Dubov. Englewood Cliffs, N. J.: Prentice-Hall, Inc., 1978. Based upon *My Thirty Years Backstairs at the White House* by Lillian Rogers Parks, with Frances Spatz Leighton. Illustrated with scenes from the mini-series mentioned above.

Death Hangs Over the White House

It Was Fun Working at the White House. Lillian Rogers Parks, with Frances Spatz Leighton. New York: Fleet Publishing Corporation, 1969.

Upstairs at the White House: My Life with the First Ladies. J. B. West, with Mary Lynn Kotz. New York: Coward, McCann & Geoghegan, 1973.

Affectionately, F.D.R.: An Intimate Biography by His Son. James Roosevelt and Sidney Shallett. New York: Harcourt, Brace and Company, 1959.

My Parents: A Differing View. James Roosevelt with Bill Libby. Chicago: Playboy Press, 1976.

An Untold Story: The Roosevelts of Hyde Park. Elliott Roosevelt and James Brough. New York: G.P. Putnam's Sons, 1973.

The Autobiography of Eleanor Roosevelt. Eleanor Roosevelt. New York: Harper and Brother, 1961.

FDR: My Boss. Grace Tully. New York: Charles Scribner's Sons, 1949.

Scandals in the Highest Office: Facts and Fictions in the Private Lives of Our Presidents. Hope Ridings Miller. New York: Random House, 1973.

Washington Quadrille. Jonathan Daniels. New York: Doubleday & Company, 1968.

The Franklin Delano Roosevelt Library and Home. Betty Jean Mueller and Edward Miller. (Hyde Park)

The Coming of the New Deal: The Age of Roosevelt. Arthur M. Schlesinger, Jr. Boston: Houghton Mifflin Company, 1959.

The Eleanor Roosevelt Story. Archibald MacLeish. Boston: Houghton Mifflin Company, 1965. Also *Reader's Digest Family Treasury of Great Biographies, Volume IV.* Pleasantville, N.Y.: Readers Digest Association, 1970.

Index

Index

Index

Index